Charles Sumner

and the Conscience
of the North

American Biographical History Series

Charles Sumner
and the Conscience of the North

Frederick J. Blue
Youngstown State University

Harlan Davidson, Inc.
Arlington Heights, Illinois 60004

Library of Congress Cataloging-in-Publication Data

Blue, Frederick J.
   Charles Sumner and the conscience of the North /
 Frederick J. Blue.
        p.   cm.—(American biographical history series)
   Includes bibliographical references and index.
   ISBN 0-88295-911-5
   1. Sumner, Charles, 1811–1874. 2. Legislators—
United States—Biography. 3. United States. Congress.
Senate—Biography.   4. Abolitionists—United States—
Biography.   I. Title. II. Series.
E415.9.S9B57   1994
973.7'092—dc20
[B]   93-46496
                                            CIP

Manufactured in the United States of America
98 97 96 95 94 1 2 3 4 5 MG

As biographies offer access to the past, they reflect the needs of the present. Newcomers to biography and biographical history often puzzle over the plethora of books that some lives inspire. "Why do we need so many biographies of Abraham Lincoln?" they ask, as they search for the "correct" version of the sixteenth president's story. Each generation needs to revisit Lincoln because each generation has fresh questions, inspired by its own experiences. Collectively, the answers to these questions expand our understanding of Lincoln and America in the 1860s, but they also assist us to better comprehend our own time. People concerned with preserving such civil liberties as freedom of the press in time of national crisis have looked at Lincoln's approach to political opposition during and after secession. Civil rights activists concerned with racial injustice have turned to Lincoln's life to clarify unresolved social conflicts that persist more than a century after his assassination.

Useful as it is to revisit such lives, it is equally valuable to explore those often neglected by biographers. Almost always, biographies are written about prominent individuals who changed, in some measure, the world around them. But who is prominent and what constitutes noteworthy change are matters of debate. Historical beauty is definitely in the eye of the beholder. That most American biographies tell of great white males and their untainted accomplishments speaks volumes about the society that produced such uncritical paeans. More recently, women and men of various racial, religious, and economic backgrounds have expanded the range of American biography. The lives of prominent African-American leaders, Native American chieftains, and immigrant sweatshop workers who climbed the success ladder to its top now crowd onto those library shelves next to familiar figures.

In the American Biographical History Series, specialists in key areas of American History describe the lives of important men and women of many different races, religions, and ethnic backgrounds as those figures shaped and were shaped by the political, social, economic, and cultural issues of their day and the people with whom they lived. Biographical subjects and readers share a dialogue across time and space as biographers pose the questions suggested by life in modern-day America to those who lived in other eras. Each life offers a timeless reservoir of answers to questions from the present. The result is at once edifying and entertaining.

The concise biographical portrait found in each volume in this series is enriched and made especially instructive by the attention paid to generational context. Each biographer has taken pains to link his or her subject to peers and predecessors engaged in the same area of accomplishment. Even the rare individuals whose ideas or behavior transcend their age operated within a broad social context of values, attitudes, and beliefs. Iconoclastic radicals, too, whatever their era, owed a debt to earlier generations of protesters and left a legacy for those who would resist that status quo in the future.

Biographers in the series offer readers new companions, individuals of accomplishment, whose lives and works can be weighed and assessed and consulted as resources in answering the nagging questions that the thoughtful in every generation ask of the past to better comprehend the present. The makers of America—male and female, black and white and red and yellow, Christian, Moslem, Jew, atheist, agnostic, and polytheist, rich and poor and in between—all testify with their lives that the past is prologue. Anxious to share his rich experiences with those willing to listen, an elderly Eastern European immigrant living in Pittsburgh boasted, "By myself, I'm a book!" He, too, realized that an important past could be explicated through the narrative of a life, in fact, his own.

When a biographer sees his or her subject in broader context, important themes are crystallized, an era is illuminated. The single life becomes a window to a past age and its truths for succeeding generations and for you.

ALAN M. KRAUT
JON L. WAKELYN

For my parents

CONTENTS

PREFACE

Americans today probably recall Charles Sumner from history texts only as the man who was savagely beaten into bloody unconsciousness on the floor of the United States Senate. Perhaps they also remember that this violence was committed by a South Carolina congressman following Sumner's bitter and personal attack on slavery and its defenders. Undoubtedly, the 1856 assault was the most dramatic experience in the senator's life, requiring three and a half years of recuperation before he was fully able to resume his congressional responsibilities.

Despite the sensational nature of these events, however, they are merely symbolic of Sumner's larger career. He should be remembered instead as a stern voice of conscience who constantly reminded nineteenth-century Americans of what many preferred to ignore: that slavery and racial injustice are immoral. Sumner worked selflessly with others to create a political system that would address these issues. He first led a revolt against the Whigs when they failed to respond and then helped to form the new Free Soil and Republican parties, all the time forcing them to focus on slavery-related issues before the Civil War and civil rights after it. This brief biography of Sumner, moreover, attempts to portray the senator's accomplishments and shortcomings within the context of issues that remain relevant to this day.

Sumner was both a reformer and a politician. In the latter role he was as eager to attain and hold office and to advance his party's fortunes as his fellow partisans, although he never shared the presidential ambitions of many of his colleagues. But as a reformer he was virtually incapable of compromising his principles to improve his political position. He was so totally committed to racial justice that he rarely understood his more pliant colleagues; nor could they appreciate his single-minded devotion to his convictions. Throughout his adult life he reminded Americans in general and government officials in particular of the need to make good the ideals of the Declaration of Independence. It is hoped that this study of Sumner will provide a window to the nation's troubled past and insight into issues that continue to confront twentieth-century Americans.

As in any such project, many people helped make this book a reality. Most especially I thank Dominic J. Capeci of Southwest Missouri State University for the many hours he spent reading the manuscript and for urging changes that he felt would improve it. He identified sections that would benefit from additional analysis to give the narrative greater insight, and his sharp pencil pointed to numerous sentences that needed to be tightened. James B. Stewart of Macalester College read the first half of the manuscript and applied his thorough knowledge of the antebellum period to help me avoid errors of fact and questionable interpretation. Jon L. Wakelyn and Alan M. Kraut, editors of the American Biographical History Series, offered valuable encouragement and suggestions. Andrew J. Davidson provided his expertise in the copy-editing process and helped me produce a more smoothly flowing narrative. David Donald, the author of the massive two-volume life of Sumner, urged me to undertake a shorter biography that might better reach the general reading public and particularly undergraduates studying American history.

Youngstown State University provided valuable support in granting me a sabbatical leave and additional time to pursue the research into Sumner's voluminous papers. Reference librarian Hildegard Schnuttgen hunted down elusive sources and acquired others through interlibrary loan. Mary Belloto formatted and proofread the manuscript. My wife Judy read much of the text and offered significant suggestions that only a layperson could provide a historian who too often assumed that what was obvious to him should be so to others. All deserve my heartfelt thanks.

FREDERICK J. BLUE

Courtesy Massachusetts Historical Society

CHAPTER ONE

The Friendship and Confidence of Judges

In 1811, the United States prepared for its second war with Great Britain. A long series of events beginning with the French Revolution had resulted in warfare between Britain and France, catching a young United States in the crossfire of two superpowers. Hence one crisis after another challenged the U.S. policy of neutrality and plunged the nation into what many beheld as another war for independence. Such a conflict, many citizens believed, was necessary to prove that the United States was a full-fledged nation worthy of respect from those countries that continued to treat it as a subordinate colony.

The people of Boston were sharply divided as President James Madison and Congress drifted toward war. The majority, members of the Federalist party, depended on trade with England and thus sought continued neutrality or war against Napoleon's France. But a significant minority supported the Republican chief executive's determination to force respect from England. Such was the thinking of Charles Pinckney Sumner. A Harvard graduate and classmate of newly appointed Supreme Court Justice Joseph Story, he was influenced by the Justice's Jeffersonian Republican sympathies. Thus despite his English roots and Puritan heritage, the young, struggling attorney agreed with those demanding that England respect his country's neutral rights. Sumner kept these leanings mostly to himself, however, not wishing to jeopardize his already precarious income in Federalist Boston.

Both Sumner and his new wife Relief Jacob traced their ancestry to English immigrants who had come to Massachusetts in the 1630s. Like many of their forebears, neither was especially demonstrative in political or personal matters, and family members rarely displayed open affection in their middle-class Boston household. The first of five boys and four girls were premature twins, Matilda and Charles, born on January 6, 1811. They, along with the remaining children who arrived over the next sixteen years, found few material comforts in a family dependent on the modest income of the father. Only later, in the 1820s, when the senior Sumner became sheriff of Suffolk County, did the Sumners move to a large home on Hancock Street and enjoy greater security.

The Boston in which Charles Sumner grew up was a complex city of 60,000 inhabitants. Lacking the ethnic diversity that would later characterize it, the city was the scene of rapid yet uneven economic growth dominated by commerce and the beginnings of industry. It contained a highly stratified, class-conscience society in which those of wealth possessed influence far beyond their numbers and expected and usually received deference from those of a lower status. With the decline and eventual disappearance of the Federalist party, Massachusetts politics were in a state of flux. The state and the nation were moving toward the second two-party system, which would eventually pit Jacksonian Democrats against their more conservative Whig opponents in the 1830s. In the meantime, the wealthy who dominated city and state politics continued to command the respect and loyalty, if not the love, of the mass of voters.

In the years between the War of 1812 and the election of Andrew Jackson in 1828, Charles and his siblings lived a typical New England childhood, although Sumner would later reveal little of his boyhood experiences. Studious and amiable, yet neither overly handsome nor adept in physical activities, he perhaps preferred to forget what had not been an especially happy time. Not surprisingly, he turned to intellectual pursuits and probably had few close boyhood friends. He received little emotional support from his parents, especially his father, a man of stiff formality whose overly harsh demands on the young boy frequently brought censure and even rejection rather than praise. But if Sumner failed to enjoy intimacy among peers or with his parents, he nonetheless was influenced by his father's humanitarian beliefs, which included a commitment to improve the welfare of the people of Boston.

Never an active abolitionist, the senior Sumner did sympathize with fugitive slaves and opposed the segregation of Boston schools. He also lectured in behalf of temperance. Perhaps due to his Unitarian beliefs, he was tolerant of Roman Catholics in an age when such attitudes were rare. His devotion to the law and equal justice impressed young Charles, although this would not be evident until after the elder Sumner died. Largely apolitical, the father revealed some of the same ambivalence toward England that would later characterize his son, the major difference being that the son extended these beliefs beyond the family to public life. Young Charles thus grew into manhood in a household committed to a humanitarianism tempered by stoic behavior.

It is not clear how young Charles got along with his brothers and sisters. His twin Matilda, with whom he was never close, died of consumption in 1832, and two other sisters died as young adults. As the oldest, Charles often lectured his brothers and sisters in an overly protective way, which they naturally resented. Yet his letters show a deep affection and concern for their well-being. He was especially close to his sister Mary, who died in 1843, and his brother George, six years his junior, with whom a rich correspondence developed. Brothers Albert and Horace died tragically in separate shipping accidents in the 1850s. With each passing, Sumner, who outlived all but his youngest sister Julia, mourned deeply and felt more and more isolated and alone. His relationship with his parents is less certain because of their own reserve and the lack of surviving correspondence. Rarely able to relate to his father, he remained deeply solicitous of his mother until her death after the Civil War, staying with her in the family home on Hancock Street whenever in Boston.

The senior Sumner lived only until 1839, but long enough to play a major role in his son's education. First taught in the private school of an aunt, Charles entered Boston Latin School at age ten. With a classical curriculum that included Latin and Greek, the school helped inspire his interest in history and literature, especially those of England, and initiated the skills and desire for a lifetime of reading and study. His classmates at Boston Latin included the future abolitionist and a close collaborator in the struggle for racial justice, Wendell Phillips, and his Whig friend-turned-antagonist, Robert Winthrop. As the five-year program neared completion, it did not appear that family income would permit Charles a college education. But it was at that critical stage that Charles's father was appointed sheriff, and he now planned to send his son to Harvard.

In the fall of 1826, the fifteen-year-old Sumner joined a class of forty freshman students with a typical admonition from his father: "Good learning and good behavior are commonly companions," which "ought never be disjoined." The teen's four years at Harvard were among his happiest, and he developed socially and intellectually. While his father kept close tabs on Charles's expenses, he nonetheless blossomed in the freedom of his new surroundings, studied long hours, and established a strong camaraderie with classmates. He did poorly in science and especially so in mathematics, which prevented a high class standing, but excelled in literature, language, and history. Most revealingly, young Sumner expanded his reading interests far beyond the unchallenging elitist curriculum. Joining one of Harvard's most popular clubs, he developed some deep and lasting friendships and with eight classmates formed a secret self-improvement society called

The Nine. Normally stern and lacking in humor, he nevertheless could enjoy a good joke and laugh at the jests of others. Not totally adverse to physical activity, he hiked from Boston to Lake Champlain and Albany with four classmates in the summer of 1829.

Graduation left the nineteen-year-old undecided and confused about a profession. Uncertain about the study of law, which many urged on him, he embarked on a year of reading at home, thereby postponing a career decision. With dedication and discipline he even studied mathematics—"my chiefest foe,"—in an effort to overcome past shortcomings. For the most part, however, he concentrated on his love of the classics and history. He briefly tried substitute teaching, only to find that he had "a natural hydrophobia towards keeping school."

Many of the values and beliefs that he would hold for a lifetime also evolved during his year of self-induced study. Under his father's influence he supported the Anti-Mason movement because he opposed the intolerance and "unwarrantable exclusion" to which the senior Sumner had been subjected by Masons. He shared his parents Unitarianism, noting that although unconvinced of Christ's divinity and "without religious feeling," he felt "an affection for everything that God created and this feeling is my religion." Then and later he attended church only sporadically but became increasingly committed to the tenets of a social gospel. Although not obvious in 1831, Sumner's faith would follow the Unitarian tradition and be one of Christian action, more intellectual than it was evangelical or personal.

In letters to Harvard classmates Sumner revealed a growing interest in the law career that they continued to urge on him, albeit a concern conditioned more by what was expected of him than by a full commitment to the practice of law. As he explained, "I look upon a *mere* lawyer, a reader of cases and cases alone, as one of the veriest wretches in the world." Therefore, Sumner's decision to enter Harvard Law School revealed his love of learning and study more than his desire to become a practicing attorney. Not given to an active social life, he could envision a career of scholarship and writing based on the law. "All empty company and association I shall eschew; and seek in the solitariness of my own mind the best companion." Yet he was much more amiable and outgoing than his father had ever been, and he charmed others in conversation and developed close male bonds among a handful of the forty students in the law school.

Even more revealing was Sumner's relationship with Supreme Court Justice Joseph Story, one of the law school's two instructors. When not in Washington, Story taught many courses, bringing new strength and prestige to the school. Biographers of Sumner and Story have noted the father-and-son-like relationship that developed between the two, a closeness that would last until Story's death in 1845. Reveling in a support that he never had from his own father, Sumner was totally devoted to his mentor; striving to satisfy Story's every expectation, he became his best pupil, revealing to Story unashamedly that "my greatest happiness is in serving you." More than a slavish devotion, his esteem was based on a respect for Story's achievements as a jurist, teacher, and humanitarian. Under his professor's guidance, Sumner's love of legal scholarship and writing matured, as did his commitment to study. Recalling his law school days in later years, he described them as "the happiest of my life."

To Sumner, "the acquisition of knowledge" exceeded "all common joys." As Story's son William noted, Sumner was "the least susceptible to the charms of women" of all the men he knew. At this stage he appeared to be totally devoted to intellectual pursuits and unconcerned with female relationships. Debate and conversation with fellow students and Story were all that was necessary to satisfy his simple yet complex needs. Devotion to study was critical, for "a lawyer must know everything. He must know law, history, philosophy, human nature . . . he must drink of all the springs of literature." Not surprisingly, he neglected exercise and health, standing over 6 feet yet weighing barely 120 pounds.

Sumner was in no hurry to begin his own law practice. Remaining in Cambridge for an extra term of study, he then accepted Story's invitation to visit Washington and see the Supreme Court in action. There he spent six weeks meeting justices and politicians alike. With the former, he was properly impressed, especially with Chief Justice John Marshall, while with the latter he shared his mentor's distaste. He had quickly accepted the political views not only of Story but of his law school peers who endorsed the Whigs' strong government, pro-business ideology, and he looked to the day when Jacksonian Democrats would lose their majority in Congress. He thus opposed the party and president in power—those who appealed more to the lower classes and championed a government that resisted granting favors to business. As he waited to hear the Senate oratory of the political giants of the age, Daniel Webster, John C. Calhoun, and Henry Clay, he wrote to his father that he would probably "never come here again," for he felt only "loathing" for politics. The more he saw of it "the more I love the law," which he expected would "give me an honorable livelihood." Ironically, his love of the law would soon diminish and eventually be replaced by a desire for a career in politics, albeit one that would leave him an outsider when he refused to conform to the accepted rules that he had found so disagreeable in 1834.

While studying law he had worked briefly in a law office and, having been admitted to the bar in early 1834, on his return from Washington entered into a partnership with his law school friend George Hillard. During the ensuing three years, Sumner built a small practice and won a reputation within the legal community as a well-read and learned attorney. Not especially adept in courtroom techniques nor attentive to the many details required of a practicing lawyer, he was still more interested in historical research and developing his literary skills. His practice thus grew slowly, and his income remained modest. Other interests diverted him from giving full attention to his practice, and in early 1835 he began filling in as a lecturer at Harvard Law School during Story's many absences. He was well suited to such a role, Story hoping that "one day you may fill the chair . . . which I occupy." Sumner thrived on the experience, telling Story that it had garnered in him a "new confidence as well as facility and perhaps capacity."

Sumner also wrote articles on legal issues for the highly regarded periodical, *The American Jurist*, which he coedited, and for the more popular yet scholarly *North American Review*. He painstakingly completed Andrew Dunlap's learned reference work on admiralty law, an opportunity presented to him because of Dunlap's declining health. As reporter for the United States Circuit Court, Sumner expertly edited several volumes of reports of the court's cases. Lecturing, writing, and editing were clearly of a higher priority to him than was the building of a successful practice. Moreover, a career based on scholarly writing could as easily give him the status he sought among Boston's elitist Whig community as could one in the courtroom.

Sumner's correspondence during these years revealed a broadening interest in reform and political affairs. His awareness of politics quickened when, with the death of John Marshall, Andrew Jackson appointed Roger Taney as Chief Justice, passing over the more experienced Story. Sumner, reflecting his mentor's political beliefs, felt only disdain for Taney and the Jacksonian Democrats. The new Chief Justice's words were those "of a demagogue," and Martin Van Buren's presidential election in 1836 meant that there would be four more years of political favoritism. Sumner's reactions reflected Massachusetts politics, in which popular participation by voters was rising dramatically as the Whigs fought to maintain their supremacy against the more reform-minded Democrats in what had become an intensely partisan battle.

Part of Sumner's discontent with Democratic domination was in aversion to the support of slavery espoused by the Jacksonians. His own growing interest in the antislavery movement is best explained by a combination of factors: his father's influence; his own Unitarian beliefs, which emphasized the need for moral reform; and his extensive study of history and its many injustices. As he told his friend, German expatriate Francis Lieber, "we are becoming abolitionists at the North fast," a claim which for Sumner in 1835 was at least a decade premature but did reflect the broadening opposition to slavery among many in Boston. Lieber, who taught political economy at South Carolina College and was soon to become a small slaveholder, would debate with Sumner over the next years as the two moved in opposite directions on sectional issues.

In the 1830s, New Englanders in general and Bostonians in particular were showing a heightened concern for humanitarian reforms of a varied nature. Both within and outside the political structure, dedicated men and women were attacking the many abuses evident in a rapidly industrializing society. Their concerns encompassed a variety of issues including temperance, the working conditions of labor, public education, prison discipline, pacifism, and the plight of the slave. The search for social justice did not recognize party lines, although the motivation of those advocating reform sometimes varied. For Whigs, it frequently included moral paternalism as a means of protecting the social order from intrusion from the lower classes—a way to induce people to behave in accordance with Whig interpretations of morality and decency. In contrast, the Jacksonian Democrats were more concerned with reforms that might force conservative economic interests to be more responsive to the welfare of the public. In the 1830s, Charles Sumner found the Whig appeal more attractive, but his conscience was stirred by antislavery advocates.

Upset by the antiabolition mobs in Boston in 1835, Sumner began to subscribe to William Lloyd Garrison's *Liberator*. He maintained his ties with the abolitionist Wendell Phillips and developed a close friendship with the Unitarian reformer

William Ellery Channing, whose antislavery views he found especially convincing. Still far from an activist on slavery-related issues, Sumner's conscience nonetheless had been further aroused in Boston's increasingly charged, reform-minded atmosphere. He also expressed the beginnings of a life-long opposition to war, the issue that had initially attracted him to Lieber.

Sumner's widening circle of friends also reflected his intellectual and literary interests and satisfied his need for male companionship. Soon after he entered the partnership with Hillard, the two joined with three other rising young Bostonians, Henry Wadsworth Longfellow, Cornelius Felton, and Henry Cleveland to form the Five of Clubs. Sumner had met Longfellow, a Harvard professor of modern languages who was soon to become his closest friend, while lecturing at the law school. The jovial Felton taught Latin at Harvard, while Cleveland was a proctor at the college before ill health forced his retirement. Each of the five aspired to a place in Boston's elitist society and styled himself a writer, although only Longfellow gained fame at it. All were under the age of thirty, and only Hillard was married when they began their regular Saturday dinner gatherings, at which, in addition to enjoying each other's company, they critiqued each other's writings and provided the kind of mutual support that they all needed and thrived on. In reinforcing each other's egos, they became what one Boston newspaper jokingly called a "Mutual Admiration Society."

Sumner's decision to travel and live for a time in Europe temporarily put an end to the weekly gatherings of the Five of Clubs. It also provided him with an escape from what quickly had become the tediousness of his law practice. His club members understood and encouraged such wanderlust, even if Story and other friends of an older generation did not. Sumner had planned and talked of his trip for months and in fact had dreamed of it for many years, declaring it a "vision of boyhood." It would be a trip of indefinite length designed to acquire "a knowledge of languages, of observing the manners, customs, and institutions of other people; most especially the English." Abroad he would discover and experience the history of Europe, which had so inspired his education. There too he would meet prominent people and perhaps become known and recognized. His need for such recognition and his willingness to give up his law practice to obtain it was an early indication of Sumner's driving ambition.

Sumner urged the dubious Story to understand that his goal for the trip was educational, to be undertaken "before the mind, absorbed in business, has lost its freshness and its capacity for receiving impressions." To Story and Professor Simon Greenleaf of the Harvard Law School, who feared that Europe might spoil him and turn him against both his profession and his country, he insisted, "Do not let it be said, then that I shall be spoiled by Europe, but rather suggest that I shall return with an increased love for my country, an admiration for its institutions, and added capacity for performing my duty in life."

Story, Longfellow, Channing, Ralph Waldo Emerson, and others provided Sumner letters of introduction so that he might meet statesmen, lawyers, writers, artists, and others of high culture throughout Europe. Sumner's ability to secure references from such a distinguished group of Bostonians is a further measure of his successful entry into the political and intellectual culture of the city. The reluctant Story and two other attorneys loaned Sumner a thousand dollars each to supplement his own savings to finance his adventure. To give up his practice and venture to unknown lands was both courageous and foolhardy, but necessary for Sumner before he could settle into his profession. He fully expected that he would "come home and be happy."

True to his word, Sumner's trip was to be anything but a holiday or the sowing of wild oats in the traditional manner of the sons of the wealthy elite. At twenty-six, more than three years removed from law school and having developed a small legal clientele, he was beyond the stage in life in which most young men undertook such adventures. And given his values, he was incapable of enjoying the carousing night life of drinking and whoring in Europe that appealed to many. As he said, he desired to study languages, laws, governments, and institutions. He wanted to meet authors and statesmen—in short to become a part of the Old World's professional society. To Lieber, he promised to speak and "write in German from Germany. There on the spot with the mighty genius of your language hovering over me I will master it. To that my nights and days must be devoted. The spirits of Goethe, Richter, and Luther will cry in my ears 'trumpet tongued.'" His almost insatiable desire to study the civilizations of Europe stemmed not only from his mastery of the classics of literature, history, and law, but also his determination to identify with what he believed to be the most cultured elements of both hemispheres.

During his twenty-eight months abroad, Sumner more than lived up to his own expectations. Leaving New York in December 1837, he arrived at Le Havre several days after Christmas following a three-week crossing that was rapid and smooth for a ship sailing in winter. Yet, as he was not one accustomed to the open ocean, he endured a week of seasickness before being well enough to eat dinner with the other passengers.

After brief travel in northern France, Sumner arrived in Paris, where he remained until June. The antiquity of the land immediately impressed him, noting at the Rouen cathedral that as an American, his "hemisphere had been discovered long since the foundation of this church." True to his pledge, he devoted himself almost exclusively to the study of the language, insisting that until he could speak and be understood he would not venture into society. Yet venture he did, attending lectures at the Sorbonne and even going to the theatre "with the play in my hand to assist me in following the actors." He confessed to his mother that despite years of studying French in Boston, "I found myself but little better than an infant" in Paris. After three months he achieved proficiency, later advising his young brother Horace to concentrate on the language, for it would be far easier to learn as a boy than as an adult.

Not surprisingly, the loose moral code of the French disturbed the self-conscious Sumner. While steering clear of the fleshpots of Paris, he cautioned Hillard to "believe everything you hear of the immorality and total depravity" of the city. "It is a perfect Sodom; without religion and without any morality between the sexes." He became annoyed at the French feeling of superiority toward not only Americans, but other Europeans, telling Story that they "believe themselves *la grand Nation.*" He thus revealed his ambivalence toward the French as he grew in respect of their culture and sought to study it more. Upset by their arrogance, he was attracted by their language and history. Outraged by their morals, he was thankful for their contribution to democratic theory as well as for the assistance they had given his country during the American Revolution.

Still, he told Story that his stay in Paris had convinced him more than ever of "the superior character" of his own country's people and institutions. On the other hand, he was not impressed with many of the Americans he met in Paris, who "degrade our just character and pervert our institutions." He was especially upset with the U.S. minister to France, Lewis Cass, a Michigan Democrat who, despite his conquering of "many tribes of Indians," had failed miserably in learning the French language. Steeping himself in French law by attending courts during his final weeks in Paris, Sumner found much to admire. He had meetings with distinguished men such as philosopher Victor Cousin and statesman-reformer Alexis de Tocqueville, who had toured the United States in the early 1830s and had written a highly acclaimed account of his impressions. The young American thus departed France "with a thousand things undone, unlearned, and unstudied which I wished to do, to learn and to study." Yet ahead lay England, "land of my studies, my thought and my dreams!"

Sumner's stay in the British Isles lasted ten months and was the highlight of his travels. Much of that time he spent in London and its surroundings, but he also explored Edinburgh, Glasgow, and Dublin. He even spent several weeks in the English countryside at the estates of London friends. Armed with assorted letters of introduction, Sumner made his way easily through the upper classes of English society. He knew English history, law, and politics almost as well as he knew those of his own country. He could "at once leap to the full enjoyment of all the mighty interests which England affords."

With no time necessary to study and learn the language, Sumner quickly plunged into London society, which he found as congenial to his interests and aspirations as the city of his birth. He felt much more at home there within a week than he had in Paris after five months. The streets, the shops, and the people reminded him of Boston. London lacked the glitter and excitement of the French capital, but even "the style of building is American; or rather ours is English." As a young, appreciative, and well-educated American who was so familiar with their way of life and who was also a friendly and ingratiating conversationalist, he was an instant hit among the English. Not only was he invited to dine with those for whom he had letters of introduction, but at such dinners he met others who immediately took to him and issued their own welcomes.

Sumner soon found himself with more engagements than there were days and evenings available. Living within a few minutes walk of Westminster Hall, he frequently attended Parliament, sat in the courtrooms of prominent judges, and even traveled on the circuits of several, "witnessing the English practice before juries." Without conceit, he noted that "it has thus fallen in my way perhaps to see more of the English bar and of its practice than ever before fell to a stranger." Surely few Americans could boast as he of being present in Westminster Abbey for the coronation of Queen Victoria in June 1839.

Despite these achievements Sumner was ever mindful of the negative way some in Boston had reacted to his going to

Europe, and he felt it necessary to defend the many benefits of his trip. In describing to Story his travels with English jurists on their circuits in the north of England, he noted: "I have the friendship and confidence of judges and of the leaders of the bar . . . And can you say that this will do me no good—that I shall be spoiled?" Surely his trip was "no vulgar holiday affair," but to learn of society, its laws, and its institutions. While envying the high status of the English barrister, he assured Greenleaf that he was nonetheless grateful "that I am an American." He concluded patriotically that he would not give up all his country represented for all that he had seen abroad.

Sumner met not only judges and attorneys, but politicians, well-known writers, scholars, and an endless parade of English royalty. He was especially impressed with the historian Thomas Macaulay, who had worked for educational and penal code reform in India as well as for an end to slavery throughout the British Empire. He was equally inspired by the Scottish essayist and reformer Thomas Carlyle, who had recently published his study of the French Revolution. He was accepted as a visitor-member in four exclusive London clubs where he occasionally dined and expanded his friendships.

Not all of those he met received his hearty approval. One who disappointed him was the flamboyant and eccentric reformer Lord Henry Brougham. Despite Brougham's outspoken opposition to slavery and his central role in England's recently successful abolition crusade, Sumner found him "vulgar beyond expression." He deemed Brougham's manner "uneasy and restless," and feared that in the future, he would "distrust his sincerity and the purity of his motives." Nonetheless, Macaulay, Carlyle, and Brougham all impressed Sumner because of their support of the Reform Bill of 1833, which had extended suffrage to the English middle class. In contrast to his reservations concerning Brougham, after meeting William Wordsworth, Sumner was left with the exhilarating feeling that he was "conversing with a superior being." The poet's manner and conversation were "simple, graceful and sincere," characteristics, "the absence of which in Brougham gave me so much pain." Life-long friendships were initiated, such as that with Lord Morpeth, the Lord Lieutenant of Ireland, "who takes a great interest in our country" and whom Sumner would later entertain in Boston.

Sumner had spent an invaluable time with his English hosts, the leaders and nobility of the nation. He understood their culture and institutions, but he had been exposed to few of the nation's poorer people and their problems. His letters and journal show little awareness of the mass of the English people. Entertained in a truly royal way during his long stay, he rarely concerned himself with those living in poverty. Carefully shielded by his overly protective hosts from intrusions from below, Sumner, true to his own elitist aspirations, failed to take note of the discontent around him. He did complain to Story of the power of the landed aristocracy maintained by the ancient law of primogeniture and of the unfair system of political representation, thus better appreciating his own nation's greater legal equality. But his concern went no further. Admiring the efforts of abolitionists like Brougham, he saw no relationship between the slave's plight with that of the poor of his own race. He had taken Story's advice to live "among the educated, the literary, the noble" and had adhered to Greenleaf's admonition to avoid "the jacobinism and radicalism and atheism of modern Europe" and to come home "a sound and liberal conservative as God made you."

By the spring of 1839, Sumner returned to the continent. After revisiting Paris, he traveled for several months each in Italy and Germany and briefly in Austria. Again, he spent more time studying language, literature, and philosophy than he did in more typical tourist activities, and his knowledge of European cultures grew appreciably. His time in Rome was saddened by the news from home that his father had died in April. Family and friends urged him not to change his plans and return early, and Sumner probably mourned only briefly for a rigid man with whom he had never been intimate. He nevertheless consoled his mother and maintained close ties with his family. In the fall he wrote to his mother of his hopes that brother Horace could be educated on the continent at schools he had seen in Geneva and Leipzig. With his father's death he felt an increased responsibility for his young brother's well-being.

Meanwhile, Sumner moved from the art and literature of Rome, Milan, Venice, Florence, and Vienna to the law of Munich, Berlin, and Heidelberg. Keeping his promise to Lieber, he studied with his usual zeal and thrived for five weeks in Heidelberg in the presence of the scholar and professor of law at the University, Karl Mittermaier, with whom he discussed legal reform. A life-long correspondence would follow with a man whom he regarded as one of the world's greatest living jurists.

While in Paris earlier in 1839, Sumner tried his hand briefly at personal diplomacy in behalf of his country. Learning that Lewis Cass was concerned about the danger of war between the United States and Great Britain over the Maine–New Brunswick boundary, Sumner shared with him that few in Britain knew or cared much about the issue. The boundary question, which had been left unresolved in the Treaty of Paris of 1783, was being agitated through bellicose statements by the governor of Maine and English journalists. As Sumner assured Boston Congressman Richard Fletcher, British officials displayed "indifference to and ignorance" of the issue. At Cass's request, Sumner wrote a scholarly study of the controversy for publication and circulation in England.

The young Bostonian's research of the boundary issue revealed a close understanding of English culture and history. It also showed that despite his respect for the law, he was intensely patriotic and loyal to the self-interest of his native New England. He thus concluded that his country was right and deserved "full *title* to the full territory." Yet he was careful not to make a blustery demand for the whole region, which could only increase tensions, for the goal must be peace at all costs.

He reminded Fletcher "that the hazards of war are not to be encountered even for some paltry acres of land." Fearing the warlike speeches even then being made in Maine, Congress, and Parliament respectively, he concluded: "I would rather give up the whole state of Maine and of Massachusetts to boot, than to go to war." To Morpeth he admitted that although "my own heart is so bound up in England," he supported his own country as "a first love," and he urged his friend to work for reason and peace among the English.

Sumner's awareness of the suffering resulting from the centuries of wars in Europe spurred his growing interest in pacifism. Still mindful of the influences of Lieber and Boston reformers like Channing, he concluded that war was "unjust and un-Christian." Still, both he and Cass were pleased with his article and the young traveler sought personally to persuade those Englishmen he met in France of the virtue of the U.S. claims. Not surprisingly, his private diplomacy brought no tangible results, and the issue remained unresolved for several more years.

As the time to leave for home approached and Sumner bade his final farewells to friends in England, he reflected "on the uncertainties to which I return," on what lay ahead in Boston. Throughout his European travels he had revealed his continuing dependence on his Boston friends with a voluminous and time-consuming correspondence. Nothing had been more welcome than their responses, which he had read and reread even as he traveled. Although the Five of Clubs had met occasionally during Sumner's long absence, all but he and Longfellow would be married or engaged before his return. Longfellow wrote of the imminent weddings of Felton and Cleveland and of his own love for Frances Appleton. Although the poet assured him that the group would be as close as ever, Sumner knew better and mourned that his friends would have less time for him on his return. But the uncertainties in his mind related as much to his career as they did to his companions. Although professing to Longfellow that he was content with his decision to travel, he was not ready to face again "long days filled with uninteresting toil and humble gains." Although he concluded that he knew his profession better than he had before and that "I can live content at home," the transition would indeed by a difficult one.

Sumner's life had been dramatically changed by his time abroad. He had fulfilled his boyhood dream, especially as he had found his and his country's roots in England. In some ways he had completed his education. He had matured yet was now more idealistic than ever. The direction in which these discoveries would take him remained unclear. The practice of law still held little attraction, and the role he would play in Boston society remained vague. He worried over how easily he could return to his former habits and lifestyle and whether the old patterns would still be desirable. He had been lionized in Europe and would find it difficult to return to the more marginal role he played in Boston. The next years would prove to be a time of profound transition, as Sumner moved from a conservative Boston attorney to a visionary reformer who demanded the end of war and slavery.

CHAPTER TWO

The Greatest Crime a Nation Can Commit

The 1840s were a time of changing priorities for Charles Sumner as he committed himself to reform and politics. His education complete, he was now finally ready to act on beliefs that had emerged only slowly. Plunging first into education and prison reform, he gained major attention with an attack on war and more spectacularly with a total involvement in the antislavery cause. Joining the Free Soil movement, he skillfully used the third party as a vehicle to political office. In 1851, he thus acquired the means to attempt to force government to face what had become his first priority—the end of slavery and the legislating of equal justice.

During his first months home from Europe, little happened to suggest that Sumner would soon change from a conservative attorney to a reformer and a politician. Arriving in Boston in time for the exciting presidential campaign of 1840, he found little to choose from between the hated Jacksonian, Martin Van Buren, and the military hero, William Henry Harrison. Like most Boston Whigs, Sumner would have preferred Daniel Webster to Harrison. His indifference also stemmed from his own Whig party's having stooped to the "vulgar appeal" of picturing Harrison as the candidate of the average

American, "the log-cabin and hard-cider representative." Of more immediate concern, Sumner struggled to resume his former lifestyle.

Sumner arrived home in March, but did not accept the daily routine of his office for six months. Greenleaf had predicted that Sumner would have little difficulty in resuming his "place in the profession," but advised him of the need to return to the "habits of business" as if he had never left New England. By fall, Sumner could finally boast to Lieber that he was at his desk by nine and that he had never been "more punctual and faithful," often working after dinner until midnight. He could not hide his discontent, however, for while he faithfully put in his time, it was anything but rewarding. "Overhauling papers, old letters and sifting accounts" left him longing "for a canto of Dante, a rhapsody of Homer, a play of Schiller." After a year's effort, he sadly concluded, "it has been the least productive year of my life." Still, he was determined to live up to others' expectations.

Sumner's difficult readjustment to life in Boston was intensified by personal problems. Although male companions were still numerous, he found relationships with women difficult. Among his new acquaintances were several European visitors whom he had met abroad, including Lord Morpeth and Charles Dickens, and he proudly introduced them to fellow Bostonians. The Five of Clubs gathered regularly, but with only he and Longfellow still single, Sumner feared a lonely future without a wife. His uneasiness became more pronounced as his closest male friends were married, and his fears of never finding a mate increased. Most especially did he fear rejection by the kind of woman that he felt a person of his social station should marry.

Sumner's friends did their best to assure him that nothing would change in their relationships with him, and they even tried to help him find the right woman with whom to share his life. Longfellow, for one, introduced him to several eligible young women and consoled him when nothing developed.

Sumner was unable to do more than mourn his lack of a wife and complain to Longfellow of his inability to "find somebody to love." For a time he courted Louisa Ward, whose sister Julia was soon to marry his friend Samuel Gridley Howe, but this relationship too came to little more than frustration. His expectations appeared too great and his lifestyle too rigid to make room for another, yet he grew increasingly unhappy. He revealed to Longfellow a short piece entitled "Misery of a Bachelor's Life," which mirrored his own plight: "Poor fellow! he returns to his lodging—I will not say to his 'home.'. . . All is dreary and repelling. No gentle face welcomes his arrival— no gentle hands meet his—no kind looks answer the listless gaze he throws around the apartment. . . ." Sumner seemed unable at first to reconcile himself to his situation. The passing of time and other interests would eventually ease his despondency, and gradually references to his lack of a wife disappeared in correspondence with his friends. Yet he never fully reconciled himself to bachelorhood.

New male friendships also helped temper his self-pity. Howe joined the Five of Clubs with the death of Cleveland in 1843 and in time became, next to Longfellow, Sumner's most trusted friend. Although Howe was ten years older than Sumner, the two shared much in common. A physician who had worked extensively with the blind and deaf, Howe was superintendent of the Perkins Institution for the Blind and became increasingly involved in prison and education reform, pacifism, and eventually the antislavery movement. The two men remained intellectually and spiritually close until late in their lives as they fought together against what they saw as the ills of society.

In part, Sumner's closeness to Howe filled the void left by the gradual drift away from dependence on the aging Story. Although his veneration for the Justice remained steady, the latter's declining health and vigor as well as increasingly conservative outlook moved Sumner into other circles. Sumner disagreed at least in part with Story's defense of a vested monopoly in the *Charles River Bridge* case (1837) and his opposition to state personal liberty laws protecting fugitive slaves in *Prigg* v. *Pennsylvania* (1842). More than the Bridge case, in which he praised the judge's legal reasoning:—"You have made a skeptic even if you have not gained a convert"—Sumner struggled with *Prigg*, privately blaming Congress for its failure to repeal the Fugitive Slave Act of 1793. Yet Story had agreed with the Court in finding the 1793 statute constitutional, and Pennsylvania's efforts to block enforcement unconstitutional. While Sumner expected a proslavery stance from Congress, he felt let down by Story's failure to come to the aid of fugitive slaves.

Friends like Howe were by then reinforcing Sumner's move to a more liberal interpretation of the Constitution in regard to slavery. Story's death in 1845 would later remove another restraint on Sumner's growing interest in the antislavery movement. Always eager to please his mentor, he hesitated to plunge into reform while the Justice still lived. At the same time, the affirming relationships with younger reformers like Howe added another powerful motive for activism. Still, to the Justice's last day, Sumner remained respectful of Story and grateful for his constant friendship and support.

In 1842, Sumner was saddened by the death of Channing, who had been so important in pointing him toward reform, particularly with regard to war and slavery. The Unitarian leader and Sumner had become close associates, especially after the latter's return from Europe. Sumner explained that "I have enjoyed his confidence in no common way," and he had assisted Channing in preparing his last treatises relating to slavery. The passing of these friends of an older generation added to Sumner's depression, as did the death of his sister Mary from tuberculosis in late 1844. Other than his brother George, Sumner had felt more affection and closeness for Mary than for any sibling. Only with them was he ever able to relate philosophically and to share his growing concern for society's ills. He had gloried in Mary's earlier successes and had on occasion escorted her in society. Her gradual decline left him devastated. As he made arrangements for her funeral, Sumner mourned that hers was "a rare blending of dignity and modesty." More important was her "character which shone transparent" and ruled "all thoughts and acts."

Mary's decline had corresponded with Sumner's serious illness during the summer of 1844 that symbolized his own depression. In late 1843, Howe had urged him to abandon "that morbid and unnatural state of mind which made you careless of whether you should live or die." Longfellow wrote words of encouragement to look to the future and "not mournfully into the Past." But Sumner's problems multiplied instead of diminishing. His boredom with his law practice inevitably added to his declining case load and created financial pressure. His lack of female companionship was a continuing frustration. Inevitably, his depressed state had made him a target for a breakdown in health.

For a time Sumner had poured himself into his work, especially in the editing of the twenty volumes of Francis Vesey's chancery reports, but rather than bringing contentment, the long hours of work, neglecting sleep and exercise, only intensified his weakness and despondency. Coughs and headaches were followed by fever and eventually total prostration, as doctors and friends despaired of his recovery. Whether it was tuberculosis, depression, or, as Sumner described it, "a slow nervous fever brought on by sitting and studying at my desk" until early morning, was not clear. The crisis had passed by the end of July, but it would be November before he was fully able to resume his work.

As Sumner recuperated during the late summer and fall under the watchful eyes of friends like Hillard, he faced the crisis of Mary's death in October. His painfully slow recovery brought with it a firm resolve to put his many problems behind him and follow the advice of Howe and Longfellow to look to the future. His escape from death seemed to be a turning point, as he now threw himself into interests in reform that he had long nurtured but had previously failed to act upon. With that decision, he began a gradual withdrawal from the practice of law and in its place looked to a future based on other concerns. He also appeared ready for the first time to give up any pretense of becoming a permanent part of the Whig elite that previously he had sought so valiantly to join. So sure did he become of the righteousness of the causes he took up that rarely if ever did he question the new direction his life was about to take.

The issue that first involved Sumner in reform was public education, a cause that he was led to by Howe in 1844. His friend introduced him to Horace Mann, secretary of the Massachusetts Board of Education, who was then in the midst of controversy with Boston's established educational leaders. For someone of Sumner's conservative background and private-school training to become interested in such a quarrel with his elders appeared unusual at first glance. Yet as he increasingly associated with young reformers like Howe and Mann, his determination to challenge the establishment in behalf of liberal causes became the rule.

In his annual report of 1844, Mann attacked the declining condition of the state's schools, which were increasingly in a dilapidated and unsanitary condition and staffed by under-trained and underpaid teachers. This in a state where the wealthy preferred to give their support to private schools. Desirous of introducing progressive reforms similar to those he had studied in Europe, Mann was opposed not only by the wealthy but also by religious leaders who feared the secular tendencies of the secretary. It was Howe who spearheaded the efforts to secure the election of Mann's supporters to the Boston School Committee in late 1844 in order to facilitate reform. Sumner agreed to be a candidate for the committee, and, although defeated, devoted himself even further to Mann's efforts by leading a drive to help fund construction of schools for teacher training.

If education was the question that launched Sumner's career as a reformer, it was the penal reform issue that first established his reputation in Boston and revealed the combative style that would characterize all of his subsequent efforts. Again, it was Howe who aroused Sumner's interest in the controversy, and the two united to wage an unremitting campaign against the efforts of conservative Bostonians for the next several years. Their methods of challenging the elite Whig establishment that controlled the city would label them as discontented radicals who failed to understand their subordinate roles. In the process, Sumner and Howe forged a seemingly unbreakable bond, with their public and private lives intersecting to create powerful motives for activism. Sumner's personal crisis that had helped launch his new career direction was about to produce its first tangible results.

Howe's concern had been raised when he discovered that the mentally ill were treated as hardened criminals, with whom they were frequently housed. For Sumner the penal reform question recalled numerous conversations he had had with European reformers during his time abroad. Closely related was the controversy over how best to house prisoners in Boston jails. As plans for a new prison developed, two conflicting approaches were considered—the separate, or Pennsylvania, system in which inmates lived and worked apart from each other, and the congregate, or Auburn, system in which they were housed together. Sumner and Howe were fully committed to the separate system, having been influenced by European reformers including Lieber and Tocqueville. The less-expensive congregate system appealed to the more practical element led by Louis Dwight, who was secretary of and long the dominant figure in the Boston Prison Discipline Society. Dwight presided at the Society's annual meetings, which had routinely endorsed his philosophy and specific proposals.

The stormy events of the Society's meeting of May 27, 1845, at the Park Street Church would thus come as an unpleasant surprise to Dwight and the rest of the conservative leadership.

As the secretary explained why the congregate system fit Boston's needs and attacked the impracticality of the opposing plan, Sumner rose in protest. In challenging Dwight's views, he demanded further study before a decision was made. Flustered by the young upstart's first public speech, Dwight agreed to permit a select committee, that included both Sumner and Howe, to visit several prisons in order to report on the efficacy of both methods. Sumner thus believed that he had successfully answered Dwight's attacks on the separate system.

Before the committee completed its report in 1846, Sumner had become much better known in Boston due to his speech attacking militarism and war on July 4, 1845. He was now regarded by Dwight and others as an outspoken rebel who knew no restraint. The prison issue had become for Sumner both a worthy cause and a symbol of his challenge to the leaders of Boston. The committee, controlled by Dwight's friends, issued its report endorsing the congregate system, while Howe's minority report found the separate system superior. Fearing that their views would not be published by the Society, Sumner wrote an article for the *Christian Examiner*, explaining the merits of the Pennsylvania plan. He noted that "the absolute separation of prisoners, so that they can neither see, hear nor touch each other is the pole-star of Prison Discipline," for under it the prisoner is "removed from all bad influences." From Lieber and Tocqueville he requested more backing and information on how the system worked in Europe.

The dispute raged through 1846 and 1847 and ended with Sumner and Howe forced to admit defeat. In the process, Sumner engaged in angry exchanges in public and in correspondence with Dwight and other Society officials. His hour-long speech at the Society's 1846 meeting arraigned Dwight and his methods. He complained that both the secretary and Treasurer Samuel A. Eliot considered "the Society as their own" and treated his protests as "an interruption." He then arranged to have an article by a German penal authority defending the separate system and attacking Dwight published in the *Law Reporter*. Even when his old law school professor Greenleaf suggested that "the subject of Prison Discipline [was] not quite in place in a Law Journal" and questioned the personal bitterness to which Sumner was carrying the feud, the young reformer was unrelenting.

The meetings of May 1847 lasted for eight evenings, with Sumner dominating the efforts to win endorsement of the separate system, incorporating the arguments of European reformers in the process, and accusing the Society of suppressing all reference to opinions it opposed. In attacking Eliot, he adopted the combative style he would later perfect, claiming he would borrow something of the treasurer's "frankness without his temper." In personalizing the issue, Sumner was displaying a personality trait that would characterize him for life; rarely would he be able to address an issue without attacking those opposed to his views. By the time of his attack on Eliot, Sumner was also involved in further conflict with conservatives who controlled the Whig party. Rebuffed in his challenge to the established leaders of the Prison Discipline Society, he had entered the fray on the more sweeping issues of war and slavery. But the prison reform movement had helped establish him as a force to be reckoned with, someone that the establishment would come to fear and loath.

Even before the prison issue climaxed, Sumner's reform interests had helped alleviate his depression over personal and professional matters. Earlier he had told Howe, "Your friendship is a chief solace of a melancholy life," but as early as 1845 his new involvements had totally changed his outlook. The event that more than any other gave his life new direction was the Fourth of July oration that he delivered in Boston in 1845. The occasion was a major city celebration held annually to bring townspeople together to relive the glories of the American Revolution. Frequently the mayor and city council invited a young and promising community figure to deliver the oration, thus the invitation to Sumner, who was just beginning to emerge in legal and Whig circles.

His announced topic, "International Peace," appeared quite fitting for the occasion and much in keeping with his interests. A supporter of Lieber's pacifism and a member of the executive committee of the Massachusetts Peace Society, Sumner had long been concerned over the horrors of war. He had been influenced by the many examples of militarism he had seen in European countries, with their large standing armies, and his knowledge of their history of recurring wars over what he considered to be trivial causes. To his brother George, he had lamented that "trial by battle" too frequently was the method of nations in settling disputes." Although hopeful that "the age of war among civilized nations has passed," he feared for the future. As mentioned, he had long been impressed by the views of Channing, an outspoken critic of the War of 1812 and a founding member of the Massachusetts Peace Society. Now, with the United States having recently annexed Texas, on the verge of war with Mexico in the Southwest, and taking an equally aggressive stand toward Great Britain over Oregon in the Northwest, Sumner recoiled against what he regarded as the dangerously bellicose attitude of the national government. It was unlikely that city officials were aware of his views, and neither they nor many in the audience were prepared for his message.

As he rose to deliver his address he presented an engaging appearance to his two thousand listeners. No longer the awkward, clumsy, and retiring youth, nor the overly slender college student, at thirty-four his features had filled out in manly attractiveness, and his long dark hair highlighted a friendly and handsome face. His audience appeared ready to adopt him as its own as he spoke in deep and resonant tones. Yet his words would please only a few, for he began by attacking the aggressive foreign policies then being pursued by the administration of Democratic president James K. Polk, policies that were generally endorsed by Whigs as well. He spared neither northern nor southern expansionist interests in his rejection of U.S. actions toward Mexico and Great Britain:

> On the one side, by an act of unjust legislation extending our power over Texas, we have endangered Peace with Mexico while on the other, by the presumptuous assertion of a disputed claim to a worthless territory beyond the Rocky Mountains, we have kindled anew, on the hearth of our Mother Country, the smothered fires of hostile strife. . . . Who believes that the *National Honor* will be promoted by a war with Mexico or a war with England? What just man would sacrifice a single human life to bring under our rule both Texas and Oregon?

Sumner continued by introducing his major theme, one rarely stated with such force or in such a setting: "IN OUR AGE THERE CAN BE NO PEACE THAT IS NOT HONORABLE; THERE CAN BE NO WAR THAT IS NOT DISHONORABLE." In outlining the fearful and inevitable outcome of war, which in the case of a conflict with Great Britain meant the end of all commerce and "social and business intercourse," he observed that war rarely accomplished its objectives. Nor did its sanction by the Christian church prove its wisdom. Historically, said Sumner, the church had distorted the message of Jesus and had "failed to discern the peculiar spiritual beauty of the faith which it professed. Like Constantine, it found new incentives to war in the religion of Peace, and such has been its character even to our own day."

Even more dangerous to a nation than a religious rationale for war, said Sumner, was the false patriotism that proclaimed "our country, be she right or wrong." In its place he called for a truer patriotism, one which transcended narrow self-worship, one which was "inspired by a loftier justice. . . . The pride, vanity, ambition, brutality, even which all rebuke in individuals" must not be "accounted virtues when displayed in the name of a country."

The young orator got his greatest reaction from the assembled throng when he compared the cost of war and of maintaining armaments in time of peace with domestic expenditures. His most telling point contrasted the cost of supporting the battleship *Ohio*, then at anchor in Boston Harbor, with the expenses of Harvard University: "For the annual sum lavished on a single ship of the line, four institutions like Harvard University might be sustained throughout the country!" Sumner followed with other comparisons of military and domestic expenses, all designed to show the folly of "the present incongruous system of *armed peace.*" He arraigned the Polk administration for devoting so few dollars to suppressing the slave trade and so many to building a navy that had become part of a "war establishment." Nor did Sumner confine his attack to the navy, but included the militia and standing army, which drained the nation's "best life-blood, the unbought energies of the youth." Rather than "the preservers of peace," the government had transformed its people into "the provokers of war."

Implicit in Sumner's attack on the nation's military establishment was his growing resistance to the annexation of the former Mexican province of Texas. Americans from southern states had brought their slaves there in the years both before and after Texas won its independence in 1836. Because Mexico threatened war if the United States annexed the region, as expansionists demanded, a military confrontation had become increasingly likely. The young orator thus effectively combined his opposition to the expansion of slavery with his loathing of war.

Politicians committed to expansion and army and naval officials in full uniform, men dependent on the military establishment for a livelihood, listened with increasing disbelief and hostility as Sumner finally neared the end of his three-hour oration. As if to answer their question of why a speech honoring independence should emphasize the evils of war, it was, he said, "because war is utterly and irreconcilably inconsistent with True Greatness." True Greatness was not measured by "the extent of territory or vastness of population or accumulations of wealth; not in fortification, or armies or navies . . . *The true Grandeur of Humanity is in moral elevation, sustained, enlightened, and decorated by the intellect of man.*" Having offered little original in ideas or solutions and guilty of an overly pedantic style, Sumner had raised issues that politicians and the military preferred not to consider. He had effectively provoked the leaders of Boston in a manner unprecedented and in a totally unexpected setting. From a little-known attorney, Sumner had become almost overnight a celebrity to peace activists and a force to be feared and shunned by the established leaders.

Reaction was swift and decisive. Many of Sumner's close friends rose in support to thank him for his message. Howe told him that he had "done a noble work" but warned that "ridicule and sarcasm" would follow. Abolitionist Lydia Maria Child praised his "eloquent attack upon the absurd barbarism of war" and suggested that even if he did nothing more "it was worth living for to have done that." The intellectual and reform community, already alert to the danger of a war against Mexico that might well expand slavery in the Southwest, rushed to Sumner's defense. James Russell Lowell, Wendell Phillips, Theodore Parker, and William Lloyd Garrison were unqualified in their support, with Phillips, a former Harvard classmate, noting "how far ahead you had strode of the CS of '32 and '33." He also thanked Sumner for "having at last redeemed our city oration from being as usual a farce."

Not surprisingly, some of Sumner's colleagues rejected the implications of at least a portion of his argument. The ailing Story spoke for many older friends in expressing his dissent "from the length and breadth of your doctrine." To Story, war under some circumstances was "not only justified but an indispensable part of public duty." Eliot, the Prison Discipline Society officer and former mayor of Boston, criticized Sumner for using a setting at which military officials were invited guests to censure as "uncivil, their profession." Several of Sumner's peers, including Mann and Felton, also registered their concerns. Mann suggested that if efforts for peace prove unavailing "then I cannot refrain from saying, *Fight!*" Felton congratulated him on having had his say, but cautioned that now it was time to return to "some literary, legal or historical subject and not to say one word on war." Sumner, said Felton, must avoid identifying himself with such extremists as Garrison and other "peace men," for they were "weaklings" and "one-idead [*sic*] enthusiasts," association with whom could only damage his future.

While the speech may not have hurt Sumner's career, it did, in fact, permanently change his career's direction. Had Story's death occurred before the oration rather than just after, the coveted Dane Chair at the Harvard Law School probably would have been offered to Sumner. Now, conservative university trustees refused even to consider him. As he explained to his brother George, "I have so many idiosyncracies of opinion, that I shall be distrusted." Yet Sumner probably would not have accepted had an appointment been tendered. Reform interests were now more consuming to him, and he feared that as a law professor "my opinions will be restrained." Unable to speak his mind, he would no longer be "a free man."

Sumner had no intention of limiting his views and instead engaged in heated exchanges with members of the Whig establishment who took issue with his pacifism. Harvard classmate Congressman Robert Winthrop insisted that defense of the country whether against Mexico or Britain was expected of all. Sumner responded by attacking those who advocated defensive wars and charged that the feud with Mexico could not be called defensive but rather was an issue over "the title of a piece of land." Sumner here referred to the land between the Nueces River and the Rio Grande, which both nations claimed and which would be the immediate issue that provoked war the following year. He argued that "the age has passed for physical force between nations"; he concluded: "the weapons of revolution and of liberty are moral, not physical."

Sumner was equally concerned by the bellicose stand toward Great Britain of elder-statesman John Quincy Adams, who demanded all of Oregon. Long an admirer of the former president because of his defiance of proslavery elements in Congress, Sumner hesitated to question Adams publicly. He was thus relieved when the matter was settled diplomatically in mid-1846 by dividing the Oregon country. But this was not before Sumner had expressed his fear that President Polk and Secretary of State James Buchanan would force the issue. He labeled Polk "a hot-house politician, vulgar, ignorant, wayward," while Buchanan, he claimed, was motivated by "a most pestilent Anglophobia." As the diplomatic settlement appeared imminent he could rejoice that "the war spirit has talked itself hoarse and feeble and the conscience of the nation is awakening."

Sumner did modify his antiwar views somewhat in light of the criticism that followed his speech. Although unable to agree with those like Mann or his friend John G. Palfrey who endorsed defensive wars, Sumner did concede privately that he could not support the complete pacifism of the Quakers. He reluctantly admitted that he believed in "the right of self defense." Rejecting the doctrine of nonresistance, he nonetheless could not conceive of Christ "as a soldier"; furthermore, war was "an unchristian institution." His partial concession was in part the result of Adams's reaction to his oration. The former president had indicated that, although he supported Sumner's "mission," the young man would be forced to modify his "theory of nonresistance" in time. Sumner could not have foreseen in 1846 that fifteen years later he would alter his views even further when he endorsed the concept of the just war in support of a struggle he hoped would destroy slavery. Instead, at this point, his concern was increasingly over a war against Mexico, which he believed was designed to seize territory into which to expand slavery.

With the slavery issue in mind, Sumner had begun working with those opposed to the annexation of Texas even before he delivered his antiwar oration. Concern for the plight of blacks had long been a priority for him, in part influenced by his father's sympathy for fugitive slaves who occasionally had appeared in Boston. He had witnessed slavery and the domestic slave trade in Washington when he visited Story in 1834 and had been shocked by the aggressive defense Southerners in Congress were quick to mount in behalf of their way of life. His travels in Europe had revealed to him a deep-seated antagonism of many against his country because it sanctioned the enslavement of millions of blacks. He had thrilled at John Quincy Adams's defiance of the defenders of slavery in the House of Representatives, as the congressman had waged a seven-year campaign climaxing in 1843 in the repeal of their gag on antislavery petitions.

Sumner's concern extended to discrimination in Massachusetts, and in late 1845 he turned down an invitation to speak to the New Bedford Lyceum because it admitted blacks only on a segregated basis. He explained to the Lyceum's leaders that he could not "sanction what is most alien to my soul" because the separation of the races defied his belief that "the children of the earth are all of one blood." Yet such feelings and actions had not required a public stance or cooperation with others of a similar perspective. Hence when the Texas question reached Congress, Sumner's views finally surfaced in the movement to contain slavery.

Although Mexico refused to recognize the independence Texas had won on the battlefield in 1836, the region had been an autonomous republic for the next nine years. The issue climaxed in 1844 when the Senate turned down a Texas annexation treaty, and presidential candidates Henry Clay and James K. Polk took opposing positions on annexation during the fall campaign. With the expansionist Democrat Polk winning a narrow victory, lame-duck president John Tyler made a final effort to annex the slave territory before leaving office in March 1845. When he urged Congress to approve a joint resolution of annexation, Northerners led by the Whigs resisted the effort. In Massachusetts, virtually all Whigs agreed in their opposition, and in January 1845, many joined with abolitionists in an anti-Texas rally in Boston's Faneuil Hall.

The meeting was dominated by a group of young Whigs led by Charles Francis Adams, son of the former president, who assumed leadership of a committee to pursue the struggle. Here Sumner had his first close contact with such men as Adams and future congressmen Palfrey, and Henry Wilson. Adams had engineered strong anti-Texas resolutions through the state legislature, and when Congress approved the joint resolution in March, the Young Whigs vowed to continue the fight. Texas had been annexed but not yet admitted to statehood; thus they continued to agitate through the remainder of 1845. In insisting on extending the fight even after Texas had gained statehood in December, they clashed for the first time with more conservative Whigs like Webster, who now argued that since the issue had been settled it should be laid to rest. The occasion for an intraparty schism was the approaching war with Mexico, which annexation of Texas had precipitated.

The developing split among Massachusetts Whigs, which was to bring Sumner to the forefront as an antislavery advocate, highlighted the turmoil that the slavery issue was creating within the national party structure. The new two-party system, which had formed in the 1820s and 1830s and had originally divided Jacksonian Democrats and their opponents over economic issues, had since shifted its emphasis to sectional questions. Especially divisive was the constitutional issue of the expansion of slavery. Southern Democrats argued that the federal government must sanction the spread of slavery into any territory acquired, while Whigs, especially those in the free states, countered that slavery could be kept out of new territories without violating the Constitution's protection of the institution. Both parties, with constituencies in the North and the South, were dependent on sectional harmony. Neither wished to be dominated either by its pro- or antislavery elements, for fear of losing the opposing faction. But the Texas question, followed by subsequent territorial issues in which the expansion of slavery was at stake, brought strains to both parties. As moderate elements of both parties labored to keep unity by remaining evasive on slavery-related issues, antislavery Democrats and Whigs began to break away from their respective bases. The Texas issue precipitated the process, and Massachusetts Whigs were the first to act. Charles Sumner would gradually emerge as the leader of Bay State antislavery Whigs who would seek to persuade party leaders of the justness of their position and, when that failed, lead fellow rebels into a third-party movement.

Just prior to Texas statehood, the anti-Texas committee had been reorganized to include Adams, Sumner, and Palfrey, as well as abolitionists Garrison and Phillips. Their coalition was cemented at a November 1845 rally, which Sumner had taken the lead in planning and for which he had helped write successfully ratified resolutions. He reminded the audience that the proposal to annex Texas had "begun in stealth and fraud, in order to expand and strengthen slavery." It was the Young Whig association with abolitionists that led established party leaders to denounce the alliance as cooperation with "dangerous radicals."

In fact, there were serious differences between the Young Whigs and the Garrisonians. In an exchange with Phillips earlier in 1845, Sumner had urged him to abandon his refusal to vote and in other ways participate in politics. To those who declined to be a part of what they regarded as an unjust and corrupt system, Sumner responded that if government sanctioned war he as a citizen must answer "by speech, by the pen, by *my vote*" to prevent such "immoralities." Phillips remained unconvinced, however, countering that he would continue to speak out against government but would not sanction the politician by voting. It was this antigovernment view of the abolitionists that the established Whig leaders seized on. Led by Congressman Winthrop and industrialists Abbot Lawrence and Nathan Appleton, the conservatives firmly controlled

Whig party machinery. Allied with cotton planters of the South, these textile manufacturers and their representatives were determined to do nothing to upset their southern friends and jeopardize their economic and political alliance. Thus when pressed to sign the anti-Texas petition being sent to Congress, they justified their refusal by claiming the danger of cooperation with abolitionists.

Sumner's differences with Winthrop accelerated as the danger of wars with Mexico and England intensified in early 1846. Having clashed with the representative over his Fourth of July oration, Sumner now questioned Winthrop's speech in Congress, which suggested that war with Britain would unite all Americans: "The *people* of this country," said Sumner, "will *not* sustain the Govt in an unjust war," for "the age has come in which Govt can claim allegiance only by keeping itself within the right." With that crisis about to be averted by a treaty dividing Oregon, war did break out with Mexico in May. It was Winthrop's vote to support the war declaration that precipitated an open break with Sumner, who now began a series of anonymous letters in the antislavery press attacking the congressman for voting for "*an unjust war, and national falsehood in the cause of slavery.*" Admitting his authorship to Winthrop and claiming "the War Bill was the wickedest in our history," Sumner again personalized their differences. He also insensitively professed disbelief that anything he had written should jeopardize their friendship.

The exchange became more bitter with Winthrop's arrogant charge that Sumner's attacks had robbed him of his "spotless reputation." Sumner responded that a congressman's conduct was "public property" and that he was thus justified in calling attention to it: "Blood! blood! is on the hands of the representative from Boston. Not all Neptune's ocean can wash them clean." When Sumner pursued his attack with another bitter letter, Winthrop charged that it was filled with "the grossest perversions" and exhibited a "fanatical and frantic spirit." Winthrop was thus compelled "to decline all further communications or conferences." Many of the socially elite of Boston followed Winthrop's lead and closed their doors to Sumner, including former Harvard professor George Ticknor, who explained that "he is outside the pale of society."

The dispute with Winthrop also provoked bitterness between Sumner and Appleton. When Sumner charged that the congressman's vote for the war was "*the worst act that was ever done by a Boston representative,*" Appleton responded in kind. To which the Young Whig replied that because "an *unjust war* is the greatest *crime* a nation can commit," Winthrop had abandoned his duty. He concluded his personal attacks in an open letter to Winthrop charging that he had made the people of Boston parties to an unjust and "cowardly" war in behalf of slavery.

In the course of these exchanges Sumner assumed much of the leadership of the "Conscience Whigs," as the Young Whigs now called themselves, in their challenge to the "Cotton Whigs." The names Cotton and Conscience fittingly represented Sumner's commitment. They symbolized the alliance of the textile interests with southern cotton planters on the one hand, versus those, like Sumner, who viewed the extension of slavery as an immoral act. In this new role Sumner again revealed a style of attack characterized by an emotional, often insensitive, and bitter personal abuse of his opponents, many of whom were among the most respected and estimable of society. The stronger his belief in the righteousness of a cause, the greater his willingness to be personal and abusive in his attacks on his opponents. He had accelerated the almost inevitable break with a party he believed had irreversibly fallen under proslavery interests.

The Cotton and Conscience factions would remain in a tenuous and turbulent coalition for another eighteen months, as they fought for control of the state Whig organization. At the party convention in late 1846, Sumner and Winthrop spoke respectively for the rival groups. Sumner called his speech "The Anti-Slavery Duties of the Whig Party," reminding his listeners that it was the obligation of all Whigs "to express themselves openly, distinctly and solemnly against slavery— not only against its further extension," but against its very existence. But the Cotton men had the last word when an appeal by Webster for party unity persuaded the delegates to reject the advanced antislavery stance that Sumner had sought.

Despite his leadership of the opposition to Winthrop, the young rebel refused to accept the dubious honor of becoming an independent candidate for Congress. Sumner did not yet see himself an aspirant, nor was he eager to challenge the powerful and respected Winthrop. Instead, he actively campaigned for his friend Howe because Winthrop could not "fitly represent" the views of Bostonians on slavery. Sumner carried his anti–Mexican War efforts into early 1847 with his argument before the state supreme court that Massachusetts troops about to be sent to the battlefront had been recruited illegally. He followed this with a public address labeling the conflict "a slave-driving war."

Sumner stepped up his efforts in behalf of the antislavery crusade with every available opportunity. Having discovered his natural ability to move an audience, the handsome and forceful speaker eagerly accepted invitations that both enhanced his reputation and furthered the movement against slavery and war. He become the foremost Conscience Whig orator at party gatherings and rallies and seized on nonpartisan occasions as well. In the late summer of 1846, he delivered the annual address to the Phi Beta Kappa Society of Harvard, using the opportunity to eulogize four recently fallen Boston leaders, including Story and Channing. Labeling his speech "The Scholar, the Jurist, the Artist, the Philanthropist," Sumner praised Story for a lifetime of judicial leadership in the court and in the classroom, but he saved his greatest accolades for Channing. Devoting himself to "the unanswerable considerations of justice and humanity," Channing, said Sumner, had insisted that northern states must abandon "all support of slavery," because what "is wrong for the individual is wrong for the state." To this Channing had added "his exertions for the abolition of the barbarous custom or institution of war."

Early in 1847, Sumner lectured before the Boston Mercantile Library Association on "White Slavery in the Barbary States." Evading the rule of the group to refrain from discussion of American slavery, he described the enslavement of whites by nations such as Algeria at the turn of the nineteenth century. Noting its milder form than that practiced even currently in America, he concluded that any variety of slavery was "a wrong and a curse." In the course of little more than a year he had come to rival Garrison as Boston's best-known and most controversial antislavery spokesman. He still professed a preference for a life of quiet scholarly pursuits, but his belief in the immorality of war and slavery were driving him to try to awaken the consciences of his fellow Northerners. His immediate goal was to reform the Whig party, or, barring that, to lead a third-party movement dedicated to stopping slavery's spread.

The Conscience Whig rallying point in early 1847 was the continuing congressional debate over the Wilmot Proviso, the proposal to ban slavery in any territory acquired from Mexico. Sumner and his cohorts agreed that support for the Proviso must be the minimum expected from their party and its next candidate for president. They implied that a failure to endorse it would mean their leaving the Whigs and seeking antislavery allies elsewhere among northern Democrats and the small, abolitionist Liberty party. Most Conscience men were in agreement with the constitutional arguments of Ohio Liberty party leader Salmon P. Chase, who believed that although the federal government could not interfere with slavery in those states where it already existed, constitutionally it could prevent its expansion into newly acquired territories. The government, said Chase, must divorce itself from any protection of slavery and preserve the territories as "free soil."

The degree of willingness of the Conscience men to consider separation from their party varied, with Sumner and

Adams in advance of many who hesitated to give up established places in the party of their fathers. Neither had appreciable influence in the Whig organization or much hope for position, given their attacks on leading Cotton men during 1846. Yet both still hoped to gain party control and realized that the fall meetings and election would be critical if they were to influence the presidential contest the following year. As 1847 unfolded they heard conflicting advice from their associates in Massachusetts and other key northern states.

Among Sumner's correspondents were two prominent Ohioans of different opinions. Chase, who had gained fame in his unsuccessful legal defense of fugitive slaves in Cincinnati, favored a new, broad-based antislavery organization that could unite Northerners of all parties. He agreed with Sumner's call for "one grand Northern party of Freedom," but felt that it would have to be an organization in which antislavery Democrats as well as Liberty men were as welcome as Whigs. In contrast, Whig Congressman Joshua Giddings from the strongly antislavery Western Reserve remained optimistic that his party could be brought to a Wilmot Proviso stance. A close ally of John Quincy Adams in the struggle against the Gag Rule, Giddings was suspicious of southern Whigs because of their support of Texas annexation. Yet he remained convinced that his party would not nominate a slaveholder for president. Sumner and Giddings corresponded weekly as the situation remained in transition.

Most discouraging to antislavery leaders was the swelling movement among Whigs to nominate Mexican War general Zachary Taylor for president. Even more upsetting to them than his military record was his ownership of slaves on his Louisiana plantation. The appeal of a heroic military leader would be difficult to overcome in the Conscience Whig drive to secure a Wilmot Proviso candidate. Thus, when Whig Senator Thomas Corwin of Ohio delivered a strong attack on the war in February 1847, northern Whigs hoped that they had found a viable alternative to Taylor. Sumner and Giddings

wrote excitedly of Corwin's attack on Polk's war policies, a reaction shared by Sumner's Massachusetts Conscience colleagues. Yet Giddings cautioned Sumner that more must be
known of the Senator's views on slavery "before we make a
move." The two men and Chase were also eager to explore
the candidacy of the politically ambitious Supreme Court Justice John McLean of Ohio.

Before pursuing the internal struggle for control of the
Massachusetts state party, Sumner received discouraging news
from Corwin. The senator had failed to follow up his antiwar
speech and had shown signs of giving in to Whig pressure to
soften his criticism. Sumner had written to him seeking his
thoughts on refusing to support the party should it nominate
a slaveholder for president. Assuming a Taylor nomination,
he asked Corwin if he "would be willing to be our leader."
Corwin's response evaded that query but did make it clear
that his primary goal was Whig unity. For him, party regulari-
ty came before the Wilmot Proviso. Sumner could not hide
his disappointment from Giddings and Chase, for he had
looked to Corwin as "a probable leader"; but his "shrinking
from the Wilmot Proviso" meant that they must look elsewhere.

Not deterred by Corwin's defection, the Conscience men
of Massachusetts set out in September for the state party convention at Worcester determined to make one last try to win
an endorsement of their views. But as in the previous year,
they met frustration. They hoped to block an endorsement
of a Webster presidential candidacy, but instead the party resolutions applauded Webster's leadership despite his failure
to endorse the Proviso. In his address to the convention Sumner charged that "with every new extension of slavery fresh
strength" is given to "the Slave Power." Massachusetts Whigs,
he urged, must "never yield support to any candidate" not opposed to slave extension. When the delegates rejected a
Wilmot Proviso plank, Sumner doubted whether Conscience
Whigs would ever "enter another convention of the party." By

year's end, the stage had been set for the formation of a new antislavery organization.

Should the Conscience men of Massachusetts move toward a third party they knew that they would not be alone. The Liberty party had already nominated Senator John P. Hale of New Hampshire for president, but many members appeared eager to become part of a larger movement if Whigs and Democrats were willing to bolt their parties and join them. The third party had originally been established in time for the 1840 presidential election and was made up primarily of political abolitionists who believed that neither major party would adopt even a moderate antislavery stance. It had opposed Texas annexation as well as the war against Mexico and insisted that the Wilmot Proviso was the minimum it could now accept as a goal in opposing slavery. Especially was Chase ready to see Hale's name withdrawn as the Liberty candidate if "a convention of all Antislavery men" could be organized for the next spring or summer. In New York, antislavery Democrats were prepared to secede if their party rejected the Proviso. Whigs like Giddings, although cautious, also appeared to be interested in joining a third party if their party refused to nominate a Proviso candidate. Sumner could thus write confidently that "the old parties are crumbling." As the process continued, "the antislavery sentiment will be the basis of a new organization."

Before the events of the spring climaxed in the formation of such an organization, two of Sumner's Whig friends in Congress became further embroiled in controversy with Winthrop and the Cotton Whigs. Withholding their votes from Winthrop for Speaker of the House in December 1847, Giddings and Palfrey almost prevented his election. Their actions brought down the wrath of fellow Whigs and mobilized Sumner. To Palfrey, he expressed his admiration for his "courage, firmness and *conscience.*" In the face of the attacks by the Whig press, "good men cannot fail to sympathize with you." Giddings became further entangled in dispute when he justified his refusal to support Winthrop because the latter had urged

Whig congressmen to vote for the Mexican War bill in May 1846. Sumner advised him on a strategy to defend his charges against Winthrop's denials. Although the dispute ended inconclusively, Sumner had one further reason to abandon hope of change among the Cotton Whigs and their allies.

Sumner found his circle of friends changing as social and business relations ended with conservative Whigs. The Five of Clubs no longer gathered, as the members' interests diverged. Sumner continued to see or correspond with Felton, but less frequently; the professor never hesitated to urge him to forgo "the madness of politics" for the "law and literature." Sumner remained on good terms with his law partner George Hillard despite the latter's conservative political philosophy, but they gradually drifted apart as Sumner became more immersed in antislavery agitation. Howe continued to be close, but his hectic schedule prevented his spending much time with Sumner, except when their reform efforts coincided.

Longfellow remained as supportive as ever, and his happy home, filled with small children, in Cambridge became a frequent refuge for Sumner, providing him with a much-needed change of pace and atmosphere. Although careful to avoid the Longfellow residence when Fanny's father Nathan Appleton was visiting, Sumner found a welcome on most Sundays, often after attending Unitarian services at King's Chapel. Although the Longfellows sympathized with his politics, and Sumner hoped they would support "a cause that can never be forgotten," they had no desire for an active role. Thus when Longfellow had written a series of poems attacking slavery in 1842, Sumner had been overjoyed at his friend's "direct tribute" to antislavery. John Quincy Adams also regularly welcomed Sumner as a guest, and the topic during these visits was inevitably antislavery politics.

As the presidential nominating conventions of the spring and summer of 1848 approached, Sumner found less and less time to devote to his law practice. In fact, he and his Conscience Whig allies used his law office for their many strategy

sessions, which they expected would lead to one last confrontation with the Cotton men before they bolted the party.
There, he, Charles Francis Adams, Wilson, Palfrey, and others
developed the tactics to be used should the Whigs select Taylor as expected.

The Democratic party was, as mentioned, experiencing similar factionalism created by the slavery issue. As with their
Whig counterparts, the Democratic antislavery faction was increasingly insistent on an endorsement of the Wilmot Proviso
as the price for its continued loyalty to the party. Centered in
New York and known as the Barnburners, this group was led
by former president Van Buren. Although slavery-related issues were their primary concern, economic reform and control of their state Democratic organization also factored into
their decision whether or not to secede from their party.
Southern Democrats and their northern allies were naturally
prepared to resist Barnburner demands and insist on a presidential candidate opposed to any congressional restrictions
on slavery. Thus when Democrats nominated Michigan senator Lewis Cass and rejected the Wilmot Proviso, they initiated
a Barnburner walkout. When the Whigs did indeed nominate
Taylor, New York and Ohio antislavery factions held statewide
rallies in Utica and Columbus respectively to plan for a national third-party convention in Buffalo in August.

Before the Conscience Whigs gathered in Worcester on
June 28, their meeting had been thoroughly planned in Sumner's office. Through the correspondence of Sumner and
Adams, it had been carefully coordinated with Ohio and New
York leaders. More than five thousand attended the Worcester
conclave, including Giddings, whose presence Adams and
Sumner had urged. Sumner's address stressed his reasons for
leaving the Whigs, arguing that a "party which renounces its
sentiments must expect to be renounced." The Slave Power,
he said, now dominated, and in choosing Taylor, an "unhal-
lowed union" had been formed "between the cotton-planters
and flesh-mongers of Louisiana and Mississippi and the cot-

ton-spinners and traffickers of New England,—between the lords of the lash and the lords of the loom." Like the Ohio convention, the Worcester meeting made no nominations, preferring to leave that to a national gathering. Although the Barnburners were prepared to insist on Van Buren's candidacy as the price for their participation, Sumner, Adams, Chase, and Giddings optimistically believed that a stronger antislavery advocate would be chosen. The Whig faction of the new party preferred McLean, while Liberty men would seek confirmation of Hale. Thus Sumner and his friends knew that harmony might be elusive.

As the Buffalo convention approached, Sumner and his correspondents continued their search for candidates capable of appealing to the broadest spectrum of northern voters. McLean remained the choice of the Conscience men, but it was clear that he would be unacceptable to the Barnburners. Chase and Sumner sought to persuade the Justice to accept second place behind Van Buren. When that appeared unlikely, Sumner urged former Harvard president Edward Everett to run with Van Buren. Not surprisingly, the conservative Whig declined, expressing his "extreme dislike of third parties." Sumner gradually reconciled himself to a ticket headed by the former president, but Van Buren's previous record on slavery-related issues left much to be desired. Most discouraging was his refusal to endorse abolition in the District of Columbia. But he had opposed Texas annexation in 1844 and now supported the Wilmot Proviso. Thus Sumner left for Buffalo believing that a Van Buren candidacy could appeal to the voters of the free states and give "our movement a national character."

Sumner naively believed that the dramatic convention that launched the Free Soil party was the beginning of a movement that could sweep the North. Following Chase's withdrawal of McLean as a presidential possibility, Van Buren edged out Hale on the first ballot. Then, in a surprise move, the delegates offered the vice-presidential nomination to

Charles Francis Adams. It was an obvious appeal to the Conscience element and partly in memory of Adams's father, who had died earlier in the year. The platform included an enthusiastic endorsement of the Wilmot Proviso, and while not supporting complete abolition, as Liberty men might desire, it contained planks to appeal to virtually all northern interest groups. It concluded with the ringing slogan: "Free Soil, Free Speech, Free Labor, and Free Men."

Sumner campaigned actively and effectively for the new party in both Maine and Massachusetts. His addresses frequently lasted three hours, with his enthusiastic audiences remaining throughout and responding with repeated applause even as the hour approached midnight. In his appeal to Whigs he realized that the chief drawback of the third party was the Van Buren candidacy, for the former Democratic leader had, as president, made his peace with the slave interests only to enhance his own power. To such reminders, Sumner told his listeners that it was not "for the Van Buren of 1838 that we are to vote, but for the Van Buren of *today*," the "champion of Freedom."

Despite their optimism and exhaustive campaigning, the Free Soilers met only limited success and did not affect the outcome of the presidential race. Taylor, remaining silent on the key issues, used his military reputation to sweep to victory. Failing to carry a single state and winning only 10 percent of the national vote, the third party did elect eight members to the House of Representatives. In Massachusetts, the showing of 28 percent of the popular vote was second only to Vermont and enough to displace the Democrats as the second party to the Whigs. Even before the vote, Sumner rationalized to Giddings that the party showing would have been "an overwhelming majority" had McLean rather than Van Buren been the candidate. He argued that the voters had been "stirred on the subject of slavery to depths never before reached." At the same time he told brother George that "the Democratic party is not merely *defeated*. It is entirely broken in pieces," and "cannot organize anew except on the Free Soil platform."

Sumner's break with the Whigs was now complete. If the reaction of Appleton to his speech at the June convention in Worcester was any indication, he had cut off any remaining ties with Whig leaders. The industrialist reacted with disbelief at the charge that a conspiracy between "the lords of the lash and the lords of the loom" had secured Taylor's nomination. When Appleton had demanded proof of such a conspiracy, he and Sumner traded indignant letters through the summer and fall. Sumner responded that his language was plain and that it was clear that there were "secret influences" that had contributed to Taylor's nomination. Appleton had the last word as he haughtily noted his sorrow that "talents so brilliant, as young and promising" had been "thrown away" in Sumner's foolish desertion of the Whig party.

Once committed to the cause of Free Soil rebellion there was no turning back for Sumner and his allies. In late October, Sumner, out of loyalty to his new party, had reluctantly accepted the Free Soil nomination to run against Winthrop for Congress. He harbored no illusions of defeating the Speaker, for, as he explained to Giddings, "we can make no effective head against the over-powering Taylorism" of Boston. To those who charged that he sought personal political glory by challenging Winthrop, he countered that the new party needed candidates to help perfect its organization. Only with an ongoing machinery could it effectively oppose the extension of slavery. Said Sumner: "We are a separate party." If pure in motive in agreeing to oppose Winthrop, Sumner nonetheless enjoyed the martyr's role, quoting John Quincy Adams's admonition that "no man is abused whose influence is not felt."

Although Sumner was badly beaten and his friend Palfrey eventually lost his run-off race for reelection to Congress, other third-party candidates were more successful. Giddings, elected many times as a Whig, now won easily as a Free Soiler in Ohio's Western Reserve. In early 1849, Free Soilers and Democrats in the Ohio legislature combined to elect Chase to the Senate. In Massachusetts, only Charles Allen was elect-

ed as a Free Soiler to the House, although Horace Mann, originally chosen to fill John Quincy Adams's unexpired term,
now was reelected with Whig and Free Soil support.

As a close friend of Mann and as the most prominent antislavery leader of his state, Sumner viewed himself almost as a
surrogate in assuming the role of a watchdog over the congressman's political activities. It was a position that Mann did
not always appreciate. Sumner was especially insistent that his
friend repudiate his Whig ties and identify solely with the new
party. Mann had steadfastly refused to renounce Taylor's candidacy, pleading that his position as the state secretary of education required him to remain politically neutral. Not
surprisingly, Sumner found the excuse unacceptable, for clearly the cause of antislavery must take precedence over his education position. He bombarded Mann relentlessly with
appeals, strongly hinting that he should resign from Congress
if unable to participate in political matters "of such magnitude." The congressman, while steadfast in his resistance to
slavery, refused either to reject the Whigs or to resign. Sumner
would renew his efforts when the new Congress convened in
late 1849, for, in what was now a distinct pattern, his conscience would permit no compromise with antislavery principle, even when it involved a friend. Ever willing to become a
martyr to the cause, he was unable to understand those who
did not share his total commitment.

Another factor in Sumner's maintaining such a careful
watch over Mann's activities was the realization that it would
be difficult to hold the third party together with the national
election over and the desire for political influence pulling
many back to their old organizations. The Barnburners of
New York were the first to yield to these pressures when they
agreed to a reunion with the Democrats with no guarantee of
party support for the Wilmot Proviso. Although Sumner was by
then showing early signs of interest in the kind of alliance with
Democrats that had given Chase a Senate seat in Ohio, he believed that such cooperation could be based only on a firm

commitment to the containment of slavery. The Barnburners' action thus sorely embarrassed him and his Ohio friends.
He noted that the Barnburners "are politicians, and do as
politicians do. I would not—I could not have done what they
have done." Again he stressed the need for a permanent "national party to promote principles of paramount importance
to the country." Any association with a major party was possible
only if antislavery principle were maintained. His commitment
to racial justice had thus taken clear precedent over the party
loyalty he had shown as a young Whig attorney less than a
decade earlier.

By 1849, few could question Sumner's total dedication to
the antislavery cause. As Free Soilers throughout the North
struggled to retain their identity, he was expanding his own
agenda to include the issue of racial justice in Boston. In so
doing he was building on a long tradition that had left his
state and city with fewer restrictions against free blacks than
virtually any other place in the North. Although still barred
from many hotels, restaurants, and theaters, African Americans could intermarry with whites, vote, hold office, testify in
court, and ride on public transportation. Since 1830, Garrison
and other abolitionists had led a relentless attack on the various forms of segregation, overcoming vehement resistance to
change. But despite these successes the schools of Boston remained segregated. In late 1849, Sumner and black attorney
Robert Morris agreed to argue the case of a black printer,
Benjamin Roberts, in behalf of his daughter Sarah who had
been denied entrance into the white elementary school because of her race. Citing the Massachusetts Constitution, Sumner concluded that Sarah Roberts's right to attend the white
school was guaranteed by the principle of "equality before the
law." State statutes had established but "one Public School . . .
equally free to all the inhabitants." To Sumner that meant
that she had a right to attend the school geographically closest
to her rather than being forced to pass five white schools to
reach the all-black school.

Sumner did not stop with common law precedent, but used arguments far in advance of the times. In so doing he effectively employed legal disputation to argue for social change and showed just how far and creatively his thinking had evolved since his law school days. Anticipating the defense's use of the separate but equal doctrine, he claimed that "the separation of children in the schools on account of race" imposed the stigma of "Caste" and was thus "a violation of Equality." In addition, whites themselves "are injured by the separation," for "they are taught to deny . . . the Brotherhood of Mankind." Schools, said Sumner, must "cherish and develop the virtues and the sympathies which are employed in the larger world . . . beginning with those relations of equality" promised to all by the Constitution.

Not surprisingly, Chief Justice Lemuel Shaw, speaking for a unanimous court in April 1850, found Sumner's thesis unconvincing. Sanctioning the separate but equal doctrine, Shaw denied that segregated schools violated the principle of equality of rights. Both the Sumner and Shaw arguments would be expanded in the late nineteenth and twentieth centuries. Sumner's reasoning, in fact, would be adopted in large part in the landmark decision of 1954, *Brown* v. *Board of Education of Topeka,* in which the U.S. Supreme Court ruled that "separate educational facilities are inherently unequal," thus initiating the long and painful process of school desegregation throughout the nation. In presenting his case, Sumner had accelerated his crusade against racial segregation as practiced outside of the slave system. He predicted to his friend Judge William Jay of New York that the legal profession would accept his position "ten years from now." To Jay, Shaw's decision denying black children equality would "foster a cruel prejudice" and was "worthy of the Daniel Webster school." Both men would be pleasantly surprised when just five years later the Massachusetts legislature prohibited the segregation of any public school "on account of the race, color or religious opinions of the applicant or scholar." Sumner had thus assumed a major role in the successful twenty-five-year struggle for civil rights in Boston. In future years he would dramatically expand these efforts, fighting for civil rights on a national level.

As he continued his antislavery efforts, Sumner also kept his antiwar views in the forefront. In so doing he frequently related the two issues, especially tying the war against Mexico to the southern demand for more slave territory. That war was not only an "aggressive" act by the United States, but, even worse, it had "foul slaveholding motives" as a cause. In his eyes, "the Institutions of War and the whole War System is outrageous, unchristian and radically wrong." In May 1849 he delivered an address to the American Peace Society in Boston, advocating a Congress of Nations and arbitration treaties between nations as substitutes for war, insisting that "the disarming of Nations would follow." While his speech attracted less response than his Fourth of July oration four years earlier, it focused more attention on practical solutions to armament and war and showed that his concern was far from a fleeting one.

With the Mexican War over and a vast region added to the United States, the government finally addressed the issue of the status of slavery in the new territories. Congress organized in December 1849, and the small band of Free Soilers made their presence felt, as their numbers prevented either of the major parties from electing a Speaker of the House. By denying Winthrop their votes, they eventually permitted the election of a southern Democrat, Howell Cobb of Georgia, when the House adopted a plurality rule. Again, Giddings, Allen, and the other Free Soilers incurred the wrath of northern Whigs, with Horace Greeley, editor of the *New York Tribune*, labeling their act a stupid betrayal of their own cause. Sumner, however, was more upset with Mann for his support of Winthrop, telling him that he had missed "a remarkable opportunity" to strengthen "public opinion which is now growing

against Slavery." When Mann responded that third-party congressmen could have prevented the choice of Cobb, "one of
the fiercest, sternest, strongest proslavery men in all the South,"
Sumner defended the Free Soilers and lamented: "Would to
God that Horace Mann would take his place among them."

Once organized, Congress devoted much of the next nine
months to consideration of the various parts of Henry Clay's
1850 proposals for sectional compromise. Free Soilers were
most enthusiastic about the bill to admit California as a free
state but especially upset over the fugitive slave bill, which denied accused fugitives a trial by jury and in other ways heavily
weighted the scales in favor of slaveowners. Overall, third-party
members found the Clay package a major setback to their
antislavery principles, including the Wilmot Proviso, but theirs
was a small voice in the face of heavy support in both major
parties for some kind of sectional settlement. Most especially
were Free Soilers dismayed by Webster's Seventh of March
speech endorsing the Clay plan, and even calling for acceptance of the fugitive slave bill. To Sumner, the speech was a
surrender whose "whole tone is low and bad." Comparing
Webster to Judas Iscariot and Benedict Arnold, he rejoiced
that so many in Massachusetts were rising up against their senator. He urged Chase and other Free Soilers to speak out and
"vindicate our fundamental positions" and rejoiced when they
did. When Mann joined in the attack, Sumner sent his praise
and offered advice on how to counter Webster's legal arguments on fugitive rights.

Webster's defense of the Clay proposals led to the loss of
one more close friend to Sumner, this time a member of the
Five of Clubs. When Felton joined a large group signing a
public letter to Webster thanking him for his speech and for
supporting his "constitutional obligations," the professor was
publicly singled out and attacked in the antislavery press. Felton replied in kind and then complained of how he had been
abused. Sumner, showing no sympathy, reminded him that

by signing the letter he had pledged himself "to surrender a panting fugitive without trial by jury" and to become "a slave catcher." Felton had enrolled himself in *"this troop of man-hunters."* Longfellow then interceded and urged Sumner not to "annoy Felton any more about politics." But Sumner persisted, and after a further angry exchange of letters he and Felton ceased all contact for the next six years.

No amount of comradeship and support over the past decade and a half could deter Sumner from personal attacks on those he felt had betrayed the antislavery cause. He told Longfellow that because of the "deep injustice" Felton had done to others, it was "impossible for me to be silent in response." Sumner's continuing friendship demanded total support for, or at the very least, acceptance of the positions he advocated. He concluded his final letter to Felton: "I break off no friendship. In anguish I mourn your altered regard for me; but more than my personal loss, I mourn the present unhappy condition of your mind and character." Once again Sumner had displayed his willingness to antagonize friends with personal insults; it would remain one of his least attractive characteristics.

Congress debated the Compromise measures until late summer, and Free Soilers like Sumner could only lament when the bills became law. With state and congressional elections looming, the third party would face an uphill battle, as Democrats and Whigs argued that sectional issues had now been settled and agitation should cease. While such an argument worked in parts of the North, in Massachusetts Webster's endorsement of the Compromise, and especially of the Fugitive Slave Act, was too controversial to allow the issues to die. Sumner's speech in Boston that fall bitterly arraigned the senator for his support of the fugitive measure. Designed to arouse the voters not only against Webster but all Whigs, it also looked to the creation of an atmosphere whereby enforcement of the fugitive law would be difficult if not impossible. Although disavowing violence, he suggested that the slavecatcher who dared come to Boston would receive anything but a friendly reception: "Men shall point at him in the streets and on the highways. Villages, towns, and cities shall refuse to receive the monster; they shall vomit him forth, never again to disturb the repose of our community." Such inflammatory words were fast becoming a standard element in the Sumner oratory.

Whigs insisted that Webster's stance be the test of party loyalty, precluding any thought some Free Soilers might have had of returning to their old party on an antislavery basis. Even Mann, having battled with Webster over the fugitive issue, found himself denied the Whig nomination for reelection to Congress. Instead, he accepted Free Soil support and was elected by third-party voters. Sumner himself reluctantly agreed to run a second time for Congress in his overwhelmingly Whig district, this time opposing Whig Samuel Eliot. Again, "the cause of Human Liberty" overcame "my general unwillingness" to seek "any political office." Chase's persuasion helped make up his mind to undertake the hopeless race, for as the Ohio senator pointed out, "if Websterism must prevail in the capital of Massachusetts—if Boston is to be yoked in with the slavehunters and their apologists, let no part of the sin lie at your door."

Chase had also pointed out that such a campaign against the Whigs might make a Free Soil coalition with the Democrats a possibility. If the Whigs could be denied an absolute majority in the legislature, Democrats and Free Soilers might combine to share the spoils, something neither could achieve by themselves. In such a union, Democrats would hold state offices, including the governorship, while the Free Soilers could gain the Senate seat in the same way that Chase had achieved his victory in Ohio. Chase had suggested the coalition idea to Sumner as early as June 1850, noting "How glad I should be to greet *you* as a Senator of Massachusetts!"

Such a union, however, was fraught with many dangers and pitfalls. Barnburner desertion of the antislavery principle had been the price in New York. With some Massachusetts Free Soilers still hoping for an eventual reunion with the Whigs, the thought of cooperating with Democrats was an anathema. Adams, Palfrey, and recent Free Soil convert Richard Henry Dana were especially vocal in this sentiment. Others, like Wilson and Sumner who had long since written off the Whigs as a hopelessly proslavery party, were more willing to consider the possibilities. Both men were more politically astute, although Sumner steadfastly maintained that he had no personal interest in political office. To Sumner, such a coalition would not be the equivalent of Mann's earlier refusal to repudiate his Whig ties. Instead, Free Soilers and Democrats would each retain their separate identities and principles and cooperate solely for the purpose of voting in the legislature. Whatever the possibilities, Sumner advised that Democrats and Free Soilers should do no bargaining before the election and wait for the results before considering a coalition. Still, he could not avoid hoping privately that the party might "influence the choice of a senator."

The election results were all that Free Soilers could have wished, for the Whigs were denied a majority in both houses of the legislature. As Sumner gleefully told his brother, Democrat George Boutwell "will be chosen governor and a Free Soil senator in the place of Daniel Webster." Still, he protested against his name being mentioned, for, as he unconvincingly told Adams, he would only unwillingly "forgo those literary plans and aspirations which I have more at heart than any merely political success." Besides, objected Sumner, there were other Free Soil leaders more qualified than he, namely Stephen Phillips or Adams himself. In fact, Sumner had by this time eagerly embraced the possibility of a political career but found it difficult to admit such an ambition. Because the coalition was unpopular with many of his fellow Free Soilers,

Sumner may still have been uncertain himself over the propriety of such a union with Democrats and self-conscious about the likelihood of being its chief beneficiary. As the coalition proceeded in early January, with Boutwell quickly chosen governor and Democrats pledging to support a Free Soiler for senator, Sumner's disclaimers continued and his difficulties mounted.

It would be almost four months before Sumner was finally elected, a tortuous period for him and all Free Soilers. With his party insisting that he was their candidate, the Whig-leaning members continued to express reservations over cooperating with Democrats. Adams gave his reluctant endorsement, but others hesitated. More serious, not all Democrats were content with what they believed was Sumner's overly radical stance against slavery. And as the balloting began, enough of them, influenced by party leader Caleb Cushing, withheld their support, leaving Sumner just short of the majority needed. His inflammatory attacks on the Fugitive Slave Law that had so endeared him to Free Soilers and abolitionists had made him unacceptable to Democrats who were dependent on their national party's patronage. To Cushing, Sumner was "a one-idead [*sic*] abolition agitator." Some tried to force a pledge from Sumner that if elected senator he would not agitate on slavery-related issues, to which he answered: "I did not seek the office"; if it were offered "it must find me an absolutely independent man."

Friends like Longfellow regretted Sumner's plunge into politics and hoped to see him soon "safe at a fireside of your own at work on that Book you dream of." The young reformer claimed to be ready to step out of the race as the deadlock continued. He rationalized that he would "retire at this moment" if it would not affect the cause, for "there is nothing in the field of politics which I covet." To Wilson, who was directing Free Soil strategy in the legislature, he played the martyr by urging the party to abandon him "without notice or apology." Said Sumner, "the cause is everything. I am nothing."

Wilson and the Free Soilers remained firm, and finally on April 24, on the twenty-sixth ballot, Sumner received the necessary majority. Although gratified, he told Longfellow's wife Fanny, "I have no joy in my new responsibilities. . . . I wish that another was in my place." Fully aware that he lacked the necessary legislative skill to perform well in a body like the Senate, he may have doubted his abilities among such a group of experienced orators and parliamentarians. He dreaded leaving those in Boston who had always understood and reassured him and had bolstered his confidence. In their place he feared he would find few friends among senators who were determined to prevent further agitation on sectional issues. But if Sumner could not rejoice, other Free Soilers did, and Adams noted that the new senator would do "himself and the country credit." Sumner begged off the victory celebration that evening and instead retreated to Longfellow's home. But he was quick to praise Wilson for his efforts: "To your ability, energy, determination, fidelity our cause owes its present success. For weal or woe you must take the responsibility of having placed me in the Senate of the United States."

Predictably, there were many who did not celebrate with Sumner's election. His friend Francis Lieber, with whom relations had cooled considerably since Sumner had become involved in the antislavery movement, feared that the presence of such an agitator in Congress might incite South Carolina secessionists to precipitous action. Sumner naturally failed to understand Lieber's inability "to rejoice" at his election. In contrast, some friends who disagreed with his philosophy, like law partner George Hillard, congratulated Sumner, noting: "You have now before you a noble career. May you walk in it with a statesman's steps." Most Whigs, however, expressed self-righteous outrage over the election, with a few even appearing on Boston streets with wide bands of black crepe on their arms.

Sumner would thus embark on a new career with the mixed blessings of his constituents and with mixed feelings. He felt "humbled by the importance" of his victory but fearful of his "inability to meet the expectations aroused." Despite his unconvincing protestations that "I do not wish to be a politician," he would now have a national forum to carry forth his moral crusade.

CHAPTER THREE

A Perpetual Speech

Senator-elect Charles Sumner embarked on his new career with both excitement and trepidation. His reluctance to join with fellow Free Soilers in their celebration of his victory in late April 1851 was based more on personal turmoil and concern over his new position than it was on false modesty. Torn between a life of scholarly research and writing and one as a political reformer, he had cast his lot with the activists during the exciting events of the late 1840s. Until now he had been able to maintain his Boston base and mix his love of quiet study with his new role in reform movements. Election to the Senate as a Free Soiler would inevitably mean turning his back on his intellectual pursuits and seeing considerably less of those whose friendship and support had always meant so much to him. As his supporters celebrated, he hurried to Longfellow's home to find refuge, feeling "more saddened than exalted." He experienced feelings of inadequacy, shaped by the high "expectation of enthusiastic friends," as well as a "distaste" for the "duties and struggles" of a senator. Legislative maneuvering in a world of competing politicians had never been his forte, but it was in such a world that he must now live and act. It was a world in which he hoped to move Congress toward his own antislavery position. Yet with few in either the North or the South sharing his moral commitment, it would be an uphill battle fraught with obstacles that only someone with his determination would have undertaken.

Sumner entered the Senate not only with the enthusiastic support of many friends but the unrealistic assumption of some that his presence would immediately make a difference in the sectional struggle. Abolitionist Theodore Parker looked for quick action: "I expect heroism of the most heroic kind." Such pressure bore heavily on Sumner in the months between his election in April and the convening of Congress in December. He told writer-reformer John Greenleaf Whittier that he was "oppressed" by his "inability to meet the expectations of friends." As others sent congratulations, he was "filled anew with the conviction of my unworthiness," and he decided to be silent until he took his seat; only in this way could he "secure a fair hearing from the country" when Congress assembled. Even then, he expected to observe before entering actively into Senate deliberations. "I regard it to be my first duty to understand the body in which I have a seat," he told John Jay, "before rushing into its contests."

Sumner thus spent the rest of 1851 quietly yet persistently preparing for his new career. As Massachusetts Free Soilers and Democrats struggled to keep their coalition together through the fall campaign, he maintained close ties with those Democrats who had supported his election. The Whigs, under Webster and Winthrop, were determined to regain ascendancy in state politics, while Sumner knew that his future depended on a continuation of the coalition that he hoped might grow into a complete "community of principles."

The new senator also realized that the Washington scene would be strikingly different from that of Massachusetts. In Congress, Democrats and Whigs would be hostile to the Free Soilers and seek to prevent any alteration of the delicate sectional balance that had been bolstered by the Compromise of 1850. As a new member, breaking into the exclusive senatorial club would be difficult in itself. But as a part of a tiny organization known for its determination to agitate slavery-related issues, Sumner anticipated a less than cordial welcome. This, along with a fear of failure, added to his determination to be silent. To New York Whig William H. Seward, one of the few from whom he expected a kind reception, he lamented that "there is nothing in the vista of politics which has any attraction for me." Again he indicated his preference for "quiet studies, books, friendships and such labors for our cause as a simple citizen may always perform."

Sumner set out for Washington in late November with heavy heart. Parting with Longfellow and Howe, "those who have been more than brothers to me," was especially difficult. "I could not speak to you as we parted," he told the poet later, "my soul was too full." Fearing what the future held, he poignantly admitted to Howe that "three times yesterday I wept like a child . . . first in parting with Longfellow, next in parting with you, and lastly as I left my mother and sister."

Sumner's first experiences in Washington were not as traumatic as he had feared, and he quickly fell into a comfortable relationship with northern and southern senators of both major parties. Unable to arrange housing with Chase, he was assigned a seat next to him in the Senate, that formerly held by Jefferson Davis of Mississippi. Chase, Sumner, and Hale were the only Free Soilers, but the trio did have at least two potential allies in Seward and the newly elected Ohio Whig, Benjamin F. Wade. The group spent much time together in both social and political settings. Determined not to appear as a radical abolitionist, Sumner made friends with Senators Pierre Soulé of Louisiana and Andrew Butler of South Carolina, both of whom were dedicated defenders of slavery and the latter, one of the authors of the Fugitive Slave Act so detested by Free Soilers. He renewed his friendship made in Paris with Senator Cass, the recently defeated presidential candidate and strong Compromise supporter. Few noted the irony when the aging Henry Clay, the Great Compromiser, made his last appearance on the Senate floor on December 1, 1851, the same day that Charles Sumner was sworn in, harboring a determination to undo the settlement on slavery that Clay and his allies had so carefully crafted.

Sumner quickly established a comfortable daily routine. He rented a bedroom and sitting room in a conveniently located New York Avenue boarding house. Rising early, following a simple breakfast he walked the mile to the Capitol to be present before the Senate convened each morning. His only other meal came in the late afternoon or early evening with a small group that met regularly at a French restaurant. Making friends easily, he enjoyed members of Congress and the diplomatic corps as they discussed the day's events. Within a month he was far from lonely, reporting to Longfellow that in a single week he had dined with the French minister on Tuesday, attended a dinner hosted by President Millard Fillmore on Wednesday, been the guest of Democratic leader Francis P. Blair on Thursday, and dined with Senator Seward on Friday. Between social and Senate activities he was rarely by himself or bored.

Initially, congressmen appeared willing to show Sumner every courtesy and assume that his earlier antislavery record had been designed for northern consumption and was to be abandoned in Washington. As a freshman third-party senator, he would have little influence and was assigned to insignificant committees, those on Revolutionary War claims and roads and canals. Surprised that he was not immediately rejected out-of-hand, especially by Southerners, he was anxious to do nothing to antagonize. Having been told by Senator Corwin that he was regarded in the South as "an ultra revolutionist and red republican," he determined that his first speeches on the Senate floor should be unrelated to slavery. He was equally desirous that his initial address come early, so that he could quickly overcome nervousness and gain stature and respect; antislavery agitation must wait.

The arrival in Washington in early December of the Hungarian revolutionary leader Louis Kossuth, who was seeking U.S. assistance for his flagging cause, gave Sumner his opportunity to address the body. Kossuth represented an issue important enough to attract attention, yet one which would allow

Sumner to avoid North-South differences. More than two years earlier, massive intervention of Russian and Austrian troops had crushed Hungary's revolution, restoring Hapsburg authority to the throne. Kossuth and his supporters had fled to Turkey, and the United States had offered him asylum. In the fall of 1851 he arrived in New York, intent on seeking support with which to reignite the revolution. Using every opportunity to evade the U.S. policy of neutrality, he found significant interest in his cause among Americans.

Thousands of New Yorkers greeted Kossuth with cheers, representing the many more who believed that their country, fresh from its victory over Mexico, had a mission to spread its democratic will over Europe. The movement, soon labeled "Young America," found proponents among journalists and politicians. Western Democrats led by Senators Cass and Stephen A. Douglas of Illinois were joined by reformers and some Free Soilers, such as Gamaliel Bailey and his *National Era*, and influential editors like James Gordon Bennett of the *New York Herald*. Although most Whigs opposed direct intervention, Fillmore's secretary of state Daniel Webster had led the drive to offer Kossuth asylum. Before assuming his seat in the Senate, Sumner himself had left the door open to some form of assistance in a campaign letter in October in which he urged that Americans extend the Hungarian a friendly reception.

Sumner's maiden Senate speech of December 10, 1851, quickly clarified any misconception about his position on Kossuth. In a brief address, after a warm welcome to the exile he declared his opposition to "encouraging any idea of belligerent intervention in European affairs." His belief in peace, his understanding of international law, and the impracticality of committing the millions of dollars necessary for such a violation of traditional U.S. neutrality made him oppose "American intervention on distant European soil." Instead, he urged the Hungarian to "leave us tread where Washington points the way." It was an effective address delivered with skill and eloquence, and one which accelerated the tide of Senate opinion against intervention that was already swelling. Kossuth went on to wear out his welcome with his incessant pleas for U.S. aid in a seven-month tour of the country and finally left for Europe in July 1852, without U.S. support and with the Young America movement in disarray.

Senator Sumner played only a minor role in this reversal of U.S. thinking, but he provoked a significant reaction in Massachusetts. On the one hand, his close friend Howe, who had championed Greek independence a quarter of a century earlier, was disappointed. He argued that there were times when force must be employed against tyranny, while Parker regretted Sumner's speech, noting "what a glorious man Kossuth is." But the senator found more supporters for his sentiments than opponents. Free Soilers like Dana and James W. Stone sent congratulations and urged him to stand by his principles. Bay State Whigs were pleased with his moderation, with Eliot relieved of much "anxiety" by Sumner's willingness to oppose the views of many "men of the party that gave you your seat in the Senate."

But Sumner had not taken his stand to please conservative Whigs. To John Bigelow, editor of the *New York Evening Post*, he argued, "Kossuth errs, all err who ask any intervention by government. . . . Enthusiast for freedom, I am for everything practical; but this is not practical." His approach had been to welcome Kossuth "warmly and systematically," but "*at the same time to plead for Peace.*" Indeed, Sumner had impressed many with his deep understanding of the issue and the moderate tone of his address. It had been an auspicious beginning.

The senator also became involved in a debate over land policy before taking up the antislavery cause. The issue involved a federal land grant to build a railroad in Iowa, a concept usually supported by western senators and opposed by Easterners. Surprisingly, Sumner endorsed the bill in a forceful speech, recognizing both the legitimate needs of western states and settlers and the political value of winning allies in

Congress from frontier areas. Predictably, many New England-ers disagreed with his reasoning, with the Whig press leading the attack. Only the Free Soil organ, the *Commonwealth* print-ed the speech, while the Whig-based *Advertiser* claimed that his stance would benefit Westerners at New England's ex-pense. Unmoved by the opposition, Sumner was satisfied that his arguments were both "original and unanswerable." Many of his friends rallied to his support, with Longfellow noting his pleasure "with your manner of answering your adversaries." Criticism had only begun, however, and Sumner would find that when it involved North-South issues, it came as frequent-ly from his antislavery supporters as it did from his opponents.

Through the late winter and early spring of 1852, Sumner determined to keep his silence on slavery-related issues. Know-ing that Senate leaders would thwart any early efforts to chal-lenge the Compromise of 1850, he patiently waited for the right moment. He explained to Palfrey in February his "de-sire by early caution and reserve" to position himself "to speak from a vantage ground when at last I do speak." He noted that in the process "many prejudices against me have disap-peared," but realized that the time would come "when I must encounter stern opposition." His approach may have pacified fellow senators, but it soon began to try the patience of some abolitionists, as well as expose him to the derision of proslav-ery Democrats.

Not surprisingly, Garrison was among the first to question the senator's silence. At an April meeting of Massachusetts abolitionists, he offered a resolution declaring Sumner's fail-ure to speak inexplicable. At the time, Phillips had rushed to defend his friend against the attack, but he explained later to Sumner that Garrison's impatience was understandable: "When he had waited two and a half months, he thought you owed us some definite statement" attacking the Fugitive Slave Act. Hurt by Phillips's explanation, Sumner defended his course and his determination "to state myself fully" but only at the opportune moment. To Howe, he claimed that "Hunker" derision was based on Democratic desire "to see me impale myself by some impracticable course." He concluded, "I shall not gratify them."

The Garrisonians had been further angered by Sumner's apparent defiance in refusing to present one of their petitions to Congress. It demanded the release from a Washington jail of abolitionists Daniel Drayton and William Sayres, accused of attempting to free a large group of slaves whom they had been transporting on the schooner *Pearl* on the Potomac River. The case had raised a considerable storm in both the northern and southern press, and any move to free Drayton and Sayres would have accelerated sectional tensions. Sumner therefore ignored the Garrisonians and instead worked quietly behind the scenes to secure their release. Cooperating with other reformers, the senator met privately with President Fillmore and agreed to avoid any public or Senate appeal. Finally, after months of delay, during which Massachusetts abolitionists accelerated their criticism of Sumner, the president issued the necessary pardon in August. Free Soilers lauded Sumner's efforts, and the senator himself boasted that had he presented the Garrison petitions in the Senate, "I should have fastened new pad locks on their prison door." Fearing further efforts by Southerners to prevent their release, Sumner then hurried to the jail and placed Drayton and Sayres in a carriage bound for Baltimore, from where they were quickly moved farther north to safety.

If Sumner had hoped that these efforts would satisfy the Garrisonians, he was soon disappointed, for they found little to praise in his actions and would be pacified with nothing short of a full-blown attack on the Fugitive Slave Act by their senator. Through it all, Sumner struggled to find the right moment and faced continuing roadblocks and self-doubt. He knew all too well the truth of the warning of Charles Francis Adams that the slave issues had been "banished from the capital by common consent . . . until the Presidential election is disposed of." He was also keenly aware that his friends were growing increasingly restive during his silence. The emotional Wilson wrote excitedly in early August: "Do not for heavens sake fail to speak, cost what it may of effort or trouble. I tell you quite frankly that our people are in a state of disappointment and almost despair," exclaiming further that Whigs and Democrats continued to ridicule him and that "nothing is so fatal to a public man as the taunt of weakness or timidity."

The pressure on Sumner was made even worse when, after he had prepared his address with meticulous care and felt himself ready for its delivery by late July, he was thwarted in his first effort to deliver it by a procedural maneuver. His motion to speak on the fugitive issue was blocked by a 32-to-10 margin, and it would be close to a month before he finally found his opportunity.

Haunted by the impatience and derision of Northerners and by the threats of Southerners who, like Senator Robert Hunter of Virginia, promised that they would continue to block his efforts to speak, Sumner devised the strategy that eventually succeeded. As the session neared adjournment in late August, a time when the Senate considered last-minute appropriation bills, he moved an amendment to a bill proposed by Hunter for paying the expenses of law enforcement officials, to the effect that no such funding be incurred in executing the Fugitive Slave Act. Sumner's proposal also included the repeal of the act. Caught by surprise, no senator attempted to block his defense of his amendment. After months of planning and frustration, Sumner finally had his chance.

He entitled his speech "Freedom National, Slavery Sectional," a precise description of the thesis he planned to prove. After tracing the antislavery nature of the Declaration of Independence and the Northwest Ordinance, he launched into an analysis of the Constitution designed to prove that the framers had intended to leave the issue of the return of fugitives to state rather than federal officials. The Fugitive Slave Act of 1850 was thus a violation of states rights because:

slavery is a local institution, peculiar to the states and under the guardianship of States Rights. It is impossible to claim for Congress any power to legislate either for its abolition in the States or its support anywhere. *Non*-intervention is the rule prescribed to the Nation.

Sumner contended that a citizen, "when oppressed may appeal" to his state for his rights. The act denied him such rights and "despoils his State of all power to protect him." It is "radically unconstitutional" because it denied the accused a trial by jury. Even worse, "it bribes the Commissioner by a double stipend to pronounce against Freedom. If he dooms a man to Slavery, the reward is ten dollars; but saving him to Freedom, his dole is five." Finally, concluded the senator, the law not only "violates the Constitution and shocks the Public Conscience," but "it offends the Divine Law." The issue should be left "in the absolute control of the States, the appointed guardians of Personal Liberty."

Sumner's was a masterful oration, although it contained little new and confined itself to a review of the arguments of those who had opposed the act's enactment two years earlier. But it had broken the silence that Congress had imposed on further debate and showed, if there had ever been any doubt, that the issue had not been laid to rest. It was a forceful four-hour address, which he had committed to memory and delivered without notes, a style to which senators were not accustomed. The galleries had filled when word spread that he had gained the floor, and senators and spectators alike listened engrossed without interruption. Even Daniel Webster, in what may have been his last visit to the Senate, sat absorbed for more than an hour. Devoid of any abuse of those responsible for the act's enactment, the speech was calm and carefully reasoned. Totally lacking in humor and filled with classical references, it stressed an argument of limited federal government authority, which Sumner would later abandon. But it was one that Congress could not ignore without peril.

George E. Badger of North Carolina led the Senate rebuttal,

calling the address an "elaborate oration, carefully written, studied and committed to memory," yet nothing more than "a tirade of abuse." Senator Douglas then summarized the arguments he and others had stated so effectively in 1850, reminding his listeners that the Constitution provided that slaves escaping into another state "shall be delivered up on the Claim of the Party to whom such Service or Labour may be due." The debate ground on for several more hours, and, to no one's surprise, Sumner's amendment of repeal received only four votes, his own and those of Hale, Wade, and Chase. Nevertheless, through skillful logic and a polished delivery, Sumner had informed the nation and the Senate that not only was his a voice to be reckoned with but, more important, that the cause of the slave had not been abandoned. While other northern senators appeared ready to acquiesce in their leaders' insistence that debate on slavery-related issues be silenced, Sumner almost single-handedly sought a renewal of the battle. Committed to the reversal of the Compromise spirit, he was thus at odds with his peers who believed that sectional harmony was more important than challenging the immorality of slavery.

Surprisingly, many of those who voted against Sumner's amendment congratulated him on the delivery and content of the speech. Even his friend Soulé of Louisiana compared it favorably with the efforts of the legendary British abolitionist William Wilberforce a generation earlier. William H. Polk of Tennessee, with apparent sincerity, called it "the greatest triumph of genius he had ever known." Many northern senators, while quick to separate themselves from his conclusions, praised Sumner warmly. Outside of Washington, antislavery leaders of all stripes, including the Garrisonians, rejoiced in his success. Phillips spoke for most by reacting with "envious admiration" for "a masterful argument and a noble testimony" that "will endear you to thousands."

The orator himself appeared well satisfied, proudly pointing out that he had only done "what I always intended to do, in my own way." He believed his arguments "unanswerable" and quickly made arrangements for the speech to be printed in pamphlet form for greater circulation. In Massachusetts some of the Whig press ignored Sumner's success, but most of his political enemies recognized the speech's significance, even while decrying its content. Ohioan Chase spoke for Free Soilers when he noted that Massachusetts "has given the cause its most faithful and eloquent champion."

When Congress adjourned, Sumner returned to New England, hoping to take a well-deserved vacation trip to Newport and Quebec. But he soon learned that Free Soilers expected his active participation in the presidential and state elections of the fall. Long before his arrival in Boston, the campaign had begun in earnest, and beleaguered Free Soilers struggled to keep their movement alive in the face of pro-Compromise efforts to eliminate the third-party challenge. Earlier in the year, Sumner had hoped that enough northern Democrats would remain true to the Wilmot Proviso concept to create a broader-based antislavery coalition. He had briefly considered support of Senator Sam Houston as a presidential candidate if the Texas Democrat continued his antislavery bent. Sumner told Adams that "the antislavery interest" under Houston "would have freer scope" than with any other nominee. But as party lines hardened during the spring, Sumner realized that Free Soilers would be on their own and in much reduced numbers in contrast to the exciting campaign of four years earlier.

With most New York Barnburners back in their old party, Democrats nominated Franklin Pierce of New Hampshire for president on a Compromise platform, and the Whigs straddled the political fence with the choice of the colorless military hero Winfield Scott and an evasive platform. To Sumner, the Democrats were more dangerous nationally, for with Pierce as president the slave power would "be fastened upon every branch of Govt." Nor could he support Scott, who he felt was not much better. More dangerous, Whig resurgency in Massachusetts could mean the end of the coalition.

Sumner and other Free Soilers reluctantly agreed on an independent course, knowing that they would lead "a forlorn hope." Because of his duties in the Senate, Sumner played no role in the August convention in Pittsburgh, which nominated his Senate colleague and early Liberty party partisan John P. Hale of New Hampshire for president. And he disappointed many in Massachusetts when he made only a brief appearance in the state during the fall. Persisting in his vacation plans, he did only token campaigning for Hale and the party's state candidates. Despite pleas from James Stone and other Free Soil leaders to speak out actively for the party, and the knowledge that he would be blamed if the coalition failed to maintain control, he remained strangely aloof. Life in Washington had so totally engrossed him that he had temporarily lost touch with the realities of state politics. He appeared to believe that his role as a senator placed him above or outside of the internal discord that was part of the Boston scene. The Whigs did regain state control, and Pierce swept to the presidency, confirming Sumner's worst fears. Despite his heroic efforts in the Senate, the difficulty of keeping public attention focused on sectional issues had increased, at least in minor part due to his own inaction during the campaign.

The short lame-duck session of Congress did little to revive Sumner's spirits, for as Washington awaited a new president, Senate leaders denied third-party members the opportunity to raise sectional issues. Refused for a time a place on any committee because he and other Free Soilers were considered "outside of any healthy political organization," Sumner again found no opportunity to speak. As critics renewed their attacks over his silence, he was clearly relieved when the session ended in March 1853. For a time his political life appeared to be floundering in the face of massive determination on the part of Democrats and Whigs to avoid controversial issues.

While recognizing that slavery "cannot be overthrown in a day," he reiterated his goal "to tame its aggressive spirit, to banish it from the national govt and to drive it into the states so that it can no longer vex our politics." Little he did in 1853 appeared to point in such a direction.

If Sumner had expected any respite from partisan factional politics on his return to Boston after Congress adjourned, he was to be sadly mistaken. Although the Whigs had regained control of the state legislature, voters had also approved the call of the Free Soil–Democratic coalition for a constitutional convention. Since its origins in 1780, the Massachusetts Constitution had become badly outdated, meeting the needs of the Revolutionary generation but not those of the mid-nineteenth century. Especially outmoded was the complex apportionment system used in determining representation in the lower house, whereby the majority Whigs could usually choose the entire forty-four-seat Boston delegation. There were demands for other needed reforms, but it was soon clear that the coalition's primary goal was to enhance its own power at Whig expense. Not all Free Soilers agreed with this aim, and Sumner soon found himself caught between the Adams-Palfrey-Dana faction, which sought only moderate change, and the Wilson group, working with Democratic boss Boutwell, whose aims were clearly more partisan.

Sumner's role at the gathering was far less effective than he had anticipated. Out of touch with the intricacies of state politics since his entrance into the Senate, he appeared at times to be little more than Wilson's puppet. For his part, Wilson never tired of reminding Sumner that he owed him a political debt for engineering his election to the Senate. At the same time, Adams failed in his contest to be a delegate, a defeat he blamed on the "rotten . . . treachery" of Wilson. Here, Sumner was caught in the middle of the ongoing feud between those like Wilson, who sought to exploit the potential of smoldering labor and ethnic unrest against their elitist Whig opponents, and the Adams faction of Free Soilers, which could not entirely divorce itself from its Whig roots. The election of delegates resulted in a large majority for reform of the kind Wilson advocated, and the *Commonwealth* confidently predicted "the final overthrow of Whiggery in Massachusetts."

The conclave produced some much-needed modernization of the state constitution, but in some of the specifics the proposed document appeared to be a brazen attempt to destroy Whig power and place the coalition firmly in control of Massachusetts politics. Most alarming were the provisions that reduced Boston and other large-city representation in the legislature to a fraction of their legitimate power. While unhappy with this violation of direct democracy, Sumner nevertheless defended the finished product both in a convention address and in the ratification struggle that fall. He told the delegates that he endorsed the apportionment clauses "not because they are all that I desire" but because they would "open the door to later reforms and eventual *Equality*." Prospects appeared strong for ratification as he embarked on a strenuous fall speaking tour in behalf of the document, combining his advocacy with a full explanation of his cherished antislavery philosophy of Freedom National. Weakening the Whig party of Massachusetts was, in Sumner's eyes, a necessary part of the struggle against slavery.

The senator's expedient course on the constitution was a source of increased tension with the Adams faction. Palfrey, who was most vehement in his resistance to ratification, even published a pamphlet attacking the changes. Adams followed with a campaign address criticizing not only the document's political motives but also Sumner for bowing to the "iron-rod of party" in his support of it. Such opposition helped turn a probable ratification victory into a 5,000-vote margin of defeat. Sumner's chagrin over the setback was based on several factors. The rejection of the constitution, he said, was "a severe calamity to the liberal cause of this state." Even worse, the Pierce administration had interfered in the coalition's efforts when Attorney General Caleb Cushing wrote an angry letter to fellow Bay State Democrats virtually ordering them to cease cooperation with "the dangerous element of abolitionism." The coalition, on whose support Sumner's power depended, had not only been defeated, but Democrats had been directed to refrain from all future collaboration with them.

Personally, Sumner's relations with two long-trusted friends had been damaged. He defended his actions in behalf of ratification to Adams and complained of the latter's public attack. A further exchange of letters revealed an inability of either to understand the other's motives, and relations remained strained until antislavery objectives brought them together again the following year. The mending of wounded feelings was much longer in coming with Palfrey, who made several tentative initiatives only to be rebuffed by Sumner's charge that he had dealt freedom "a deadly blow" by his opposition to the constitution's ratification. Even after resuming communications, neither could put the issue fully behind him. Perhaps frustrated by his failure to bring change in either Washington or Massachusetts, Sumner, once again, appeared incapable of avoiding the extension of political differences to the personal level.

Finally able to put state issues aside, Sumner gladly returned to Washington at the end of 1853 for the first session of the Thirty-third Congress. He still longed for the intellectual life he had given up in Boston for "the cares and responsibilities" of serving in Congress. Corresponding frequently with William W. Story, the son of his former mentor, who was a sculptor living in Rome, Sumner noted that he could "no longer feel at ease with a book." With envy he imagined Story "enjoying letters and art! No such days for me!" But in the Senate he could expect to play a significant role in critical sectional issues, especially those involving territorial slavery.

Most immediate were the plans to open vast western regions in the Louisiana Territory to settlement, areas in which slavery had been prohibited north of the parallel 36°30' by the Missouri Compromise of 1820. The ensuing debate would touch off a major North-South confrontation and eventually lead to the realignment of national parties that Sumner had long sought. It would also come at a time when the two-party system of Democrats and Whigs appeared to be crumbling in the face of the ineffectiveness of the Whigs as an opposition party. Following its shattering defeat in the presidential election of 1852 and the death of its two greatest national leaders, Clay and Webster, the party was ill-prepared to face the complex sectional issues that had placed southern Democrats and their northern allies, led by Franklin Pierce and Stephen Douglas, firmly in control in Washington. In addition, the Whigs appeared incapable of responding to the religious and ethnic issues represented by the influx of large numbers of Irish-Catholic immigrants and the growing resentment against them led by nativist elements. Sumner hoped that a Whig decline and a subsequent realignment of parties might place him and his antislavery colleagues in a position to influence change in a decisive way.

The bill to organize the Nebraska Territory quickly mushroomed into an explosion that ended the lull in antislavery agitation that had prevailed since the enactment of the Compromise of 1850. After numerous modifications, the measure, introduced by Senator Douglas, emerged in January 1854 as the Kansas-Nebraska bill, a proposal to divide the territory in two and repeal the Missouri Compromise ban on slavery there. While not ensuring that either part of the territory would approve slavery, the bill left it up to the respective residents to decide through a process known as popular sovereignty. It thus gave Southerners the hope that the southern portion of the territory, Kansas, might opt for the institution. Douglas firmly maintained that such was not his objective, but many northern members of Congress saw it differently. Most assumed that Douglas also had a personal motive in introducing his measure. Eager for the Democratic presidential nomination in 1856, he might, if his bill was perceived as beneficial to the South, garner the support of Southerners. Thus he might attain a nomination and election with the support of voters throughout the nation.

Most outraged by the Douglas proposal was the small band of Free Soilers led by Chase, Sumner, and Giddings, who, frustrated by their enforced silence during the previous session, at last saw an opportunity to provoke debate on slavery. Hoping to delay and eventually prevent the bill's passage, they introduced petitions from northern voters against it. When that tactic failed, they joined with three others in an impassioned public letter entitled "Appeal of the Independent Democrats in Congress to the People of the United States," which labeled Douglas's bill "an atrocious plot" to exclude free settlers from Kansas "and convert it into a dreary region of despotism, inhabited by masters and slaves." By repeal of the ban on slavery, Douglas, they claimed, was willing to "subjugate the whole country to the yoke of slaveholding despotism." As the bitter debate continued into the spring, Sumner no longer had to struggle to present his views. Instead, he played a central role in the resistance to what many Northerners regarded as a total surrender to proslavery interests.

Speaking several times during the extended debates, Sumner delivered his major address, "The Landmark of Freedom," in late February. Using an Old Testament text, "Cursed be he that removeth his neighbor's landmark," [Deuteronomy 27:17] his major thrust was to prove that the Missouri Compromise ban against slavery north of 36°30' was a sacred trust that Southerners had willingly supported at the time of its enactment in 1820. The Douglas bill was "an infraction of solemn obligations, assumed beyond recall by the South on the admission of Missouri into the Union as a Slave State." Listing prominent southern slaveholding legislators and cabinet members who, thirty-four years earlier, had backed it, including William Crawford and John C. Calhoun, and concluding with President James Monroe, who had signed the measure, Sumner reminded the Senate that the Missouri Compromise "takes its life from the South." Now, the next generation of Southerners refused to accept the obligations of their fathers: "The Prohibition of slavery in the Territory of Kansas and Nebraska stands on foundations of living rock, upheld by the early policy of the Fathers by constant precedent and time-honored compact."

Sumner's address struck a responsive chord among antislavery Northerners, and letters of praise poured in. Abolitionists and Free Soilers, along with numerous Whigs and Democrats, sent congratulations. The most prominent African-American leader, Frederick Douglass, editor of the abolitionist journal *The North Star*, rejoiced that "all the friends of freedom in every state and of every color may claim you just now as their representative." The senator's old Whig nemesis, Samuel Eliot, praised his effort, and James Russell Lowell exclaimed, "you have put yourself in support of the moral sense of Massachusetts." But few of his correspondents could vote with him in Congress, and Senator Douglas pushed relentlessly toward passage of the bill. The Illinois Democrat stepped up his vicious attacks on Sumner and Chase, calling them "the abolition confederates" pleading "the cause of Niggerism." Sumner complained to Adams that "our force of effective workers against this wickedness" was being overwhelmed. After six weeks of debate, antislavery forces were crushed 37 to 14 in the initial Senate vote in early March.

There followed two months of further legislative maneuvering, during which time the House narrowly endorsed the measure and antislavery leaders desperately sought to block final approval. Clashing personally and bitterly with Douglas and his southern allies, Sumner prepared to fight on until the bill was enacted. After midnight on the final day of debate, he introduced petitions against the measure from several outraged northern groups, including New England clergy, and explained that the bill about to be approved was "at once the worst and the best on which Congress ever acted." Worst, because it was a "victory of Slavery" that "defied every sentiment of justice, humanity and Christianity." Best, because "it puts

Freedom and Slavery face to face and bids them grapple." In the struggle to follow, "the Slave Power will be broken." Concluded Sumner dramatically: "Sorrowfully I bend before the wrong you commit,— joyfully I welcome the promise of the future."

The clash that Sumner had predicted began immediately, for in Boston on the day following enactment of the Kansas-Nebraska measure, antislavery activists assembled to protest the seizure of Anthony Burns, a fugitive slave from Virginia, under the terms of the Fugitive Slave Act. Fiery speeches by Phillips and others led the crowd to storm the courthouse where Burns was being held. That confrontation left a guard dead. Inside, attorney Richard Henry Dana defended Burns, but on June 2, the court ordered the accused returned to his master. Following an attempted street assault on Dana by proslavery guards, federal troops were ordered to escort Burns to the dock where a ship bound for Virginia awaited him. Having draped their buildings in black and hung their flags at half-mast, solemn Bostonians watched in anger as the deed was completed. Again, Boston retained its central role in civil rights struggles, as it had since 1830. Advocates of racial equality had used the Burns case to call attention to the continuing presence of injustice, and again Sumner's role would be central to the controversy.

The Democratic press of Boston immediately labeled the senator as the provoker of the violence surrounding the Burns case, for he had given "the word which encourages the assassin" by "inciting his constituents to resist federal laws, even to the shedding of blood." The *Washington Star* spoke for many outraged Southerners when it warned that if the safety of those pursuing fugitives could not be protected in Boston, northern agitators would need to be more careful themselves "in their walk, talk, and acts." The paper threatened that "*Sumner and his infamous gang*" would not be permitted to "counsel treason" and "incite the ignorant to bloodshed and murder" and expect to be tolerated in "this city which he has done so

e, especially those eager to exploit other issues
e used as a springboard for their own political
ict, there were other matters of concern to voters
ry. Most pressing in Massachusetts were the re-
of temperance and nativism. As mentioned, the
rowing Irish population, and it was becoming po-
ent as a faction of the Democratic party. It was
ited in the popular mind with excessive drinking
papal influence from Rome. Resentment against
immigrants was growing among various native-
ts. Job security of many appeared threatened by
d temperance advocates were finding willing ears
against the newcomers. Inevitably, the political
exploiting such sentiments became obvious. In
ts and elsewhere, the American, or Know Nothing
gun to emerge by late 1853. The growing appeal
it movement to Massachusetts voters also included
sentiment. Such resentment was directed against
organizations, including the Free Soilers and both
s.

er, nativism represented a challenge that he and
lust meet squarely, for not only was he strongly op-
movement on moral grounds, but its success in
ention away from sectional issues was immediate.
pportive of some form of temperance legislation,
any effort to discriminate against foreigners, and
speeches that fall he urged voters to welcome
is of the present." Attending the Worcester con-
created the state's new Republican party, Sum-
le delegates not to scatter their votes but to "unite
consistent phalanx" and "to cooperate with the
reedom in other states. As REPUBLICANS we go
ounter the *Oligarchs of Slavery*."

ts of the election of 1854 in Massachusetts were
o the senator, for the issues of fugitives and slavery
roved less appealing to voters than did nativism.

much to vilify." Sumner's response was to plan a renewed Senate attack on the Fugitive Slave Act. He saw the situation as made to order to present additional petitions for the repeal of the infamous law. He would seize the opportunity, for the atmosphere in Boston and Washington had ended any hesitancy about his role.

The Burns case set the stage for a prolonged Senate debate in late June, in which Sumner pressed for repeal of the fugitive law. When Southerners tried to block him from introducing petitions from his constituents, he launched into a comparison of the Fugitive Slave Act with the British Stamp Act of 1765. The latter "was at most an infringement of *civil* liberty only, not of personal liberty;" an "unjust tax of a few pence" had been levied. But, he said, by the act of 1850 *"the right of a man to himself"* was violated. Surely, no one could deny "how far the tyranny of the Slave Act is beyond the tyranny of the Stamp Act."

But it was Sumner's promise that he could not obey the act that provoked the greatest excitement. When South Carolinian Andrew Butler charged that Sumner thus defied the Constitution, the latter retaliated: "Does the honorable senator ask *me* if I would personally join in sending a fellow man into bondage? Is thy servant a dog that he should do this thing?" As passions heated, Butler again accused Sumner of rejecting the Constitution and suggesting "that you regard it the office of a dog to enforce it." Sumner's response cited as precedent earlier arguments of John Quincy Adams and slaveholder Andrew Jackson, each of whom had pledged himself to support the Constitution "AS HE UNDERSTANDS IT, and not as it is *understood by others*." Thus the senator was bound "to oppose all enactments by Congress on the subject of fugitive slaves as a flagrant violation of the Constitution."

Effectively turning the argument against his attackers, he exploded: "Until some one rises and openly confesses his willingness to become a Slave-Hunter, I will not believe there can be one." As he paused and no one rose, he concluded that much to vilify." Sumner's response was to plan a renewed Senate attack on the Fugitive Slave Act. He saw the situation as made to order to present additional petitions for the repeal of the infamous law. He would seize the opportunity, for the atmosphere in Boston and Washington had ended any hesitancy about his role.

The Burns case set the stage for a prolonged Senate debate in late June, in which Sumner pressed for repeal of the fugitive law. When Southerners tried to block him from introducing petitions from his constituents, he launched into a comparison of the Fugitive Slave Act with the British Stamp Act of 1765. The latter "was at most an infringement of *civil* liberty only, not of personal liberty;" an "unjust tax of a few pence" had been levied. But, he said, by the act of 1850 "*the right of a man to himself*" was violated. Surely, no one could deny "how far the tyranny of the Slave Act is beyond the tyranny of the Stamp Act."

But it was Sumner's promise that he could not obey the act that provoked the greatest excitement. When South Carolinian Andrew Butler charged that Sumner thus defied the Constitution, the latter retaliated: "Does the honorable senator ask *me* if I would personally join in sending a fellow man into bondage? Is thy servant a dog that he should do this thing?" As passions heated, Butler again accused Sumner of rejecting the Constitution and suggesting "that you regard it the office of a dog to enforce it." Sumner's response cited as precedent earlier arguments of John Quincy Adams and slaveholder Andrew Jackson, each of whom had pledged himself to support the Constitution "AS HE UNDERSTANDS IT, and not as it is *understood by others.*" Thus the senator was bound "to oppose all enactments by Congress on the subject of fugitive slaves as a flagrant violation of the Constitution."

Effectively turning the argument against his attackers, he exploded: "Until some one rises and openly confesses his willingness to become a Slave-Hunter, I will not believe there can be one." As he paused and no one rose, he concluded that

Senate, Sumner had established himself as by far the most outspoken critic of the southern way of life. His moral and political values had led him to challenge all forms of proslavery rhetoric and action.

Thus while Sumner's popularity soared in Boston, he was viewed throughout the South and by many in Washington as the most dangerous adversary of slavery. In the Senate, those who had been on friendly terms with him or at least had tolerated his presence now shunned him entirely. Ostracized socially, he had made himself a marked man against whom Southerners and their nonslaveholding northern allies would guard themselves, ignoring him when possible, and striking back in kind when he dared attack their cherished institution.

As the most prominent congressional opponent of slavery, Sumner would also play a pivotal role in the realignment of parties, which the Kansas-Nebraska Act and subsequent debates had precipitated. He, Chase, and Giddings had viewed their "Appeal of the Independent Democrats" as much a device to mobilize a new antislavery party as a statement of opposition to the Douglas bill. Arguing that the Democrats were responsible for the measure and that Whigs had been totally ineffective in preventing its enactment, they believed that a new party, uniting the small Free Soil group with the antislavery elements of the major parties, was the answer. Resisting such a possibility were numerous antislavery politicians who feared the loss of influence in the major parties. Most prominent among them was Seward, who believed that his presidential prospects depended on his dominant position among Whigs. Little beyond preliminary meetings of interested congressmen in May and June occurred in Washington to launch a new party during the spring and summer of 1854, and it would be on the state level that organizational efforts would develop before the fall elections.

Sumner firmly believed that the only question of significance in party realignment was slavery. Consequently, he failed to understand the goals of those more politically ambitious than he, especially those eager to exploit other issues that could be used as a springboard for their own political agenda. In fact, there were other matters of concern to voters besides slavery. Most pressing in Massachusetts were the related issues of temperance and nativism. As mentioned, the state had a growing Irish population, and it was becoming politically potent as a faction of the Democratic party. It was often associated in the popular mind with excessive drinking and loyalty to papal influence from Rome. Resentment against these recent immigrants was growing among various native-born elements. Job security of many appeared threatened by the Irish, and temperance advocates were finding willing ears in their case against the newcomers. Inevitably, the political potential of exploiting such sentiments became obvious. In Massachusetts and elsewhere, the American, or Know Nothing party had begun to emerge by late 1853. The growing appeal of the nativist movement to Massachusetts voters also included an antiparty sentiment. Such resentment was directed against all political organizations, including the Free Soilers and both major parties.

To Sumner, nativism represented a challenge that he and his friends must meet squarely, for not only was he strongly opposed to the movement on moral grounds, but its success in diverting attention away from sectional issues was immediate. Although supportive of some form of temperance legislation, he rejected any effort to discriminate against foreigners, and in campaign speeches that fall he urged voters to welcome "the Pilgrims of the present." Attending the Worcester convention that created the state's new Republican party, Sumner urged the delegates not to scatter their votes but to "unite in one firm consistent phalanx" and "to cooperate with the friends of Freedom in other states. As REPUBLICANS we go forth to encounter the *Oligarchs of Slavery.*"

The results of the election of 1854 in Massachusetts were distressing to the senator, for the issues of fugitives and slavery in Kansas proved less appealing to voters than did nativism.

They elected Know Nothing gubernatorial candidate Henry J. Gardner and chose a legislature dominated by his party. Sumner blamed the election results on the failure of embattled Whigs to support the newly formed Republicans. More dangerous was Wilson's endorsement of Gardner and the Know Nothings in his successful effort to use their movement to win the other Massachusetts seat in the United States Senate. Although glad to have Wilson as a colleague in the Senate because of his support of antislavery causes, Sumner was fearful of the potential of the movement that had placed him there.

Thus Sumner's political problems at home continued. While still opposed to nativism on firm grounds of ideology, he soon found that it had become a movement of such magnitude that it might threaten his Senate seat if he dared to attack it too strongly. Temporarily, he adopted an expedient course of silence on immigrant issues while struggling to keep the focus on sectionalism. With so many antislavery politicians like Wilson openly or quietly supporting nativism at home, his dilemma increased. His greatest fear was that the movement "promises to break up the whole Northern combination" against slavery.

The lecture hall proved as effective a forum for raising sectional issues as the Senate. In Washington again for the short session of Congress beginning in December 1854, Sumner found limited opportunity to renew the agitation that had centered around him during the previous session. Instead, he was forced to wait until Congress adjourned to renew his assault on slavery. In May 1855, he delivered a major address in New York, in which he presented the issues closest to his heart. Calling his oration "The Anti-Slavery Enterprise," and speaking before a huge audience, he outlined the duties of antislavery Northerners. It was a dramatically effective appeal, revealing Sumner at the peak of his oratorical skills. Waving aside the practical objections of those opposed to agitation, he urged unity among Northerners for the assault on slavery: "mutual sympathy, trust, and alliance" must replace "mutual criticism, crimination and feud." Only then would the "Slave Oligarchy" be conquered and the national government rescued "from degrading thraldom." If effective oratory alone could have united the North, Sumner's speech would have achieved its goal.

Americans in those years understood speech-making proficiency in a very different light than later Americans would, and they were willing to sit for several hours in rapt attention to those most skilled in the art. The public lecture had by then become an important form of instruction throughout the North, with small towns and cities alike inviting those with regional or national reputations to speak on topics ranging from science and travel to moral issues. The lecture became a public occasion, and, while not usually partisan or political in nature, reformers such as Emerson and Phillips were among those most in demand. Americans in the 1840s and 1850s sought to be instructed, inspired, and entertained, and the lecturer needed to possess the qualities of a performer. The best known, led by the scholarly Everett, delivered their orations entirely from memory, with dramatic voice, diction, and gestures. Sumner, who had been developing these oratorical skills for more than a decade, fit easily into this mold, and he soon found himself among those most eagerly sought on the lectern.

It was thus a rhetorical culture in which Sumner operated, one in which he was not simply orating or spewing invective as a ritualistic exercise to feed his own ego or to send a thrill through his restive constituents. He might in fact enhance his limited political power through public speaking, gaining by words what he could not through legislation. He did, of course, hope to persuade his listeners to his perspective through his arguments, but he also used public lectures to polish an ability that he had first developed in school and had begun to practice publicly in the 1840s. In an age of oratorical giants in which the public venerated those skilled in the craft, Sumner saw himself as a worthy successor of the generation of

Clay and Webster. Yet while they spoke in behalf of compromise on North-South issues, Sumner believed that only by confronting slavery and its adherents directly could bondage ever be overcome.

So impressive and popular was "The Anti-Slavery Enterprise," that he delivered it in cities throughout the Northeast that spring. He then embarked on a lecture tour of the Old Northwest, which also brought him south of the Ohio River for a first-hand look at the institution that he was determined to undermine. At each stop he consulted with and was sometimes hosted by antislavery leaders. In Cincinnati, he stayed with Chase, then in the midst of a successful campaign to become Ohio's first Republican governor. In Milwaukee, he visited abolitionist Sherman Booth, who had recently challenged the Fugitive Slave Act in Wisconsin courts. Throughout, he urged his hosts to the cause of Republicanism against the rising Know Nothing tide. But his visit to the slave states of Kentucky and Tennessee affected him most deeply. In Lexington, he was entertained by antislavery advocate Cassius Clay and saw the condition of slaves on the plantation of Clay's brother Brutus. He witnessed "a slave sold on the steps of the court house" and concluded that the more he saw of slavery "the more indefensible does it seem."

Sumner returned to Boston in time for the fall state campaign. He was even more aware of the seriousness of the Know Nothing challenge than he had been the previous year because the movement had achieved a significant legislative record. He thus no longer evaded the issues it raised. Rather, he directly attacked the nativists and their gubernatorial candidate Gardner and urged antislavery unity behind Republican opponent Julius Rockwell. He warned voters against the Know Nothing organization, "a party which beginning in secrecy, interferes with religious belief" and bases its "discrimination on the accident of birth." Said Sumner, it "is not the party for us," for while "professing opposition to Slavery," it was not "wedded to Freedom." Only by pure antislavery emphasis could the distracting and dangerous nativist influence be defeated. In the immediate election, Gardner defeated Rockwell, but as time would show, the Know Nothing movement had already peaked, and the voters of Massachusetts and other northern states would soon be ready to turn their undivided attention to the sectional issues, as Sumner had urged.

Relieved to return to Washington and escape the turmoil of state politics, Sumner prepared for another session of Congress that promised to be dominated by the ongoing Kansas conflict. Still fearing that Gardner and the Know Nothing legislature might try to force a new election for senator a year before his term ended, in order to secure the Senate seat for the Governor, Sumner knew that he must again be vocal in his attacks against proslavery efforts in Kansas.

Although the Gardner threat proved to be exaggerated, the situations in Kansas and Congress were building toward a crisis. With 1856 being an election year, Democrats and Republicans each sought to maneuver the territorial situation into one from which they could benefit politically. Violence had erupted in Kansas, and Sumner received a constant stream of letters from antislavery settlers there asking for his help and telling of an impending invasion of proslavery forces. Actively encouraging the New England Emigrant Aid Company, which assisted antislavery settlers in moving into the region, Sumner received numerous pleas for his support in the Senate. Said one settler after describing the unrest in Lawrence, Kansas, and "the shameful attacks upon the ballot box" and free soil press there, "We are expecting open warfare. . . . What will you do for us in Congress?"

By late February 1856, Senate debates on the various proposals for Kansas statehood had begun in earnest. Sumner's new Massachusetts colleague Wilson initiated the defense of free-state interests, and Sumner predicted that the debates would drag on for weeks. "You will hear nothing but Kansas from this time forever," he told Parker. Fearing that Southerners and their northern allies would dominate the proceedings and prevent the admission of Kansas as a free state, he resolved to bend every effort "to plead for the distant plundered territory." In March, he clashed again with Douglas, who had attacked the antislavery motives and methods of the Emigrant Aid Company and labeled its members as "defiant revolutionists" supported by "black Republican traitors." Sumner rushed to the company's defense, noting that its only offense was that "its agents love Freedom and hate Slavery." Like many, he believed that the Illinois Democrat was eager to please the South not only because of his proslavery sentiments but because he needed their support come the presidential nominating convention of his party in June.

As news from Kansas told of further outrages, the settlers there being "trampled down far beyond our fathers," Sumner planned "the most thorough and complete speech of my life. My soul is wrung by this outrage and I shall pour it forth." He would thus answer Douglas and his southern allies. Prophetically, his Kansan friend Eli Thayer, organizer of the Emigrant Aid Company, warned Sumner of the repercussions of such a speech. "There will be gnashing of teeth among the defenders of Slavery," he said. "Be prepared, therefore for the worst of their endeavors."

Sumner designed his two-day oration, "The Crime Against Kansas," more to arouse public opinion than to affect the legislative process of the Senate. With Southerners and their moderate northern allies in control of the body, there was little chance that he could persuade the Senate to approve admission of Kansas as a free state. But he could arouse the northern public to rally behind his view that what was happening in both Kansas and Congress was indeed a crime. Not incidentally, he might also enhance his own reputation as the leader of the antislavery forces in Congress. On May 19, 1856, the chamber overflowed, as virtually every senator and many House members were joined by large numbers of the press and the public, all sweltering together in the ninety-degree heat. The crime that Congress had committed, began Sumner, was opening the territory to slavery when it passed the Kansas-Nebraska Act two years earlier. Before detailing the offense, he prefaced his attack by indicting those senators responsible for the "championship of human wrong." Especially guilty were Senators Butler and Douglas, "who tho unlike as Don Quixote and Sancho Panza, yet, sally forth together in the same adventure." Butler, he said, had:

> chosen a mistress to whom he has made his vows, and who tho ugly to others is always lovely to him, tho polluted in the sight of the world, is chaste in his sight; I mean the harlot Slavery. For her his tongue is always profuse in words. . . . The frenzy of Don Quixote in behalf of his wench Dulcinea de Toboso is all surpassed. . . . As the Senator from South Carolina is the Don Quixote, so the Senator from Illinois is the squire of Slavery, its very Sancho Panza ready to do its humiliating offices. This Senator in his labored address vindicating his labored report— piling one mass of elaborate error upon another mass—constrained himself as you will remember to unfamiliar decencies of speech.

But, continued Sumner, Douglas would not prevail, for "against him is immortal principle . . . ; against him is Nature with all her subtle forces; against him is God. Let him try to subdue these."

Sumner then moved to the actual crime, reminding his listeners that the slaveholding congressmen of 1820 were responsible for the 36°30' demarcation between slave and free territory—the landmark of freedom which Congress had repealed in 1854 in "a swindle of God-given, inalienable rights." Since the bill's enactment, southern Congressmen had conspired to extend slavery into the territory. Outlining the fraudulent actions to elect a proslavery legislature there, he arraigned the Missouri invaders organized "*before any counter movement from the North*" was conceived. The remedy, he urged, was the restoration of the original prohibition against slavery in the area. If Congress would enact Seward's bill "for the immediate admission of Kansas" as a free state, it would be upholding "the prayer of the people of the Territory." Only in this way could the crime against Kansas be revoked and free-dom and democracy there be protected.

Sumner concluded his oration with one further insensitive personal thrust at Butler. It was the sixty-year-old South Car-olinian, he suggested, who "overflows with rage" at the mere mention of statehood for a free Kansas, "and with incoherent phrase discharges the loose expectoration of his speech." He "touches nothing which he does not disfigure with error. . . . He cannot ope his mouth, but out there flies a blunder." The senator concluded by maligning Butler's state by suggesting that if South Carolina's entire history were "blotted out of ex-istence" civilization would lose "less than it has already gained by the example of Kansas in that valiant struggle against op-pression." When Sumner finally relented, all were aware that they had witnessed a most remarkable performance that could not long remain unanswered.

Sumner's former friend, the conservative Cass, was the first to respond, labeling the address "the most un-American and unpatriotic that ever grated on the ears of this high body." Others, including Mason of Virginia, joined in attacking Sum-ner, but it was reserved for Douglas to offer the major rebuttal, remarks that were equally insulting to those of his assailant. Appealing again for the support of southern Democrats, he re-minded his audience of Sumner's defiance of the Constitu-tion in regard to the Fugitive Slave Act and sarcastically noted that "we have had another dish of the classics served up—clas-sic allusions, each one only distinguished for its lasciviousness and obscenity." Sumner, said Douglas, had his speech "com-mitted to memory, practiced every night before the glass with a Negro boy to hold the candle and watch the gestures" until the "vulgar terms" were perfected for delivery. Defending his Kansas-Nebraska measure, Douglas was most incensed that Sumner had persisted in calling it a "swindle and a crime." Concluded the Illinois Democrat, Sumner must "whisper a se-cret apology" in Senator Butler's ear "as satisfaction for a pub-lic outrage on his character."

In response, Sumner showed no regret. Instead, the verbal sparring concluded with one final insulting jab at Douglas: "No person with the upright form of man can be allowed without violation of all decency to switch out his tongue the perpetual stench of offensive personality. Sir, that is not a proper weapon of debate at least on this floor. The noisome, squat, and nameless animal to which I now refer is not the proper model for an American Senator. Will the Senator from Illinois take notice?" In a body known for abusive language and vilification, Sumner and Douglas had engaged in an unprecedented exchange and had accelerated sectional tensions and animosities to new heights.

Sumner told abolitionist William Jay immediately after delivering his address that he had "been through a terrible battle." On hearing that the free-state town of Lawrence had suffered heavy damage at the hands of a proslavery mob, he could only conclude that "my soul bleeds for Kansas." He believed that the abuse of free-state settlers there was unparalleled. In fact, partisans of both the North and the South had turned Kansas into a raging battleground, as each side sought to see the Kansas Territory become either a free or slave state. As John Brown prepared to inflict his pro-abolition vengeance at Pottawatomie Creek, leaving five proslavery settlers dead in his wake, Sumner was about to endure his own ordeal of violence in the Senate, one which numerous Southerners had threatened but few believed would actually be carried out.

Sumner's oration was received in a predictable fashion. Friends like Whittier called it a "grand and terrible philippic" that "has *saved the country.*" Greeley's *New York Tribune* found it "the most masterly, striking and scathing production of the session"; Sumner had "bravely denounced the Kansas swindle from first to last." While questioning Sumner's language because of Butler's popularity, Carl Schurz, the German-born Republican leader from Wisconsin, concluded that the Senator's words "in point of acerbity and personal offensiveness"

were "far behind the brutal insults which had been frequently hurled from the proslavery side of the Senate at him and his
political friends." The Free Soil *National Era* strongly agreed,
and noted that Sumner, "who had been ridiculed by Mr. Butler," had merely returned "the battery of ridicule upon him
with tremendous force."

Yet, as Seward's abolitionist wife Frances cautioned Sumner, "cutting personal sarcasm" seldom produced anything
but bitterness. Animosity was the rule throughout the South
with the *Columbus Enquirer* (Ga.) speaking for many in condemning "with unmitigated censure the low and undignified
language of the Senator from Massachusetts" who chose "to
degrade the dignity of the whole Senate by insulting one of its
members with blackguard ribaldry." There were predictions
that Sumner would soon be called to account for his abusive
tirade.

In the past as Sumner had delivered Senate speeches,
Southerners had attempted to disrupt his efforts by talking
loudly or milling around the floor and in general being uncivil. Following his "Crime Against Kansas" address, rumors
spread that a violent attack on the senator was also a possibility. Republican John A. Bingham of Ohio told Wilson that he
had heard such threats. Wilson in turn consulted Anson
Burlingame and Schuyler Colfax, both members of the House,
about plans to escort Sumner to and from the Capitol and to
live with him until the threat had passed. But Sumner had dismissed the idea with, "None of that, Wilson!"

Apparently oblivious to the danger, Sumner sat quietly
working at his desk in the Senate chamber on the afternoon of
May 22, some thirty minutes after the Senate had adjourned.
With few people close by, he was approached by Preston
Brooks, a handsome young congressman from South Carolina,
the son of Butler's cousin. Sumner later testified that Brooks
exclaimed: "I have read your speech over carefully. It is a libel
on South Carolina and Mr. Butler who is a relative of mine."

Before finishing, he launched into a series of blows on Sumner's head with his cane. When the stick broke in pieces, he continued the assault with one of the fragments. Attempting to rise from his seat, Sumner wrenched up the desk "which was screwed to the floor," and then fell to the floor in bloody unconsciousness.

During the beating a *New York Times* reporter, James W. Simonton, had tried to intervene but was stopped by Representative Lawrence M. Keitt of South Carolina, who, "with his cane raised, cried 'Let them alone, Let them alone.'" Finally, Brooks was seized by Ambrose S. Murray of New York after the shouted warning "Don't kill him" from another brought him to his senses. Brooks, who had planned with Keitt only to teach Sumner a lesson, had instead lost control. He later told his brother that he had given the senator "about 30 first rate stripes. Towards the last he bellowed like a calf. I wore my cane out completely but saved the Head which is gold." He concluded proudly that "every lick went where I intended."

After several minutes Sumner regained consciousness and recognized others at a distance including Douglas and Robert Toombs of Georgia who merely watched, offering no assistance. Bystanders then carried him out of the chamber, where a doctor had been summoned to dress his wounds. Shortly thereafter, Wilson took him, still in his blood-soaked clothes, in a carriage to his lodgings. There the physician, Cornelius Boyle, ministered to him again but indicated that he could not yet assess the extent of the injuries. Clearly, however, there would be no quick return to Congress for the senator from Massachusetts.

While Sumner remained heavily sedated in his rooms, the nation responded with shock upon learning of what had occurred. Initially the Senate appeared ready to act and the next day approved a motion by Seward that a committee of five be appointed to investigate the assault. But with Southerners unwilling to trust the appointments to the chair, a Mason amendment to elect the members was approved. Election meant that all of those chosen were Democrats; those elected included three Southerners and Cass: none were Sumner allies. The debate leading to the vote included an angry exchange between Wilson and Butler, the latter defending Brooks for "acting under the dictates of high honor." Predictably, the Senate committee chose to do nothing. Instead, it concluded that it was up to the House to investigate and take action since the assault "was committed by one of its members."

The House, under Republican control, could be expected to probe more deeply, although any finding it rendered would be controversial. It was the House committee that interviewed Sumner in his quarters shortly after the assault and then, by strict party vote, recommended the expulsion of Brooks. After extended debate, the whole body approved the committee recommendation 121 to 95, far short of the two-thirds required for expulsion. The committee's call for censure of Keitt was narrowly approved. Both votes followed party and sectional lines, with all Republicans voting with the majorities and virtually all slave state representatives opposed. Brooks quickly resigned after an emotional defense of his action, but he withdrew with the assurance that his constituents would return him to Congress with a unanimous vote of confidence. Federal court proceedings in early July added to the heated emotions, although Brooks's only penalty was a $300 fine. Sumner declined to testify at the trial, but Butler, Mason, and other Southerners were present to support their friend. Admitting to the charge of assault, the thirty-seven-year-old South Carolinian compared his action to that of a husband avenging his wounded honor against his wife's assailant.

While Congress and the court deliberated, public opinion in both the North and the South reacted with fury. With few exceptions, Southerners applauded Brooks and his deed. One South Carolina extremist promised Sumner an even "worse thrashing" if he dared "insult our little state" again. Brooks was embraced as a hero throughout the slave states. Said the *Richmond Enquirer*, the assault was "good in conception, better in execution and best of all in consequences," while the *Charleston Daily Courier* exclaimed that the proper response to Brooks was "to reecho the words 'well done' from Washington to the Rio Grande." Even the conservative *Columbus Enquirer* (Ga.), while declining to endorse the violence, suggested that those "who indulge in vituperative personalities must not be surprised if they arouse passions which it is not always possible to restrain. . . . They who sow the wind may expect to reap the whirlwind." The paper also decried the protests of "puritanic descendants and negro worshippers" in Massachusetts who now support "this martyr of foul language."

Southern members of Congress were equally vehement in their reactions. Mason of Virginia found Brooks's action "one of painful duty" necessary to protect "the honor of his friend" Butler, while Jefferson Davis of Mississippi added that the assailant had been wrongfully made "the subject of vilification, misrepresentation and persecution, *because he resented a libelous assault upon the reputation*" of South Carolina. When Congress adjourned in late summer, receptions and testimonial dinners were held in Brooks's honor throughout his state. He received numerous live-oak canes from admiring Southerners, in recognition of the act and the cause he had defended. The South appeared united in believing that Sumner had got what he deserved. Southerners agreed that they must continue to defend themselves, with violence if necessary, against those who would threaten their way of life. Yet by defending Brooks for his assault on a man they feared and despised, they played into the hands of antislavery advocates. Inevitably they allowed Northerners to depict the attack as representative of the violence of the slave system and of the southern spirit.

Northern reaction was one of bitter hostility to the South in general and to Brooks in particular, coupled with a realization that the beating made Sumner a martyr to the cause of freedom. Astute politicians were quick to realize that the incident might result in added support for the Republican party and its position on Kansas. Among the first to write to Sumner was Ohio governor Chase, who wished that he had been near to offer aid "when the dastardly ruffian struck you down." J. S. Rock spoke for the black citizens of Boston in expressing confidence in him "as a faithful friend of the slave." Reformer Richard Cobden represented Sumner's many English friends in decrying "the use of the bludgeon as a mode of replying" to a political opponent. Sumner heard from countless obscure Northerners who had never written to him before, such as a man from Keokuk, Iowa, who noted that the senator had the "painful privilege to be the first martyr in the cause of *Freedom*" in Congress. The Republican press was equally strong in its defense of Sumner and attack on Brooks. The *National Era* asserted that "the assault is one without mitigating circumstances" and concluded that "there was nothing in the speech to justify or excuse violence."

A recurring theme in the North emphasized that the beating served as a useful weapon against slavery. Abolitionist Henry Bowditch explained, it would "awaken our people from the lethargy which they have sunk." The cause of freedom, whether it be in resisting proslavery activists in Kansas or aiding fugitives in Boston, had been advanced dramatically. As Republican leaders prepared to circulate thousands of copies of "The Crime Against Kansas" in pamphlet form, Massachusetts legislator Stone suggested that when Sumner returned to Boston as the hero of a great cause, "we can bring together a large class of influential people who would not be so likely otherwise to step within our ranks."

Many of Sumner's political opponents in Massachusetts and elsewhere were as eager to denounce Brooks and the South as Republicans were. Conservatives Everett and Winthrop, who had been deeply upset by the senator's speech, were even more outraged by the beating and appeared willing for a time to work more closely with Republicans. The political potential of the situation was dramatically promising. Public meetings of protest were most common in Sumner's home state, including a mass demonstration of support in Faneuil Hall, but they occurred in cities and small towns throughout the East and the Old Northwest. In New York, five thousand shouted their protests at a rally at the Broadway Tabernacle, while in Kansas, free-state settlers joined their voices to the rising chorus. Northerners now found it easier to believe what Sumner and other Republicans had long claimed: Southerners, or the "Slave Power," as they preferred to call those who dominated Congress, were guilty of an arbitrary and unrestrained exercise of authority. Antislavery advocates believed that this southern influence was achieved by an alliance with weak-willed and conservative Northerners in Congress and a presidency that allowed them to dictate the actions of the national government in an undemocratic and oppressive way.

Related events further hurt the southern image and played into northern hands. Butler himself added to the Republican momentum when, in a Senate speech in mid-June, he complained of Sumner's absence and suggested that "the minor flesh wounds" Brooks had inflicted "ought not to have detained him." The southern press even charged that Sumner had acted cowardly in the face of the beating. The *Columbus Enquirer* claimed that Brooks had given him ample time to respond before striking him, but that the senator was "too irresolute or terrified to defend himself manfully."

Brooks intensified the northern fury when he challenged Wilson to a duel after the latter's verbal attack on Butler in the Senate. Wilson contemptuously dismissed Brooks's reaction as the "lingering relic of a barbarous civilization." Bitter criticism of Brooks by Massachusetts Congressman Burlingame, in which he compared the assault on Sumner to Cain's killing of his brother Abel, brought another Brooks challenge to duel. But when Brooks refused to travel north for such a showdown, Northerners could picture him as a coward, and the further violence that Sumner had feared was averted.

Sumner and his Republican cause gained additional stature when the senator requested that proposed private financial assistance for his medical expenses should instead be given to antislavery residents in Kansas to further "the security of freedom" there. Yet as important as Republican momentum was to Sumner, it would mean little if his injuries were too severe to prevent a quick return to the Senate.

Rather than the quick recovery and return to the Senate that he had hoped for, Sumner's full restoration to health was slow and painful, stretching over the next three and a half years in a process that became almost as controversial as the speech and caning had been. Inevitably, his recuperation became entwined in both national and state politics, an issue in the 1856 presidential election, and a divisive factor among Massachusetts Republicans, several of whom coveted his Senate seat should he prove unable to continue.

Initially, Sumner's injuries, while serious, did not appear to be the kind that would keep him out of the Senate for more than a short time. In testimony to the House committee, Dr. Boyle reported that "the scalp had been cut through to the bone in two ragged cuts two and one-quarter inches long and one less than two inches." In addition, Sumner had suffered "bruises on his head, neck, shoulders and hands," and there had been a heavy loss of blood. The attack had occurred on Thursday; by Saturday, the senator's brother George arrived from Boston to care for him during his recuperation. The following day Marshall S. Perry, a prominent Boston physician and friend of Sumner, came to supervise whatever additional treatment might be necessary.

Recovery appeared to be progressing normally, and on Monday the senator was able to give his testimony to the House committee that visited his boarding house. Sumner had already begun talking of appearing in the Senate when on Tuesday a major setback developed. Perry later reported that "during the night the pain became very violent," and when he saw his patient on Wednesday his fever was high, he felt "extreme nervousness," and "the scalp above the right ear was inflamed." For the next three days "he was in a critical situation." After the immediate crisis passed, Sumner suffered "neuralgic pain in the back of the head" and extreme pressure on his brain. With loss of appetite, his weight and strength fell, and he was unable to sleep. He could not walk without pain; "every step he took seemed to produce a shock upon the brain."

In early June, friends moved him to nearby Silver Spring, Maryland, to the home of Republican leader Francis P. Blair, where they hoped an escape from the Washington heat would speed his recovery. Experiencing little relief, Sumner sought a more complete change of scenery and was placed under the care of Dr. R. M. Jackson in the Allegheny Mountains at Cresson, Pennsylvania. There, the combination of mountain air and a carefully prescribed diet and mild exercise regimen brought the first signs of recovery, although many of his painful symptoms persisted. Jackson concluded that "the brain and spinal cord had been the seat of a grave and formidable lesion" with a resulting "inflammation of the brain." Yet after five weeks under the doctor's care, Sumner was convinced that he was ready to resume a normal life. Jackson believed otherwise and indicated later that Sumner "left the mountain prematurely before he was hardened and his body restored."

The senator's impatience with his slow recovery was natural, for he longed to return to the volatile Kansas debates and vindicate his honor. Friends like Phillips urged him to give up any thought of a quick return to the Senate and assured him that the legislature "will give you six more years to work in." Sumner finally abandoned any hope of resuming his Senate work before the late summer adjournment, despite his strong desire to return and expose "the brutality of the slave oligarchy." He told Chase that "never before could I have spoken with so much effect," but he concluded reluctantly, "I must submit."

When the senator left Jackson's care in September he was tormented, not only by a reoccurrence of many of his debilitating symptoms, but also by a rising chorus from southern Democrats that his injuries were far from serious and that he was using them for political purposes. Early in the summer, the *Washington Daily Union* had suggested that he "sought to be martyrized into a reelection" to the Senate. In the course of congressional debates, Butler and other Southerners implied that he was shamming, a charge aired frequently in the next months in the Democratic press of both the North and the South. In response, Sumner and Wilson collected and published letters from the attending physicians attesting to the severity of his wounds, which had affected both his brain and spinal cord, injuries from which he could recover in time "unless he allows himself too soon to enter upon his Senatorial duties."

Sumner was naturally infuriated by this "assault on my character" which, he said, only intensified "the character of the original act" of Brooks himself. Adding to his depressed state and his very real pain and suffering was the haunting fear that he was not recovering and that he might never return to a normal and active life. In October, he despondently told Bigelow that "I am still an invalid, with weeks if not months of seclusion still before me. . . . My brain and whole nervous system are still jangled and subject to relapse."

Sumner was too weak to campaign for his party in the presidential campaign of 1856, but his silence did his party's cause greater good than any active role he might have played. Republican orators kept the Brooks beating and the senator's precarious health constantly before the electorate. The Democrats and their nominee James Buchanan were hard pressed to counter the Republican themes of "Bleeding Kansas and Bleeding Sumner," which together revealed the continuing aggressiveness of the Slave Power. Seward reassured Sumner that he had done "more than any other" for the party and the antislavery cause.

By any objective measure, Sumner's injuries and sufferings were entirely genuine. Yet Massachusetts Republicans appeared overly eager to exploit his presence by planning an elaborate celebration on his return to Boston to vote. Despite the senator's expressed opposition to "all such receptions" and his desire "to come home in privacy," he reluctantly agreed to accept the cheers of Bostonians at a public gathering. Traveling in a carriage, he was cheered by throngs of supporters along the route. At the statehouse, a crowd of six thousand strained to hear his response to their rousing welcome. After a few words, spoken "with feeble voice," he was forced to give his written comments to reporters. The event, billed as a celebration of his return, was in effect a Republican rally. Sumner's own comments attacking his Democratic opponents as tools of slavery added to the partisanship. The senator also confidently assured Bostonians that he would soon be able to resume his full duties in the Senate. Yet the festivities had taxed Sumner's feeble strength, precipitating a relapse, adding doubt as to when he could resume his Senate duties.

Complicating the issue, the legislature would convene in January 1857 to consider Sumner's reelection, although his martyrdom meant that there would probably be only token opposition. Recognizing the inevitable, Governor Gardner had sought and won reelection rather than challenging Sumner for his senate seat. With Republicans controlling the legislature and an atmosphere of support and sympathy for Sumner prevelant, he was easily chosen. The House gave him all but twelve votes and the Senate its unanimous support, this in sharp contrast to the prolonged struggle of six years earlier. Sumner's acceptance letter described his reelection as a sign that the state was uniting "in fraternal support of a sacred cause." Eight months after the Brooks beating, state politicians recognized that Sumner's popular appeal was too great to challenge and that they must give him further time to recuperate. As 1857 opened, it appeared likely that Sumner would not be healthy enough for some time to serve his state in more than a token fashion. Yet his absence from the Senate would continue to speak loudly for Republican interests.

Sumner's valiant efforts to resume his duties in Washington after his reelection proved frustrating. Until late in the session, which was scheduled to end in early March, he had remained in Boston. "Urgent counsel" from his physicians suggested that an additional six to twelve months of rest away from Washington would be necessary "before I shall be thoroughly well." He continued to feel extreme pressure on his head when tired or exerting his mind in any great effort. His friends unanimously advised him to make no Senate appearance during the short session of early 1857, and Wilson urged that he announce that under doctor's advice he would not attend at least until the new Congress convened in December.

Sumner was determined, however, to be present, at least briefly, when his vote could be most useful. Accordingly, late in February he appeared in the Senate chamber to be greeted warmly by Republicans and ignored by Democrats. Too weak to sit through a day of debate, he returned to his lodgings, where he waited to be called when his vote was needed on a tariff reduction bill beneficial to New England woolen manufacturers. He explained that he was "in torment" much of the time and that "a cloud began to gather over my brain." He had abandoned all thought of speaking, for Dr. Perry had warned that he would probably have a "congestion of the brain if I made the attempt." Shortly after being sworn in for his second term in early March, he left for Europe in search of recovery, lamenting to Blair, "This condition must end. What is life without health? Ten months of mine have nearly gone and I am still an invalid."

Even before he sailed, events were occurring that might help him put his torment behind him. The death of Preston Brooks at thirty-seven in early 1857 would have been little noted had it not been for his singular act of violence. Wilson reported to Sumner the details of Brooks's funeral service in the House, which included the "frantic" efforts of Southerners to outdo each other in his praise. The eulogy given by John Savage of Tennessee compared Brooks's act with Brutus's stabbing of Caesar, an event which he suggested history had applauded. To Wilson and other Republicans, Brooks's demise revealed instead that "God has avenged the blows of May last."

But Sumner felt no vengeance then or later that same year at the death of Andrew Butler. Longfellow noted that rather than as an object of hatred, Sumner saw Brooks "as a mere tool of the slaveholders." Always eager to confront slavery and engage its proponents in bitter acrimonious debate, Sumner had nonetheless remained forgiving in the face of the attack and the ensuing insults. So too would he be silent and conciliatory at the death of his two antagonists.

Sumner's first trip abroad had occurred twenty years earlier, when, as a young man of twenty-six, he had gone to study European societies, people, and institutions. Now he sought to renew many of the friendships he had made, although his primary hope was to improve his health in order to expedite his return to the Senate at the end of the year for a renewed assault on slavery. His eight months in Europe appeared at first to be accomplishing that goal, for his health did improve, albeit with setbacks along the way. He divided his time primarily between England and France, and although his schedule was hectic at times, he wisely kept his focus on rest and relaxation. Travel and personal contacts served both to reinvigorate him and increase his desire to return to the Senate.

For a time he believed that his recovery was progressing satisfactorily, but it was never total and there were frequent relapses. In June, he became so weak that he could not leave his room for ten days. Headaches persisted, as did the "sensitivity" in his spine. It was the opinion of several English doctors, including Queen Victoria's physician, that if the senator returned to political activity in less than a year, "he will become a permanent invalid." This additional psychological obstacle to recovery guaranteed that the fear of a relapse would haunt him even after his return.

Sumner had gone abroad hoping to forget sectional politics, but in this he failed completely, an additional factor slowing his recovery. His desire to be kept abreast with developments in Washington and Boston along with his friends' eagerness to supply regular updates meant that he was seldom out of touch. Howe, Adams, Chase, and Wilson continually provided him news of U.S. politics, which included the Supreme Court's Dred Scott decision denying the federal government the power to ban territorial slavery. Reports of further turmoil in Kansas and Congress and of the Buchanan administration's efforts to gain statehood for Kansas on a proslavery basis added to the senator's discomfort, and he told Howe that he feared that Kansas was "a doomed territory." Most discouraging was Adams's assessment that "the Slave Power rides triumphant" in Washington and "makes the President bow to its supremacy." Such views only confirmed Sumner's "renewed determination to give myself to our great cause." He thus sailed for home in early November ever fearful of a relapse but eager to reenter the sectional fray.

Sumner's arrival in Washington in December for the new session of Congress was a totally unhappy experience. He faced the added concern of his own safety due to threats such as that from a Southerner who promised that "you shall not occupy a seat in the Senate," adding that the senator's "scalp in South Carolina would bring quite a price." Sumner told Whittier of his desire to speak against slavery in the Senate "and liberate my soul," but added that he was alarmed that if he did he might be shot. Such fears accelerated the return of his old symptoms, and he endured several weeks in Washington of renewed pain and agony. Unable to serve on any committee because of his condition, he remained "a passive spectator" in the Senate until finally retreating to Boston at the end of December. With Wilson's urging, he returned again to Washington several times to be on hand for key votes on Kansas. On the final Senate vote approving the proslavery Lecompton constitution, all he could do was "to cry out in a loud voice, 'No.'" After each vote, he retreated to New York or Philadelphia, close enough to hurry back when Wilson wired him of a pending vote, but far enough away to avoid the pressure of the Washington scene. Much to his relief, the Northern-dominated House rejected the bill and the Kansas issue remained stalemated.

In April 1858, Sumner suffered a major relapse. In addition to a kidney complication, he endured renewed back pains and "pressure on the brain attended with lameness and exhaustion," so severe were his symptoms that friends had to help him return to his quarters. His physician now confirmed the English doctors' prognosis of the need for further rest to prevent permanent disability: "The recurrence of these symptoms at such slight notice and without sufficient cause" meant that Sumner's system was "still that of an invalid."

Frustration and discouragement best described Sumner's mood as he made plans for a return to Europe in late May. He told Howe that "all my plans are clouded. I had hoped to do something—indeed to strike a blow before this session closed." Almost pathetically, he asked: "When will it all end?" As he boarded the steamer *Vanderbilt* in New York, he released a letter to his Massachusetts constituents explaining the need for further time away from the Senate as recommended by his American and English physicians. But he was now more eager than ever to expose "the hideousness of Slavery" as soon as could return to his duties. Even more important, he concluded, was that supporters had assured him that "my vacant chair was a perpetual speech."

Sumner's second effort at recuperation abroad began inauspiciously, and his prospects for a full recovery appeared at a lower ebb than at any time since the caning. His letter to Massachusetts voters was seized on by opponents as a means of derision among Democrats, North and South. The *New York Herald* led the chorus by questioning how Sumner's constituents liked being "represented by an empty chair." As the attacks accelerated, few were willing to come to Sumner's defense until Greeley's *Tribune* countered that his "vacant chair is more useful to the country than many of the full ones in the chamber." There were demands from some that he resign, and for the first time his tenure in the Senate appeared to be in jeopardy.

Physically, Sumner's condition matched his political outlook. On his arrival in Paris, he was in intense pain, both to his head, with the least mental exertion including reading, and to his back, with any attempt to walk. Near desperation, Sumner was willing to try any treatment that promised relief. Unlike his visit a year earlier, which he had spent resting and traveling, he now subjected himself to the most controversial of medical experiments. On the recommendation of a Boston merchant, he consulted a well-known physician in the field of nerve disorders, Charles Edward Brown-Séquard. After a lengthy examination, the doctor concluded that the remedy was "fire" to absorb "the excess fluid" around the brain. A special moxa would be applied, burning the skin of his neck and back. Sumner accepted the diagnosis and treatment without hesitation, even turning down the chloroform that could ease the pain, because he had been told that it might lessen the treatment's effectiveness.

Brown-Séquard administered six such moxas during the next two weeks, later noting that he had "never seen a man bearing such fortitude as Mr. Sumner has shown, the extremely violent pain of this kind of burning." For two months the senator was in intense agony, spending most of his time in bed, frequently unable to sleep, and seeing few people. The doctor assured him that the more he suffered, the greater his "chance of being cured." Adding to his misery was the onset of chest pains, which the doctor called "neuralgia," and a later generation would diagnose as angina pectoris, most probably induced or at least intensified by the shock of the burning.

Many of Sumner's friends were horrified by his reports from Paris of his treatment and the suffering that it required him to endure, and they were not reassured by his explanations. He told Longfellow that "the torment is great," but even worse was "the succession of blisters, inflammations and smarts." But he assured him of Brown-Séquard's belief "that without this

cruel treatment I should have been a permanent invalid."
With the Paris correspondent of the *New York Tribune* providing an even fuller coverage of Sumner's treatment to American readers, there could be little doubt of his real suffering
and his determination to be cured. Longfellow responded
simply with the injunction: "No more fire! No more moxa!"
Howe, a doctor himself, felt nothing but distrust for Brown-
Séquard's methods, while Sumner's Boston physician Perry
believed that total rest would have helped more than "the ap-
plication of hot irons."

In fact, there is no evidence that the treatment did anything
physiologically to speed his recovery. Nonetheless, Sumner did
begin a gradual healing process that, while taking another year
and a half to complete, may have been aided by the effect the
treatment had on his mental state. Never doubting the success
of the fire treatment, Sumner and his French physician believed that it had hastened his recovery immeasurably.

Sumner's summer of suffering in 1858 was followed by a
lengthy stay at the mineral springs of Aix-les-Bains, with its
daily treatment of hot and cold baths, and a quiet winter in
southern France. Through it all Sumner finally began to heal,
both in mind and body, content that Americans now believed
that he had not been shamming. There were still minor relapses that brought the return of some symptoms, but with as-
surances that further rest away from Washington would fully
restore his health, he reluctantly agreed to remain abroad
through 1859, until the next Congress convened in December. Toward the end of his stay he announced to Adams "that
I am to return a well man." After visits in London, his last
weeks in Paris were spent shopping for books, bronzes, porce-
lain, and other art works, purchases which may have helped
his psyche but which would leave him in debt for months to
come. His adjustment to the rapidly changing political scene
at home would present an even more difficult problem.

By the time Sumner returned to Boston in November 1859,
he had been out of the country and out of direct touch with

U.S. politics for more than a year and a half. Most Republicans greeted him warmly, for the reports of his extended suffering had increased his popularity. During his absence, his conservative alma mater Harvard had extended him an honorary doctor of law degree, an announcement that Longfellow reported "was received by the assembly with a cordial burst of applause." Old friendships such as that with Felton had been restored to their former warmth. And his health appeared to be increasingly strong, all important in light of continuing political storms in Boston and Washington.

Massachusetts politics remained fluid, and there were still those who coveted Sumner's seat in the Senate. Chief among them was Nathaniel Banks, elected governor in 1857 as a Republican, the center of party dissension because of his apparent willingness to compromise antislavery principle to forward his own interests. From a distance Sumner had found such factionalism incomprehensible. In the fall of 1858, Banks had tried to use his position as governor to force Sumner's resignation by engineering a resolution at the party convention that "the first duty of a representative" was "to attend the session of the body of which he is a member." Although Banks claimed that this resolution was not aimed at Sumner and backed away from a confrontation when the senator's friends rallied in his behalf, Sumner now recognized the need to keep up his guard. He knew he must show himself healthy enough to convince doubters that he was again capable of an active role in the Senate.

As in the past, Sumner found the sectional conflict in Congress much more to his taste than the intrigues of state politics. Yet his return to Washington would tax all of his strength and resolve as the nation drifted toward the secession crisis. Further threats on his life alarmed both the senator and his friends. Republicans, although still a minority in the Senate, had increased their strength considerably, and they now controlled the House. It was thus a far different scene from his first session in 1851 when he had been one of three Free Soilers whom others feared and despised. Although Democrats were anything but cordial to him upon his return, he was assigned to the Committee on Foreign Relations, a position that later gave him the opportunity to exert influence in an area of his special interest and expertise. In the immediate session, however, with Mason chairing the committee, it would be a scene of conflict rather than deliberate debate. Still, Sumner expected to ease himself back into his duties gradually and to refrain from major Senate speeches until he was sure of his strength.

During his long months away from Washington, the sectional crisis had continued to intensify. The Kansas issue remained unresolved, with Republicans using their control of the House to frustrate the prosouthern policies of Buchanan and the Democratic-controlled Senate. The Supreme Court had entered the fray in March 1857 with its ruling in the Dred Scott case, which legitimized territorial slavery and challenged the key platform plank of the Republican party. The president's determination to satisfy the South by admitting Kansas as a slave state had antagonized even Senator Douglas, who finally broke with the administration over its refusal to permit a fair vote on slavery by the residents of the territory. In the midterm congressional elections of 1858, Douglas survived the challenge of Republican Abraham Lincoln and won reelection with a spirited defense of his popular sovereignty doctrine. He hoped to ride his victory into a Democratic nomination for president in 1860. Thus little had been resolved during Sumner's long enforced absence, and North-South relations had become even more strained.

Sumner's hope for a quiet return to the Senate proved even more difficult because of the political uproar following John Brown's raid at Harpers Ferry in October 1859. The assault on the federal arsenal there had been designed to free and arm the slaves of the Upper South and had indirectly involved several of Sumner's friends. Initially, Sumner stayed out of the Senate debate and privately deplored Brown's act. But he could not help but admire "the singular courage and character shewn by its author." Among those who had provided financial aid to Brown was Concord journalist Franklin Sanborn, who resisted his summons to appear before the Senate investigating committee. With the help of Sumner and others, Sanborn successfully challenged that body's authority to force his testimony. Sumner's several short speeches in March and April helped get Sanborn's case referred to the Judiciary Committee where the matter died. It also marked Sumner's first active participation in Senate debates, and in a bitter exchange with Mason, he revealed that he had lost none of his old passion on slavery-related issues.

Sumner planned a more thorough attack on slavery in the Senate, but the opportunity would not arise until the nominations for the 1860 presidential race were almost complete. As in the past, with no personal ambitions either to be a candidate or to participate actively in Republican politics to name a nominee, he played no role in the process. In part, this was due to the competition between two of his friends, Chase and Seward, to be the candidate, for he desired to offend neither. He was closer personally to Chase, but he recognized the greater popular appeal of Seward. With the Democratic party dividing into northern and southern wings and nominating Douglas and John Breckinridge of Kentucky, and a third party choosing John Bell of Tennessee, Sumner assumed that whomever the Republicans nominated at their Chicago convention would be elected. He believed, as did most, that Seward would be the choice but determined to "keep aloof from personal questions."

Sumner remained in Washington rather than attending the convention and was thus surprised to learn that the delegates had rejected Seward and had nominated dark-horse candidate Abraham Lincoln. He quickly consoled the New York senator over his defeat and explained to an English friend that as a prominent and controversial senator, Seward was "too much known" to be nominated. Lincoln, he believed, was "a good honest Anti-Slavery man" but one with "little acquaintance with government" and "uninformed on Foreign Affairs." Nonetheless, he concluded, "we think he will be the next President."

With the critical presidential campaign of 1860 underway, Sumner concluded that the time was ripe to deliver a thorough attack on slavery. Several factors motivated him. Since his return to Congress he had played only a secondary role in debates, and some still wondered if he was strong enough to participate on the same level that he had before his caning. When the session opened in late 1859, friends reminded him that "much is expected of you." He must make "one great speech" so that all would be convinced of his recovery. Such an effort would also convince himself of his ability to resume his old role and end any lingering doubts about his strength and stamina.

Sumner's long absence had made him even more radical on slavery-related issues. Three and a half years of enforced silence had served only to make him more determined to expose the moral wrongs of the southern way of life. He also feared that some of his Republican colleagues were too willing to compromise on slavery-related issues in the face of southern aggressiveness. Alarmed that such backsliding resulted from the need to appear moderate in order to win the presidential election, he complained to Longfellow that "our own republicans are often hollow in their professions." Clearly they needed to be reminded that "slavery barbarizes everything here" and that they must stand firm. His address, to be called "The Barbarism of Slavery," would meet that need.

When news spread of Sumner's plans to speak in the Senate on June 4, interest mounted and the galleries filled. In contrast, many Democrats absented themselves or made a point of appearing not to be interested as they contemptuously busied themselves with other activities in the Senate chamber even as he spoke. Rather than committing his speech to memory as in the past, Sumner thought it wiser to read it, perhaps forfeiting some of the dramatic effect in favor of not overtaxing himself. The bill under debate would admit Kansas to the union as a free state, but he referred to that issue only briefly in his four-hour indictment of slavery and its defenders.

Sumner began by quoting the eighteenth-century English religious leader John Wesley that slavery was "the sum of all villanies." He then launched into a detailed description of its cruel and inhuman effect. By "its conversion of a human being into chattel or a piece of property," it abrogated marriage and parental relations, closed "the gates of knowledge" and appropriated "all the toil of its victims" to the exploitation of slaveowners. Outlining its brutalizing effect on the slaveowner, he quoted an advertisement from a Georgia newspaper:

> 'Runaway—My man Fountain; has holes in his ears; a scar on the right side of his forehead; has been shot in the hind part of his legs; is marked on his back with the whip. Apply to Robert Beaseley, Macon, Georgia.' Hole in the ears; scar on the forehead; shot in the legs; and marks of the lash on his back; Such are the tokens by which the slave Master identifies his slave.

Sumner then indicted the three agents "by which the Barbarism is maintained—the Slave-Overseer, the Slave-Breeder and the Slave-Hunter," together "constituting a triumvirate of Slavery in whom its essential brutality, vulgarity and crime are all embodied."

The senator concluded with a defense of the Republican party's position on the relationship of slavery to the Constitution, hoping to steel his brethren to stand firm during the approaching campaign. Here he reviewed the ground he had covered in earlier speeches. He did not question the right of each state to control "its domestic institutions." But neither Congress nor a territory could "give legal existence to slavery in the United States." Finally, addressing the bill before the Senate, he concluded that Congress must admit Kansas as a free state: "Then will the Barbarism of Slavery be repelled and the pretension of property in man be rebuked."

Sumner was convinced that his speech had met his objectives, and his many friends agreed. As he made plans for a massive distribution of the address, he sent one of the first copies to candidate Lincoln, with the explanation that he had "endeavored to expose the true character of the assumptions now made by Slave-Masters." He added his "hope that what I said may help our great cause." Schurz congratulated him and expressed his delight "to hear again the true ring of the moral Antislavery sentiment," while Frederick Douglass rejoiced "at the tremendous exposure of the meanness, brutality . . . and barbarism of American Slavery." Giddings, Garrison, Phillips, and Chase were among the several hundred who sent congratulatory letters regarding the speech, while candidate Lincoln responded that he anticipated both "pleasure and instruction from it." In sharp contrast, others in both the North and the South reacted with shock, horror, or abuse.

That Southerners would treat his speech with contempt and anger surprised no one. Senator James Chestnut of South Carolina spoke for many, complaining that when Sumner had left the Senate four years earlier, "we had hoped to be relieved from the outpourings of such vulgar malice." Yet, said Chestnut, Southerners must not respond to him: "Let him remain in the solicitude of his own irremedial and ineffable infamy." The *Charleston Daily Courier* leaped to Chestnut's defense when it exclaimed that he had "effectively answered the mendacious and malignant" senator "who through the madness of the hour disgraces a Senatorial chair of Massachusetts."

After a drunken Virginian confronted Sumner in his boarding house, accusing him of having slandered all slaveholders and threatening to return with others to cut his "d—d throat," northern congressmen Burlingame and John Sherman insisted on staying with him to protect him until tensions eased. The *Richmond Dispatch* claimed that Sumner was "the mouthpiece of a powerful party" and "the spirit in which the South is regarded" by all Republicans. It was their design "to make uncompromising war upon the South—to destroy its institutions at any cost of blood." The paper concluded: "this is nothing more nor less than a proclamation of civil war." Southerners felt their charges confirmed when, less than two weeks after his attack on slavery, Sumner presented antislavery petitions from his black constituents. When the Senate rebuffed his effort because of the petitioners' race, he attacked southern attempts to deny them "*the liberty to pray*," arguing that "in the history of misfortune or of tyranny nothing can surpass this final act of robbery."

Much of the northern press was equally negative in its response to Sumner's efforts. The Democratic *New York Herald* urged its readers to the conclusion that his attack on slavery proved that the Republican party could not be trusted with the presidency. Much of the Republican press and party leadership feared that voters might react just as the *Herald* predicted. Greeley's *Tribune* found the speech "strong and forcible," but "ill-timed" because it could lead to a Senate rejection of Kansas statehood. The *Springfield Daily Republican* agreed that while the speech effectively attacked slavery, its "usefulness" to the party's cause was doubtful. Sumner's response to such criticism was to label it an effort "to read me out of the party" for speaking the truth. Rather than bending, he would redouble his efforts to circulate the speech to an even larger audience.

Many Republican party leaders would have been happier had Sumner remained silent, both in the Senate and during the ensuing campaign. The party was composed of a delicate coalition of disparate factions: former Whigs interested in economic issues that would favor business; nativistic elements still hoping to revive the antiforeign sentiments of the Know Nothings; antislavery Democrats antagonized by the pro-South policies of the Buchanan administration but insistent that the party avoid any implication of interference with southern slavery; and the more radical antislavery wing led by Seward, Chase, and Sumner. Party leaders were naturally eager to steer a middle course to appeal to the broadest cross section of the northern electorate. They feared that Sumner would jeopardize their efforts to portray the party and its candidates as representing moderation on sectional issues. They also worried lest Southerners, impressed by Sumner's words, believe that he spoke for the whole party and conclude that a Republican president would forsake their interests, forcing their decision to secede the Union.

But Sumner's strength and determination had been renewed, and he would not be stifled. Soon after Congress adjourned he delivered a campaign oration at Cooper Institute in New York to three thousand cheering enthusiasts. In addition to a ringing endorsement of Lincoln and an attack on Douglas's "popular sovereignty dodge," he repeated much of his Senate attack on slavery and the need for Republicans to stand firm against it. During the late summer and fall he spoke widely in Massachusetts and Maine, most notably with a powerful appeal to his state's party convention in Worcester. Again he singled out Douglas and his fellow northern Democrats, who "by dishonest, audacious theories on Slavery, both morally and constitutionally" have "put all who truly love their country on the defensive." As the election approached, he was far from the reluctant politician mourning the abandonment of scholarly pursuits that he had been when first elected to the Senate. His commitment to the antislavery cause had intensified since his caning and recovery, and he enthusiastically campaigned for his party.

Sumner's vigorous efforts in the Senate and on the campaign trail convinced him that his health was fully restored and that he had regained his antislavery prominence. He wrote to Brown-Séquard that he had completed his Senate address "without any touch of my old perverse complaints" and his New York speech "without any sensation beyond that of simple fatigue and not much of that." As he looked ahead to the November election, he confidently noted, "I do not doubt the result. Lincoln will be chosen." But then would begin "a new class of perils and anxieties." While he felt that the threats of secession "have no force," the new president's competency in organizing the government remained to be tested. He concluded: "Idealist as I am, I shall prepare myself in advance for many disappointments."

CHAPTER FOUR

Spokesman of the Antislavery Conscience

The presidential election of 1860 set in motion a series of events that kept Charles Sumner in the political spotlight. He rejoiced with the victory of Abraham Lincoln, believing his long-sought goal of abolition had moved closer to realization. But the times were fraught with immediate dangers. More imminent than emancipation was the threat of the secession of the slave states and a bloody civil war that could have major international implications relating to foreign neutrality. Soon to chair the Senate Committee on Foreign Relations, Sumner knew that he would play a major role in the congressional response to the new administration's diplomatic policies. Even more pressing was the danger of war itself, for, given his commitment to peace, the prospect of bloody strife among Americans placed the senator in a terrible dilemma. As Sumner explained to the Duchess of Argyll, "Much as I desire the extinction of Slavery, I do not wish to see it go down in blood." Yet as Sumner faced the issues of secession and war, he concluded that emancipation was worth whatever it might cost. He would thus exert his influence in seeking to persuade the president to the same conclusion and then to take the next step of encouraging the enlistment of freedmen in the Union army. Throughout the war years he thus remained an ever-steady voice of moral conscience, seeking to persuade others to accept the racial implications of a war against slavery.

Sumner remained almost totally preoccupied with official senatorial duties, even as he became deeply involved in Civil War issues, but his personal relations with friends and family continued to be as large a part of his life as they had ever been. Although his dedication to antislavery principle got in the way of close ties with Charles Francis Adams, other relationships, such as that with Lieber, were happily restored. Sumner had, as mentioned, broken with the professor in the early 1850s because of Lieber's tolerance of the slaveholders of South Carolina, where he lived. At the start of the war, Lieber taught at Columbia College in New York, and the two resumed an important correspondence. During the war and Reconstruction years, Lieber, an expert on military law, advised Sumner on many critical issues relating to legal technicalities. Sumner, in turn, was instrumental in securing a commission in the Union army for one of the professor's sons.

Sumner's closest friends continued to be Longfellow and Howe, and with them there were few ideological differences. The poet's agreement with the senator's stance on public questions and his apolitical nature had permitted their friendship to ripen and strengthen. Tragically, early in the war Longfellow's wife Fanny had died in a fire, a shock from which her husband took months to recover. When he was finally ready to be consoled, Sumner became a solid rock for him in his loneliness. As Longfellow's grief gradually lessened, Sumner was instrumental in getting his friend's mind focused on other things and was especially supportive when his son was injured in battle late in the war.

Sumner's family ties also strengthened during the war. His brother George had returned from years abroad in 1852 and had helped nurse Sumner during the first months after his beating. The two remained in close touch thereafter, and Charles grew increasingly solicitous as George's health de-

clined early in the war. With the tragic death at sea of brother
Albert in 1856, his only other surviving sibling was Julia. He
had been overly protective in the 1850s when she had married
a young physician. Now Sumner maintained close contact with
both Julia, who had moved to California, and with his aging
mother, who still lived in the family home on Hancock Street.
During his long months in Washington, he constantly sought
news from Howe of her health and that of George. He worried
especially that during his absence the care of George would
prove overly taxing on his mother. His return to Boston each
time Congress adjourned allowed him to strengthen those
family ties, which now seemed more important than when he
was younger.

But the dramatic public events of the early 1860s demanded that Sumner turn from personal concerns. Four months
of drift preceded Lincoln taking office, for lame-duck President Buchanan presided over a government that refused to
act in the face of the secession crisis. Shortly after Congress
convened in December, South Carolina became the first state
to secede from the Union. It was followed shortly by six other
states of the Lower South, which together had formed the
Confederate States of America even before Lincoln arrived in
the capital. Buchanan's indecisiveness was almost equalled by
the indecision within the Republican party, which even Sumner reflected. At first the senator appeared ambivalent over
the severity of the situation and how the government should
respond to secession. Unsure over whether to force the states
back into the Union, he believed they could not survive on
their own, especially if the federal government remained firm
in keeping the Upper South in place. He told Howe that "four
or five [states] should go out *long enough* to be completely
humbled and chastened and to leave us in control of the Government." Yet he could also tell newly elected Massachusetts
Republican Governor John Andrew that in order to avoid war,
he would give up "territory and state."

If the use of force to perserve the Union troubled Sumner,

he never considered backing down on slavery. He was thus appalled to learn of the plans of many in Congress, some in his own party, to compromise on the issue. Such ideas soon centered around the proposals of Senator John J. Crittenden of Kentucky, which included constitutional guarantees of slavery in the territories south of 36°30' and restricted Congress's right to legislate on the subject. Sumner's determination to resist such plans was bolstered by friends like Giddings, who expressed outrage "to find so many cowards even among Republicans." As House and Senate committees formed to work out a way to accommodate the secessionists, sentiment for compromise emerged even in Massachusetts. When three of his former Whig antagonists, Everett, Amos Lawrence, and Winthrop came to Washington to present a giant petition in favor of the Crittenden proposals, Sumner grew more adamant in his protests. At a meeting with the president in early February, Buchanan urged Massachusetts to adopt the compromise, to which Sumner replied that his constituents "would see their State sunk below the sea and turned into a sand-bank before they would adopt propositions acknowledging *property in men.*"

Even more threatening to Sumner were the proposals of fellow Republican Seward. The New York senator favored modification or repeal of the personal liberty laws of the North, a constitutional guarantee that Congress would not interfere with slavery in the states, and the possibility of the creation of a new slave state in the Southwest. Seward had told Sumner of his plan before presenting it, and the latter had "protested with my whole soul." Telling Governor Andrew of his opposition, he explained that he could never "become party to any proposition which sanctions Slavery directly or indirectly." Instead, he had urged Seward to indicate that no action should be taken until Lincoln was inaugurated, for any step other than expressing total confidence in the new president would "demoralize" the North.

Equally disturbing to Sumner was the support for placating

the South given by his old Free Soil colleague Adams. A member of the House committee seeking compromise, Adams was among those urging Massachusetts participation in the Washington Peace Conference called by Virginia Unionists for early February. Opposed even to sending delegates to the conference, Sumner urged Governor Andrew to refuse to appoint any. He was equally vehement in calling on Andrew and other state officials to block repeal of the Massachusetts Personal Liberty law. Such an action, he said, would set a "bad example" for other states. It was critical that Andrew keep the legislators firm: "Don't let them undo anything they have done for Freedom." Warned by friends in Boston of appeasement sentiment, Sumner kept up the pressure through letters to supporters in Massachusetts.

Sumner's adherence to firm antislavery principle was again at the expense of a long personal friendship, in this case with Adams. The two had feuded in 1853 over the proposed revision in the state constitution but had since resolved their differences. Now, in 1861, Adams believed that secession and war could only be avoided by seeking an accommodation with Southerners, seeing in Sumner's stance an "almost grim satisfaction at the prospect of civil conflict." Clearly he misread Sumner's motives, for the senator was as eager as he to avoid war. Hence, when Adams learned of Sumner's efforts to block the appointment of delegates to the peace conference, the two exchanged "rather warm" words and ceased all but formal communication. Ill feelings intensified with the prospect of Adams being named by Lincoln as minister to England. It is likely that Sumner would have welcomed the appointment himself, and some of his friends, including Governor Andrew, worked quietly to secure the place for him. Adams's appointment in mid-March left their relationship even more strained, although it was their differences regarding the secession crisis more than who went to London that caused the breach.

Thanks in large part to the determination of both Sumner and Andrew, Massachusetts remained firm against compromise as the time of Lincoln's inauguration approached. The governor reluctantly appointed delegates to the peace conference, although the men Andrews chose were all opposed to concessions. Sumner was thus "relieved to know that there is not a single weak joint in them." He had earlier spoken in the Senate against the Massachusetts petitions supporting the Crittenden proposals, saying they would "foist into the National Constitution guarantees of Slavery which the framers" had never intended. It was through the efforts of Sumner and like-minded opponents of compromise that neither the Crittenden nor the Peace Conference proposals received congressional approval. Instead, the Sumner principle of "inauguration first, adjustment afterwards" prevailed, and the country tensely waited for the swearing in of the new president. Optimistic that compromise had been rejected, Sumner told Andrew that "if Mr. L *stands firm*, I do not doubt that our cause will be saved."

Lincoln's inaugural address of March 4, 1861, strengthened Sumner's hope that there would be no sacrifice of principle. Although the new president promised not to interfere with slavery where it already existed, he reminded Southerners that the Union was "perpetual," secession unconstitutional, and that "the laws of the Union [would] be faithfully executed in all the States." Although interpretations of Lincoln's words varied according to party and section, Sumner and most Republicans were satisfied. The president had pledged himself not to interfere with slavery, but neither would he tolerate secession to sustain it.

Although Lincoln and his party faced the immediate crisis of secession, Republicans at first appeared preoccupied with dividing the spoils of office. Sumner, like all party members in Congress, was inevitably drawn into the struggle as office-seekers besieged him for the rewards that went with control. He soon found "the scramble for office to be both "enormous and sickening," telling Longfellow that he wished he "could fly away to some other planet." Nevertheless, he quickly accommodated himself to it by actively seeking appointments for those he felt deserving. One of the most important political plums was the position of postmaster of Boston, who would have the duty of appointing more than a hundred clerks. Much of Sumner's early correspondence revolved around the person he would recommend, for tradition dictated that Lincoln ask the senior senator to recommend the appointees for this and many other (Massachusetts) positions. Before making his choices, Sumner consulted closely with party leaders such as Francis Bird and Andrew, who advised that "we must be bold. We must *use* power when we have it." The senator's decision to recommend Palfrey for postmaster indicated that any resentment against the former Free Soiler over his opposition to the proposed state constitution in 1853 had been forgotten.

Equally significant in terms of patronage control was the post of collector of customs for Boston, and again Sumner's input was critical in Lincoln's appointment of John Z. Goodrich. Numerous diplomatic posts were part of the Massachusetts share of patronage, and for the most part Secretary of State Seward honored Sumner's recommendations. Still swamped by requests from other "deserving" Republicans and their friends and relatives, Sumner despaired that patronage concerns were taking too much of his and Lincoln's time; he told Longfellow that the president "ought to be mediating the condition of the country and his great public duties, instead of listening to the tales of office seekers." Indeed, he secretly longed "for my old place" in the minority, "free, open and unembarrassed" by those seeking favors.

Sumner was soon satisfied that Lincoln could rise above patronage feuds and face the seccession crisis boldly. Against cabinet advice, the president ordered reinforcements to be sent to the beleaguered Fort Sumter in Charleston Harbor. By April 14, before the supplies arrived, the Confederates forced the surrender of the fort, and the war had begun. Few could predict then the terrible bloodshed to follow, but for Sumner it was a time of deep torment. Long an opponent of war, he regretted being "called to take such great responsibility in a direful ghastly civil war!" Yet he could honestly justify a war that he believed secessionists had provoked to protect slavery. As the two sides prepared to battle, Sumner, like most Northerners, believed the Confederacy would give in after a brief struggle. In his eyes, the president's resolve had prevailed over the "insincerity and duplicity" of many in Washington: "As I see more of him I like him better."

Sumner would not always feel so positively about Lincoln in the years ahead as he attempted to influence him in both domestic and foreign policy questions. Perhaps their greatest difference, although one which they eventually resolved, concerned the ultimate purpose of the war. Agreeing for the most part with the president's handling of military strategy, Sumner grew increasingly appreciative of the enormous complexities the chief executive faced in handling men and armies. Yet for the senator, the goal of saving the Union could only be achieved by abolishing slavery and guaranteeing equality to the freedmen. The president, with more immediate military issues to face and responsible to a people who did not share Sumner's emancipation goals, pursued a more hesitant policy and came to Sumner's position only slowly and somewhat reluctantly. Lincoln's desire to colonize outside of the country any blacks freed further complicated their differences. Furthermore, emancipation issues would inevitably become intertwined with foreign policy because of the need to prevent European assistance to the Confederacy. Sumner's ongoing differences with Secretary of State Seward compounded his difficulties with the administration. Yet as the war evolved, the president and the senator, despite their vast differences in personality, perspective, and responsibility, came to appreciate each other's better qualities and developed a close working relationship.

How to resolve the status of close to four million slaves in the face of divisive civil war was the greatest challenge facing both president and Congress. In part, Lincoln's policy toward slavery was shaped by the need to keep the four border slave states loyal to the Union. After Virginia and three other Upper South states had joined the Confederacy following the beginning of hostilities, only Maryland, Delaware, Kentucky, and Missouri remained in the Union as slave states. Their importance to the Union strategically and psychologically was clear, and any precipitous move against slavery might force their secession. In addition, many Northerners who supported a war to preserve the Union might balk at one whose goals included emancipation; Lincoln and party leaders in Congress acted with full awareness that an attack on slavery might strengthen the Democratic opposition. To Sumner, such concerns were of far less magnitude than the opportunity the war presented for a frontal attack on the peculiar institution itself. Many of the government's internal differences during the first year and a half of the war revolved around these competing policies.

The specific process of emancipation was not as important to Sumner as freedom itself. While preferring that Congress take the lead in advancing his goal, he readily accepted whatever steps Lincoln might take. Complicating the situation were the attitudes and actions of military commanders in the field. As the fighting accelerated, Sumner hoped that the Union defeat at Bull Run in July 1861 might bring about a greater determination to resist the Confederacy and thus make the "extinction of Slavery inevitable." In August, Congress responded with the first Confiscation Act, authorizing the seizure of slaves used directly in the Confederate war effort. At the end of that month General John C. Frémont, commander of the Union's Western Department, ordered the freeing of the slaves of all Confederate sympathizers in Missouri, thus going far beyond the intentions of either Congress or the president. Sumner hailed Frémont's invoking of martial law to free the slaves as a logical and necessary step. Thus when Lincoln revoked the general's order, fearing its repercussions among border state Unionists and seeing it as a challenge to his executive authority, Sumner reacted with dismay: "Our Presdt is now dictator." He possessed "the power of a God," yet he failed "to use it God-like."

The revoking of Frémont's order finally provoked Sumner publicly to advocate abolition by the federal government. Earlier in the year, he had believed that the president was moving toward emancipation, albeit at too slow a pace. Shortly after his inauguration, Lincoln had told the senator: "You are only six weeks ahead of me." The two consulted frequently on foreign policy matters, and Sumner frequently used such meetings to maintain his gentle pressure toward emancipation. But clearly Sumner had little understanding of the difficult position Lincoln was in, and by fall his patience had worn thin.

Sumner chose the Republican state convention in Worcester in early October to make his position public. Because slavery was the "sole cause and main strength of the rebellion it must be struck down. The means available to the president was a solemn Proclamation" invoking "the War Power," a method that was "positively recognized by the Constitution." Loyal slaveowners might even be compensated for freeing their slaves, for "never should any question of money be allowed to interfere with human freedom." The speech also hinted at the use of blacks as troops in the Union army. Although many convention delegates received his address with enthusiasm, others did not, and the resolutions adopted were silent on emancipation. Clearly Sumner was far ahead of much of his party concerning what he believed to be the central issue of the war.

Sumner, among the first in Congress to call for emancipation, was determined to press on despite resistance. Shortly after the Worcester address, he told Phillips that it was "not in my nature to retreat. My special object will be to shew Slavery" to be the basic cause of the war. His Boston address on October 18, which he called "The Rebellion: Its Origin and Mainspring," expanded on the Worcester themes, again emphasizing that the rebellion was "reinforced by slavery." Because "the fields of the South are cultivated by slaves," the "white freemen are at liberty to play the part of rebels." Thus the slaves, "without taking up arms, [are] actually engaged in feeding, supporting, succoring, invigorating those battling for their enslavement." He proposed a several-step process whereby the president should declare martial law and in effect proclaim emancipation "as a MILITARY NECESSITY, in *just self defense . . . as our armies advance in the Slave States or land on their coasts.*" He repeated the address in at least six locations throughout the Northeast, culminating with a November appearance at Cooper Institute in New York.

The importance of Sumner's appeal cannot be overestimated, for although he was much more than six weeks ahead of Lincoln on emancipation, he had laid down almost precisely the stance the president would adopt the following summer. Effectively linking the war with abolition in the public mind, he advocated a national policy that Lincoln could not yet endorse but one for which Sumner's advocacy would help prepare the way. Schurz later concluded that while differing with Sumner, the president "listened to him as the spokesman of the antislavery conscience." Sumner's influence on Lincoln's thinking was in fact substantial. Others like Treasury Secretary Chase were also influential in shaping the president's direction, but Lincoln always suspected the secretary of ulterior political motives. In contrast, he understood that Sumner had no higher political office in mind; thus could he respect the senator's views as genuine and sincere. Above all, he recognized that Sumner was promoting "an act of justice."

For Sumner, 1862 brought both victory and further frustration, as Congress and the president moved gradually to implement emancipation. Each step seemed to Sumner excruciatingly slow, and members of his own party often resisted his goals. The Republican wartime coalition included a variety of factions ranging from conservatives and moderates who viewed the war primarily as a means to preserve the Union—even leaving slavery intact if necessary—to radicals who demanded that abolition was at least as important a goal as forcing the Confederate states back into the Union. When the Thirty-seventh Congress convened for its second session in December 1861, the radical element had further consolidated its control, forcing the president to consider racial change as seriously as he did the efforts of border state conservatives and Democrats to maintain the status quo. Many of the key committees in both houses were chaired by radicals led by Sumner, Wilson, Hale, Zachary Chandler, Benjamin Wade, and Thaddeus Stevens.

In December, Lincoln told Sumner of his plans to introduce a proposal for gradual, compensated emancipation in the border states. While not agreeing with some of the plan's details, Sumner recognized that events were carrying the president in his direction. With New England in the lead in exerting pressure toward emancipation, he urged Governor Andrew to proclaim emancipation "as an essential and happy agency in subduing a wicked rebellion." This added incentive would, he hoped, move Congress and the president to follow.

Sumner himself was under strong pressure from New England abolitionists to bend every effort in behalf of the slaves. Howe reminded him that the policy of permitting generals to return fugitives to their owners was "unjust and cruel." In his eyes, Lincoln was "a greater slaveholder than the King of Dahomey" for tolerating such treatment. Sumner needed no such reminder, however, for in Senate remarks he had already attacked Massachusetts Brigadeer General Charles P. Stone for the implementation of this policy. It was especially evil, he said, because Stone "sees fit to impose this vile and unconstitutional duty upon Massachusetts troops." Congress responded to the urging of him and others in March 1862 with an act prohibiting the practice by army officers, but Sumner continued to be a watchdog over attempted violations of the act. In May, he attacked General Henry W. Halleck, commander in the Western theatre, for his directive prohibiting fugitive slaves from being admitted into his lines without his approval. Said Sumner, such an order was "inconsistent, absurd, unconstitutional, and inhuman."

Lincoln introduced his plan for gradual emancipation in the Union slave states in early March. The proposal included compensation for owners who freed their slaves; it also urged the colonization outside of the country of those freed. At a breakfast meeting with the president on the day he sent his proposal to Congress, Sumner endorsed the concept, although he complained about the idea of gradualism and rejected outright any plan of colonization. Although Congress endorsed the gradual emancipation and compensation aspects, the border states, whose continued loyalty Lincoln depended on, showed little interest in the plan. Despite Lincoln's efforts to persuade and pressure them, they rejected the idea, a factor in the president's ultimate decision to take more immediate steps. Yet even as Lincoln was urging his moderate approach on the border states, Sumner was already working for the implementation of a much more sweeping plan of emancipation for the seceded areas.

Almost a month earlier, Sumner had introduced resolutions in the Senate outlining the state-suicide concept as a means of accelerating the end of slavery and establishing congressional control of the terms under which states could return to the Union. Before introducing his proposal, he had first to try to nullify Lincoln's pledge not to interfere with slavery. The senator thus reasoned that because the Confederate states had renounced "all allegiance to the Constitution" by seceding, they had forfeited "all functions and powers essential to the continued existence of the state as a body politic." In so doing, they had reverted to territorial status and all "peculiar local institutions," including slavery, that "derived from local law," would "therefore cease legally and constitutionally." Congress would have complete jurisdiction because the states, through secession, had in effect committed suicide. The law-

makers should thus establish "provisional" or "territorial" governments and govern them as such.

Not surprisingly Sumner's proposals found only limited
favor in Congress, and the bill encompassing his plan was
quickly tabled. He was well aware that the time was not yet
ripe for such a drastic concept, and he had readily agreed to
tabling the motion, so that it could be resurrected later rather
than be buried in committee. By presenting his resolutions,
Sumner hoped to force the president and Congress to commit
to some plan of emancipation, even if it were not as sweeping as his.

In the Senate, moderate Republicans William Pitt Fessenden of Maine and John Sherman of Ohio led the attack
on the state-suicide concept. Fessenden refused to "look upon
the States of this Union as gone and destroyed," while Sherman charged that to "strike the States out of this system of
Govt" would destroy American democracy. The *New York
Evening Post* spoke for much of the northern press in arguing
that the Sumner proposal "prostrates our whole peculiar political organization in order to save the poor slaves." Sumner
responded that when the states died "the territory remains
and the Constitution . . . remains." Most important, "Slavery itself has lost its *slender legality* in this suicide." Abolitionist
friends like John Jay could agree that "the Southern States
have ceased to be States of the Union," and "the slaves in the
eyes of the Constitution are freemen." But it appeared unlikely that either the president or a majority in Congress would
ever agree. Nonetheless, Sumner's proposal had helped prepare the way for less drastic means to the same end.

Sumner's first success in pushing the government toward
emancipation was a minor treaty with England pledging the
cooperation of the two nations in a more effective suppression
of the Atlantic slave trade. He was in close consultation with Seward as the treaty was being negotiated; he arranged for its
quick consideration and approval by the Senate Committee
on Foreign Relations and successfully urged its ratification by

the entire Senate on April 24, 1861. As he explained to Lieber, following approval he "hurried from the chamber to Seward who was asleep on his sofa at the Department. He leaped, when he heard the news . . . 'Good God! The Democrats have disappeared. This is the greatest act of the Administration.'"

Sumner was even more instrumental in securing Senate approval of a bill recognizing the independence of the black republics of Haiti and Liberia and authorizing diplomatic relations with them. The president had invited congressional action, long blocked by Southerners who had feared the precedent of recognizing areas that had formerly been slave colonies. Many Republicans had balked at the idea of black diplomats in Washington and had delayed the bill for weeks. This "act of justice" came the same day as did the ratification of the treaty with England, and Sumner concluded happily: "Rarely has the Senate done so much in a single day."

Also in April, Congress accepted Wilson's compensated emancipation plan for the District of Columbia. While Sumner had originally balked at the concept of rewarding slaveowners, he now embraced it, arguing that since Congress had tolerated slavery there for so long, it was "responsible for the manifold wrong." Sumner's support of the bill brought praise from Frederick Douglass, who suggested that "to you more than any other American statesman belongs the honor of this great triumph of justice, liberty and sound policy." Sumner also pleaded for the repeal of the Fugitive Slave Act, but with Congress not yet ready to agree, he urged a compromise resolution to protect blacks "in Washington from unconstitutional seizure as fugitive slaves." He was also instrumental in legislation to establish schools for African-American children in the District and to permit blacks to testify in Washington courts.

The bill to end territorial slavery received an enthusiastic Sumner endorsement, although by the time of its enactment in June 1862, the issue, which had been the source of so much North-South bitterness in the 1840s and 1850s, had lost much

of its relevance. Such action now affected relatively few bonds-
men, but Sumner attacked on other fronts. At the request of
black constituent William Nell, for example, he sought to de-
segregate the post office by removing the decades-old ban on
black employment. Although his bill passed the Senate it was
tabled in the House, requiring its reintroduction later. More
important, however, were the congressional efforts to strength-
en the process of confiscating slaves from their owners and
the president's continuing movement toward a more general
emancipation policy.

Just prior to that, however, Lincoln again angered radicals
by revoking the order of Major General David Hunter that
freed the slaves within his command. Lincoln argued, as he
had the previous year regarding Frémont's policy, that such
authority belonged only to the president. Sumner "deplored"
Lincoln's action, but he realized that emancipation was now
inevitable. "My faith is fixed," he told Phillips.

The second confiscation act of July 17, 1862, authorized
presidential seizure of rebel property and provided that slaves
coming within Union lines "shall be deemed captives of war
and shall be forever free." Sumner had delivered a lengthy
speech in support of the measure in May, calling secessionists "*criminals*" and "*enemies*" subject to all wartime "penalties,
seizures, contributions, confiscations, captures and prizes"; in
regard to slaves "confiscation becomes emancipation." He concluded that taking slaves would deny to "the Rebellion its
mainspring of activity and strength . . . its chief source of provisions and supplies," removing "a motive and temptation to
prolonged resistance."

In the debates on confiscation, Sumner became the leading proponent of the bill as proposed by Illinois Republican
Lyman Trumbull. In part, his advocacy reflected a growing
impatience with the president, for in effect the bill told Lincoln that if he failed to act Congress would. Some in the Senate feared that the taking of such a power would reduce the
president "to pitiable dependence upon the will of Congress,"

but a growing number of congressional Republicans now appeared willing to exert additional pressure on Lincoln to persuade him to cooperate with lawmakers. Sumner believed that emancipation should occur through the cooperative effort of the president and Congress. His role here revealed how he had moved from a prewar insurgent to a wartime consensus-builder among fellow Republicans. Furthermore, confiscation was "a step to Emancipation," not a challenge to presidential authority. To ease the president's concern over the legality of property confiscation, he noted that "to give freedom is nobler than to take property." At the same time, Sumner argued that confiscation was a constitutional power granted to Congress as a war measure. Nor were such war powers limited to the president:

> The President, it is said, . . . may seize, confiscate and liberate under the Rights of War but Congress cannot direct these things to be done. Pray, Sir, where is the limitation upon Congress? Read the . . . Constitution and you will find the powers vast as all the requirements of war. Confiscation and liberation are other War Powers of Congress incident to the general grant of power, which it remains for us to employ. So important are they, that without them I fear all the rest will be in vain. Yes Sir, in vain do we gather mighty armies and in vain do we tax our people unless we are ready to grasp these other means through which the war can be carried to the homes of the Rebellion."

The president signed the confiscation bill, which required that legal proceedings be initiated by the executive branch to determine whether slaveowners had engaged in rebellion. Lincoln made minimal effort to employ the measure, for he had already decided by mid-July to accomplish emancipation by a presidential proclamation. Among the factors that led him to his decision were the questionable status of fugitive slaves who were coming in large numbers into Union army camps, the indirect aid slaves were providing the Confederacy by growing food and building entrenchments, the border states' rejection of his plan for compensated emancipation, the value of foreign neutrality should a proclamation be issued, and the pressure on him for emancipation from radical leaders like Sumner.

On July 22, Lincoln informed the cabinet of his decision to use his war power to free slaves behind Confederate lines. On the advice of Seward, such an order was to be postponed until it could be issued in conjunction with a military victory, so that it would not be seen as an act of desperation. The policy was officially announced on September 22 to take effect on January 1, 1863. Both Treasury Secretary Chase and Sumner had some input in suggesting how the president should justify emancipation in the Proclamation's final form. The senator recommended that the concluding sentence should say "something about *justice and God*," while the secretary proposed the actual wording: "And upon this act, sincerely believed to be an act of justice, warranted by the Constitution, upon military necessity, I invoke the considerate judgment of mankind, and the gracious favor of Almighty God."

Sumner had deplored the delays, first in issuing the Proclamation and then in its implementation, saying he "wished it to be put forth—the sooner the better." But once Lincoln acted, Sumner gave the policy his enthusiastic support, hoping also to see it include the use of blacks as troops against the Confederacy. He had long tried to persuade the president to encourage black enlistment. The Confiscation Act had authorized him to take action "in such manner as he may judge best." But on this point, too, Lincoln was hesitant, having earlier told Sumner of his fears concerning the reaction of Union troops. If blacks were enlisted, he said, "half of the army would lay down their arms and three other states would join in the rebellion." He thus preferred at first to interpret the act's authorization to include the use of contrabands as laborers only rather than as troops. Sumner complained in August that Lincoln "still holds back from the last step to which everything irresistibly tends." Yet here too, Lincoln displayed flexibility, and by the end of the year not only had he authorized Secretary of War Stanton to begin such recruitment but had become an enthusiastic proponent of it. Sumner now optimistically believed that the change in policy would quickly "put an end to the war."

Lincoln's change in direction came at a politically opportune moment for Sumner, who used the recently announced emancipation policy to beat back the challenge from conservative Republicans in Massachusetts. This group, led by Dana, had claimed that Massachusetts radicals like Sumner and Governor Andrew were hurting the war effort by forcing the president to take drastic actions that alienated northern moderates. There was even talk of organizing a "People's party" to block Sumner's reelection when the legislature balloted in early 1863. Although Sumner's skillful supporters outmaneuvered their adversaries at the Republican convention and won him the party's endorsement, the opposition appeared ready to bolt and form a separate party. But with the president and the senator coming to apparent harmony on emancipation and the latter using his patronage power adroitly, Sumner was able to seize the initiative. He could confidently tell a Faneuil Hall rally in early October that "Surely this is no time for the strife of party. . . . Its clamors of opposition are more than ever unpatriotic." The People's party concept quietly collapsed in October, and Governor Andrew easily won reelection. In January, the new legislature sent Sumner back to Washington by a more than five-to-one margin over his nearest opponent. As the Republican party moved toward a greater consensus on slavery-related issues, Sumner's leadership in that direction allowed him to consolidate his own power base in Massachusetts as he began a third term in the Senate.

On his return to Washington, Sumner stepped up his efforts for the recruitment of black troops. Some such steps had been taken before Lincoln officially sanctioned the formation of black units in the Emancipation Proclamation. The senator had already spearheaded the efforts to persuade not only Governor Andrew but military commanders to take the initiative.

In early 1863, Sumner seized on the Proclamation to justify a bill to organize up to 300,000 black troops. He found Secretary Stanton especially receptive to such a policy, even predicting that by the middle of the year 200,000 blacks would be under arms. Thanks in part to the commitment of Andrew and Sumner, Massachusetts played a prominent role in the creation of black Union army regiments. The first such unit, raised by General Rufus Saxton, was commanded by Thomas W. Higginson of the Bay State, while that of Robert Gould Shaw was the first to see extensive battlefield action.

Sumner was also instrumental in securing equal pay for black troops. Initially, they received three dollars less per month than white soldiers, despite Sumner's argument that the Union could not afford to refuse "justice to colored soldiers whom it has allowed to shed their blood in its cause." Higginson, in defending his troops' role, had emphasized that they served "for the redemption of their race." Most Republicans readily accepted these arguments, but some resisted Sumner's insistence that equal pay be granted retroactively to the day they enlisted. The senator retorted that the country should resist "doing injustice, least of all injustice to a people of a race too long crushed by injustice." Under extreme pressure from advocates of equality like Sumner, Andrew, and Higginson, Attorney General Edward Bates finally ruled in July 1864 that African-American soldiers were entitled to equal pay. By then blacks had become a major component of the Union army.

Sumner's efforts in behalf of black troops was a continuation of his commitment to racial equality that had first emerged in the 1840s as a young Whig fighting against the expansion of slavery into territories won in the Mexican War. At that time he had brought the issue closer to home with his attack on Boston's segregated schools in 1849 and his defense of the fugitive Anthony Burns in 1854. Now, during the Civil War, he was revealing again the consistency of his commitment to racial egalitarianism, first as he urged the president into a firmer stand in behalf of emancipation, and then as he fought for the use and equal treatment of black troops. His efforts were already pointing beyond immediate war issues to a postwar U.S. society in which he would seek civil rights in the South for the same African Americans he had helped to free.

Sumner and other radicals also worked in Congress to persuade the president to extend his emancipation policy to include slaves originally excluded, those in Union slave states and Confederate states already controlled by Union armies. Sumner was aided by petitions sent to him by Susan B. Anthony of the Women's Loyal National League bearing 100,000 signatures seeking emancipation of "all persons of African descent." To facilitate Senate action on this and related issues, he persuaded the body to create the Select Committee on Slavery and Freedmen with him as its chair. He rejoiced in the changed atmosphere of the Senate, noting that until recently the concept of accelerating emancipation "would have created a storm of violence." Now he confidently hoped "to report a bill sweeping away all Fugitive Slave Bills—also an Amendment of the Constitution abolishing Slavery" everywhere.

Sumner did not play a major role in the actual drafting of such an amendment, a process assumed instead by the Senate Judiciary Committee. But his Select Committee did initiate legislation designed to repeal the remaining "odious provisions in support of slavery," especially those relating to fugitive slaves. As slavery began to crumble, the issue of runaway slaves became largely academic, for now the fugitive laws were rarely if ever enforced. Nonetheless, Sumner was determined that they be expunged in order "to clear the statute-book of all support of slavery."

Even here there was resistance from Democrats as well as from conservative members of his own party. When the Senate voted on the issue in April 1864, a motion made by Republican John Sherman to exclude the Fugitive Slave Act of 1793 from repeal passed 24 to 17. That ten Republicans could join the opposition led Sumner to conclude: "This nation does not deserve to be saved." Yet two months later the Senate, recognizing the inconsistency of allowing such a measure to stand even as emancipation proceeded, reversed itself and followed the House in approving Sumner's motion to revoke all fugitive slave laws. When Lincoln signed the measure on June 28, the issue had finally been laid to rest. Sumner's first effort in 1852 to repeal the act of 1850 had received only four votes; now he rejoiced with Longfellow that, "Thus closes one chapter of my life. I was chosen to the Senate in order to do this work." The poet responded, "Your hour of triumph has come at last!"

Sumner also took advantage of the changed atmosphere in Congress to secure the removal of other discriminatory measures affecting both enslaved and free blacks. On July 4, President Lincoln signed bills that the senator had championed outlawing the coastal slave trade and opening federal courts to black witnesses. Sumner described the latter as "of immense practical importance," for its repeal brought to an end one of the "curiosities of an expiring barbarism." Sumner also persuaded the Senate to approve the desegregation of Washington's streetcars. Until then African Americans had been forced to ride in segregated cars or on the exposed platforms of all-white cars. In winning narrow Senate approval Sumner argued that "the rights of colored persons must be placed under the protection of positive statute" to prevent continued abuse. Less than a year later he secured the discharge of a conductor who had persisted in segregating blacks.

In each such attack on discrimination, Sumner had to overcome the formidable opposition of other senators. A significant minority of conservative Republicans led by Sherman and Fessenden joined with Democrats in defending the segregated society that Sumner was bent on dismantling. They frequently resented his tactics and lofty moral rhetoric but only managed to effect a holding action against a spreading tide of sentiment for equality. In the midst of his efforts in the Senate, Sumner pointedly rejected an invitation to deliver an address on the Marquis de Lafayette to the Young Men's Association of

Albany, an organization that excluded African Americans. Said Sumner: "I cannot speak of Lafayette who was a friend of universal liberty under the auspices of a society which makes itself the champion of caste and vulgar prejudice." Sumner's consistent efforts in behalf of biracial egalitarianism faced major obstacles, as he labored to overcome racist ideas and practices long accepted by much of white America.

Sumner was also among the most outspoken proponents of the formation of a federal agency to assist former slaves in finding a place in the rapidly changing society of the South and to protect them from the possibility of falling again under the domination of their former masters. While the war continued to rage, his chief concern was for the formation of a relief agency that would help provide food and shelter for a displaced and sometimes starving population. As peaceful conditions were restored, such a freedmen's bureau would take on the added role of helping to find land and employment for the former slaves. While most in Congress could agree on the immediate need for relief for the freedmen, many could not endorse such a continuing governmental role in time of peace. This would be especially so if it meant land redistribution, which Sumner and a few others advocated, for many argued that the sanctity of property precluded confiscation of the lands of former slaveowners. Although Congress would not fully address this issue until after hostilities had ended, there was much debate beginning in 1864 over the nature of the agency to be established. Here Sumner met significant delay and frustration.

A House bill establishing the bureau under the jurisdiction of the War Department was referred to Sumner's Select Committee on Slavery and Freedmen in February 1864. The committee favored Treasury Department jurisdiction instead because it already controlled the lands of the South. The Senate accepted that recommendation, but when the House balked, the bill was allowed to die. It was not until the next session of Congress in early 1865 when, after long deliberation, the House insistence on War Department control prevailed and the Freedmen's Bureau was established. Although in the final measure Sumner's role in the creation of the Freedman's Bureau was minor, he optimistically believed that the new bureau would be able to address a most critical aspect of the postwar South. Emancipation must "not be nullified," he argued, and the former slaves must be "protected in the rights now assured to them." Above all, they must be "saved from the prevailing caste which menaces Slavery under some new form."

One way to guarantee the permanency of Sumner's war goals was to persuade the president of the need for a radical Republican to head the Supreme Court. Chief Justice Taney, who had so antagonized Republicans with his Dred Scott ruling in 1857, had been in declining health long before his death on October 12, 1864. Sumner immediately wrote to Lincoln that Taney's death "is a victory for liberty and the Constitution. Thus far the Constitution has been interpreted for Slavery. Thank God! It may now be interpreted for liberty."

The senator's candidate to replace Taney was his long-time friend Salmon P. Chase, who had resigned from his Treasury post in June. Lincoln had been considering Chase for Chief Justice ever since the previous spring, when Sumner first began urging it. For his part, Chase had made no effort to hide his desire for the post, but when Lincoln delayed the appointment Sumner and Chase became concerned. In late October, Sumner reminded the president that "Anti-Slavery men are all trembling lest the opportunity be lost of appointing a Chief Justice who . . . would deal a death-blow to Slavery." A month later, with still no decision from the White House, Sumner wrote a third letter urging Chase's appointment because he would "not need arguments of counsel to convert him." Lincoln had delayed in order to give consideration to other more moderate Republicans, but in early December he finally endorsed Sumner's recommendation and nominated Chase.

The long-term ramifications of Chase's appointment could not immediately be seen, but Sumner was gratified by an early action of the Chief Justice that he had urged. John Rock, a black attorney from Boston whom Sumner had worked with in the school desegregation case of 1849–50, had enlisted the senator's backing in seeking admission to practice before the Supreme Court. Sumner urged his appointment on Chase, pointing out that with Rock as the first African-American attorney so honored, other race restrictions would also fall. Less than a decade earlier, Taney had declared that blacks were not citizens. Sumner's role in securing Rock's appointment symbolically tied together his prewar and wartime efforts in behalf of civil rights for African Americans. Chase's appointment of Rock in January 1865 appeared to Sumner to mean that a new era had begun, one that he was determined to see through to complete equality.

Such a new era, while elevating the freedmen, must not, thought Sumner, include harsh treatment of Confederate prisoners of war. On this issue the senator was closer to President Lincoln than he was to many of his fellow radicals in Congress. Cruel abuse of Union prisoners by Confederates, especially as stories and pictures of the deplorable conditions at the Andersonville prison in Georgia circulated, led many in Congress to demand revenge. In January 1865, the Senate debated a resolution that the president should, in the treatment of Confederate prisoners of war, "resort at once to measures of retaliation . . . in respect to quantity and quality of food, clothing, fuel, medicine, medical attendance [and] personal exposure."

Sumner found such an approach deplorable and countered that "any attempted imitation of Rebel barbarism" was not only impractical and useless, but would also be "immoral inasmuch as it proceeded from vengeance alone." It would, said Sumner, "have no other result than to degrade the national character and the national name." Having attacked the barbarism of slavery in earlier addresses, he concluded: "The Rebellion is nothing but that very barbarism armed for battle. Plainly it is our duty to overcome it, not imitate it." Citing a letter from Lieber opposing retaliation, he worked with Senate Democrats and a small group of Republicans to remove the offending sections of the resolutions. Criticized so frequently for the harshness of his attitudes toward the slaveholding South, Sumner proved more humane than most Northerners on the all-important question of the treatment of Confederate prisoners.

Although domestic issues involving slavery took most of Sumner's attention, foreign policy questions were also important to him and, in his mind, closely related. Communication with the many friends he had met in England and France on earlier visits, along with long study of European history and diplomacy and his knowledge and love of Old World culture and society, made him a natural choice to chair the Senate Committee on Foreign Relations. Party leaders had originally urged his appointment to the committee with these considerations in mind, and his elevation to the chair when Republicans assumed control of Congress in 1861 had followed as a natural consequence of his recognized expertise and knowledge of foreign affairs. The next decade would reveal his success in elevating the importance of his post to unprecedented heights. As Schurz explained: "Next to the advancement of the antislavery cause, he had no object more nearly at heart than the maintenance of an honorable friendship with foreign nations."

Secretary of State Seward had gotten off to an unfortunate start with the president by sending him a memo shortly before the fall of Fort Sumter in April 1861. In it he suggested that Lincoln "demand explanations" from various European nations, including France, Spain, and Britain, for allegedly hostile actions. Should the explanations not be "satisfactory," the United States should declare war, for the secretary believed that such a foreign crisis would unite Americans and prevent civil war. The president had quickly rejected this approach as foolhardy and had made it clear that he, not the secretary, was responsible for all critical foreign policy decisions. Thus Sumner quickly realized he would need to influence both men if he were to play an important role in foreign policy.

The primary task of U.S. diplomacy during the Civil War was to prevent the powers of Europe, especially Britain, from assisting the Confederacy, a policy Lincoln initiated on April 19, 1861, when he proclaimed a blockade of Confederate ports. Ironically, such a step in effect granted to the Confederacy belligerent status, much as Lincoln and Sumner tried to deny it. Less than a month later, Britain, to be followed shortly by France, issued a proclamation of neutrality, thereby granting belligerent status to the Confederacy and allowing it to seek loans and purchase war supplies from neutral nations. Although Europe's action was tantamount to an acknowledgement of the legality of the Union blockade, many in Washington feared that the European response was also a step toward recognizing the Confederacy as a sovereign nation. Recognition in turn could mean extensive aid to the rebels, although such a possibility may have been more imagined than real. On this issue, Lincoln, Seward, and Sumner agreed: every effort would be made to prevent Europe from treating the Confederacy as an independent nation. The success of the Union war effort might very well depend on foreign neutrality.

Britain and France harbored decidedly mixed feelings toward the American war. Prime Minister Lord Henry Palmerston and Foreign Secretary Lord John Russell, along with the British minister in Washington, Richard P. Lyons, had to evaluate carefully both the economic and political ramifications that would result from an independent Confederacy. Equally significant would be a decision by Lincoln to adopt emancipation as a war aim, for it would have made more difficult a pro-Confederate policy among Europeans. Their dilemma gave Sumner additional ammunition to persuade Lincoln to attack slavery. To the senator, preserving European neutrality and challenging slavery were linked.

Throughout much of 1861, Sumner felt his task as chairman of Foreign Relations was to counter what he believed were the misguided policies of Secretary Seward. Not only had the New Yorker sought to compromise with Southerners before the war began, but he had urged Lincoln to adopt a warlike stance against Europe. Once hostilities had begun in April, Seward continued to take a combative stand toward Europe, and thus Sumner had felt it necessary to temper the secretary's influence. "The fruits of *Sewardism*" included "demoralizing our energies and planting distrust everywhere," especially among foreign ministers in Washington.

Sumner's fears concerning Seward were reinforced when his friend, the Duke of Argyll, a member of the British cabinet, urged him in early June "to induce your government and especially Mr. Seward," to act in a "less reckless spirit." As the prospect of an immediate confrontation with Britain eased, Sumner could tell his English friends that while Seward's impact had been "sinister," he believed that the danger had passed due to his own efforts and because "the President is honest and well-disposed." In late May, when Seward prepared to send a hostile note to the British in response to their recognition of Confederate belligerency, Lincoln enlisted Sumner's advice. Agreeing with the senator's emphatic reaction that Seward's note was too threatening, the president excised several of its offending passages. In the process, Sumner won new respect from Lincoln, who increasingly came to trust his advice on foreign policy issues.

Sumner believed that British interests were tied closely to a Union victory. Even indirect assistance to an area controlled by slaveholders would be both a grievous error and an immoral act. As he told the Duchess of Argyll, "nothing can protract the crisis more than sympathy with the rebels." Although relations between the two countries improved slightly by mid-1861, they drifted precariously through the rest of the year. Hostile statements from British officials, including those of Russell and Chancellor of the Exchequer William Gladstone, led Sumner to complain again in November of the pro-Confederate policy of the British. Why all Englishmen did not share his feelings about slavery was incomprehensible because "we are fighting the battle of civilization." Instead, "this wicked rebellion has found backing in England." A new crisis at the end of the year came precariously close to provoking the British intervention that Sumner direly feared.

In early November, a Union warship captained by Charles Wilkes stopped the British mail packet *Trent.* When a boarding party discovered that Confederate commissioners James Mason and John Slidell were aboard en route to Europe in search of foreign assistance, Wilkes quickly arrested them and forced them to a prison in Boston. The immediate northern reaction was one of celebration. Governor Andrew and Navy Secretary Gideon Welles were among those who congratulated the captain, while a House resolution thanked Wilkes "for his brave, adroit and patriotic conduct." When the news reached London, however, there was an immediate outcry. With the militant British press calling for retaliation, Palmerston's cabinet debated his proposal to send a fleet to U.S. waters. The official British response was more tempered, in part due to the intervention of Sumner's friend, British Liberal leader Richard Cobden. The resulting protest demanded a release of the prisoners and an apology, but not as an ultimatum. Prince Albert's suggestion that Wilkes's action had not been authorized by the administration might allow the Lincoln Government to disavow it if it so chose.

Sumner's initial response came while he was in Boston: "We shall have to give them up." Yet on his return to Washington for the new session of Congress, he provided Seward with precedents to defend Wilkes's action. His indecision ended, however, when he received letters from Cobden and other English friends urging a U.S. backdown. He now realized that there was an imminent threat of British retaliation if the United States persisted in its course. Cobden pointed out that "the capture of Mason and Slidell can have little effect in discour-

aging the South compared to the indirect encouragement it
may hold out of embroiling your government with England."
The British reformer John Bright urged that the case be submitted to arbitration; he was especially alarmed by the war
spirit in his country that was being fed by the London *Times*
and other journals. Sumner quickly showed the correspondence to the president, who was "much moved and astonished
by the English intelligence." The senator now assured his
British friends that Lincoln, whom he described as "essential-
ly honest and pacific," believed that "there will be no war unless England is *bent* upon having one."

Sumner's efforts had an important effect in the ultimate
decision to release the Confederate commissioners. The president invited him to a Christmas Day cabinet meeting at which
he read the Cobden and Bright letters. On the following day
Seward informed Lyons that because Wilkes's actions had not
been authorized, Mason and Slidell would be released. In effect he argued that the captain's mistake was in taking the
commissioners off the ship, for had he brought the ship, its
passengers, and cargo before a prize court for a decision, his
action would have been legitimate. In thanking Bright and
Cobden for their roles, Sumner urged that the settlement "be
accepted sincerely and in the Name of Peace." He further insisted that "if England and France had not led the Rebels to
expect foreign Sympathy, our work would be easily accomplished." Although neither Lincoln nor Seward issued an official apology, the British accepted the release as tantamount
to one.

Sumner continued to defend the U.S. response and his role
in it in the days ahead. When militants in Congress, led by
Senator Hale criticized the prisoner release, Sumner was quick
to remind his friend that he had "spoken too swiftly," for the
administration had acted honorably. As Senate debate continued, Sumner silenced the critics with an elaborate speech
on January 9, 1862. His main thrust was to show how immoral
an act Britain had committed in offering protection to two

"arrogant, audacious, persistent, perfidious" envoys who sought to forward their cause of "treason, conspiracy and rebellion" through their European mission. But in forcing Mason and Slidell from the *Trent*, the American captain had erred because they could not be seized without a trial. Therefore, continued the senator, "the conduct of Captain Wilkes must be disavowed while men who are traitors, conspirators and rebels, all in one, are allowed to go free." Yet, he concluded, it was better "that criminals, tho dyed in guilt, should go free" than "that the Law of Nations should be violated" and peace endangered. As Sumner explained to Bright, his "earnest desire" in presenting these arguments "was to do something for peace."

By the time Sumner delivered his address, emotions on both sides of the Atlantic had cooled, but he nonetheless had effectively defended the administration against its many critics who had opposed the release of the envoys. The fact that Mason and Slidell would spend the next three years futilely trying to win Confederate recognition in London and Paris could not be known in January 1862, yet Sumner's explanation helped convince most Northerners that Lincoln had done the only thing possible.

Sumner's many correspondents as well as the press lauded his words. Numerous U.S. diplomats in Europe sent their congratulations, and Greeley's *Tribune* found the address worthy of rank as a state paper "side by side with the dispatches of Madison and Jefferson." Even the usually hostile *New York Herald* praised Sumner for delivering a "dignified rebuke" to Great Britain as "a genuine statesman." The *Boston Transcript* concluded that the speech was "a masterpiece." Sumner also believed that his remarks had "satisfied the country," but many in England were angered by what they felt was the speech's anti-British tone. There were months of difficult diplomacy still ahead between the two nations, and Sumner could not rest on what he feared was only a temporary easing of tensions.

Relations with Britain improved during the next months, as evidenced by the success of Seward and Sumner in April 1862 in completing the treaty forcing the suppression of the slave trade. But it was a temporary improvement in atmosphere only, and when the Union suffered major military defeats in Virginia in early summer at the hands of Robert E. Lee's armies, the British again began seriously to consider recognition of the Confederacy. As Cobden told Sumner, "there is an all but unanimous belief" in England "that you *cannot* subject the South to the Union." Bright added that Lee's victories created "pleasure among your enemies." Most dangerous were the pro-Confederate attitudes of Foreign Secretary Russell and Chancellor of the Exchequer Gladstone, the latter suggesting that Jefferson Davis had succeeded in creating a nation.

As Union troops continued to falter, British officials debated whether to accept a French proposal to offer joint mediation to the two American sides. In mid-September, Russell told Prime Minister Palmerston that Britain ought "to recognize the Southern states as an independent State." Bright wrote Sumner of Gladstone's "vile speech in Newcastle, full of insulting pity for the North and of praise and support for the South." Sumner reacted with predictable fury against a nation that he believed was turning its back on the struggle against slavery.

The Union military success at Antietam in September 1862, followed closely by Lincoln's preliminary proclamation of emancipation, ended any immediate threat of British collaboration with the French or recognition of the Confederacy. Palmerston, who had remained more cautious than Russell and Gladstone, now rejected the French offer of joint mediation. With emancipation an official Union objective, Britain would defer to public opinion at home and delay further any thought of recognizing a proslavery Confederacy. But relations with the United States remained far from friendly, and by mid-1862, Confederate ships built in British shipyards had begun to prey on Union shipping. Senator Sumner would again play a central role in the U.S. protest against this latest British provocation.

Before this new crisis with Britain came to a head, the Lincoln administration faced an internal crisis of its own, one that revolved around the secretary of state. Again, Sumner was deeply involved. The midterm elections of 1862 had not gone well for the Republican party (called the Union party during the war). Democrats gained thirty-two seats in the House and won key governorships in New York and New Jersey. Republicans did retain control of the House, and while their losses were not as serious as partisans on both sides suggested, the results reflected both war weariness and discontent over the administration's emancipation policy. A major military setback at Fredericksburg, Virginia, in mid-December added to the crisis atmosphere in Washington.

In their frustration, radical Republicans found a scapegoat in Seward, who could be blamed not only for the ongoing problems in foreign relations but also for exerting a conservative influence on the president in regard to slavery-related issues and on Lincoln's appointment of key military leaders. Sumner told Bright that despite his "talent and prodigious industry," Seward had "neither wisdom nor courage." The political ambitions of Secretary Chase also played a key role in the efforts of a group of senators, led by Sumner, who met with Lincoln to demand a reorganization of the cabinet and the ouster of Seward. His removal would probably result in the treasury secretary becoming the dominant cabinet figure. Chase's close friendship with Sumner meant that the senator also would benefit from Seward's demise, with some even suggesting that he replace Seward as chief of the State Department.

As the senators laid out their concerns to the president, Sumner emphasized the foreign policy problems that had characterized Seward's leadership. Others talked of Seward's support of General George McClellan, whose delaying tactics on the battlefield and lack of support of emancipation had antagonized radicals and had led to their call for his removal. Sumner, too, saw Seward as "one of the protectors of McClellan who has been the author of our delays." Two evening meetings resulted in Lincoln adroitly outmaneuvering the Senate delegation. The chief result was the embarrassment of Chase, who, when put on the spot by the president, meekly endorsed administration policies. For his part, Sumner revealed no desire for Seward's job and told Longfellow that "I much prefer my present place." With the party often divided on critical questions, the president and the senator needed and depended on each other; neither could afford to jeopardize that relationship by antagonizing the other. Less than a week later, on Christmas Day, Lincoln called Sumner to the White House to confer about the final wording of the Emancipation Proclamation.

If Sumner could not appreciate Seward's better qualities the president could, and as foreign relations remained tense, the feuding senator and secretary would have to work together as best they could to curb objectionable British acts. By mid-1862, two Confederate naval cruisers built in British shipyards had begun preying on Union merchant ships, eventually sinking more than a hundred vessels. These raiders, the *Alabama* and the *Florida*, built at Liverpool and manned mostly by British sailors, were allowed to leave England despite strong U.S. protest and conclusive evidence that they were built in violation of British law. As their depredations increased, evidence emerged in mid-1863 that two ironclad warships, the Laird rams, were also about to be launched from England for the Confederates. Yet even as Minister Adams protested vehemently and threatened war if they were released, British officials had determined to seize the rams and prevent their sailing.

Throughout the crisis Sumner, Seward, and Adams had kept up a relentless attack on British policies, and together their protests may have been a factor in the ironclads being detained. In the process, Sumner's disgust and outrage with British actions reached a boiling point. As early as the fall of 1862, he had complained of "rebel ships built and equipped" in England and of the government's willingness to support an "oligarchy of slave drivers." He now told Bright that "the feeling here with England is most bitter."

Still, Sumner was unwilling to go as far as many militants in Congress, and he strongly opposed a Seward-backed bill authorizing the president to issue letters of marque, permission to private citizens to capture and confiscate merchant ships of other nations. He explained to Secretaries Welles and Blair that such letters would "give us a bad name" and serve no good purpose: "They will be mischievous and discreditable; and all the good they can do can be better done in some other way." In a Senate speech Sumner repeated these points, but the bill authorizing the issuance of the letters passed by large margins. Still, he did not give in and remained in Washington after Congress adjourned to try to persuade Lincoln not to implement the policy. Again he emphasized that the use of letters of marque was not practical and could "*possibly* involve us with Foreign Nations . . . without any corresponding good." At the same time his differences with Seward accelerated when the secretary gloated over the bill's passage. Ultimately, the president found Sumner's arguments more convincing and actually refused to authorize such privateering in the remaining two years of the war.

While Congress and the administration struggled over the proper response to European aggression, Sumner successfully led the Senate to reject an overly belligerent response to French meddling in the Western Hemisphere. Early in the war, Napoleon III had taken advantage of the Civil War to intervene in Mexico, allegedly to collect debts, but in reality to establish a puppet regime there. Some senators, led by James A. McDougall of California, sought a U.S. ultimatum condemning the occupation in Mexico and demanding an immediate French withdrawal. While outraged over the French action,

Sumner saw the McDougall resolutions as poorly timed and destined to divert attention from the Union's struggle against the Confederacy. Through his efforts the Senate tabled the House-approved resolutions concerning the French action.

Similarly, Sumner succeeded in deflecting a unilateral French effort to mediate between the North and the South, a process that might force Union recognition of the Confederacy with slavery left intact. The senator's resolutions described such interference as "an unfriendly act" and added that the war would continue "until the Rebellion shall be overcome." The Senate approved 31 to 5. Thus while patient with the French concerning their presence in Mexico, Sumner would not tolerate their mediation attempt for a moment for fear that it might jeopardize the Union and its drive toward emancipation.

It was the British ships, however, that posed the greater challenge to a Union victory in the Civil War. So determined was Sumner to accelerate the ultimate success of the war that he did not hesitate to rally his countrymen against the continuing British actions. He therefore planned to deliver an address in New York in early September 1863, at a time when the possibility of the British release of the Laird rams still remained likely. With the *Alabama* and *Florida* wreaking havoc on Union shipping on the Atlantic, additional foreign assistance appeared to many to be the only hope of a Confederate victory. Union victories at Gettysburg and Vicksburg in July had given new life to Union hopes for an end to the war, but European recognition could revive Confederate fortunes, as could the release of the rams. Thus Sumner hoped not only to rally Americans to the recognition of these dangers but also to confirm Union determination in European minds. Again he would spare few feelings, even those of his closest British friends, with the emotion of his address. He explained to Lieber that he feared Americans "were groping from ignorance of what England has done" and that "the country needed light." He also hoped to convince the British and French of the danger and immorality of their ways.

Sumner's address before three thousand cheering supporters at Cooper Institute emphasized the distinct danger of European intervention. He attacked the British proclamation of neutrality of May 1861, and then questioned the Russell and Gladstone prophecies of Union failure, significant, he said, of their hopes and wishes. Beyond recognizing Confederate belligerency, Britain had committed the highly objectionable act of allowing Confederate cruisers, "all built, rigged, armed and manned in her shipyards," to prey on Union shipping. He tied this policy closely to the character of Confederate officials, whom the ships' owners represented. He spoke "not merely of slaveholders, but of people to whom Slavery is a passion and a business, therefore Slavemongers—now in rebellion for the sake of Slavery." Surely, he concluded, all nations must "obey the rule of morality—that it will 'shun fellowship with the wicked,' that it will not 'enter the service of barbarians'" or "enter into alliance to 'help the ungodly.'" By linking the evil nature of the Confederacy to the immorality of the British for assisting it, Sumner intended his speech as "a warning—with a pleading for peace" issued "*by a friend* who meant peace and not war."

Even Sumner's English friends were unhappy with the address, although some questioned its timing more than its substance. Cobden wondered whether it was wise to attack Britain at a time when the hopes of the South depended on "a rupture between yourselves and Europe." The Duke of Argyll reacted more harshly: "I read yr last speech with sorrow . . . feeling sure that it wd do nothing but harm here." Government officials, led by Foreign Secretary Russell, rejected Sumner's charges categorically and attacked the senator for his militancy.

The northern reaction was positive with few reservations. Seward recognized the speech as "a very important public service," while Sumner's many friends were more lavish in their praise. Greeley found it a "cogent demonstration of the systematic injustice which we as a people have been subjected." The *New York Herald* called the speech effective in its "exposure and denunciations" of the "false pretence of the British Government."

Although Sumner later learned that Russell had already detained the Laird rams, the senator suggested that his warning to Britain had been a factor in preventing intervention. Russell, he claimed, "was pushing England into war" at the time. How important this warning was in preventing that intervention is debatable. Yet Sumner again had expressed the spirit of his fellow Americans and had made them more alert. He had hoped to bring about "*a change of British policy,*" and "restore good feelings." In fact, British policy had already changed and the government was no longer considering direct aid to the Confederacy. Bright assured him that the British were "content now to watch your contest without wishing to interfere in it." Nonetheless, Sumner's harsh indictment of British policy had done little to restore the good feelings he claimed to be seeking and may even have hurt them.

Throughout the war years Sumner devoted equal attention to foreign and domestic issues, although in his mind the two were inseparable. Both must be directed not only to the defeat of the Confederacy but also to the completion of emancipation. In the midst of the debate to establish a freedman's bureau, Republicans faced a presidential election and a challenge to their direction of the war effort. In seeking to reelect Abraham Lincoln, the party faced what at first appeared to be an insurmountable task because the president had shown his vulnerability. With no immediate victory in sight and Democrats exploiting the unpopularity of his military and racial policies, Lincoln's reelection was in jeopardy. Continued stalemate on the battlefield following further Union setbacks and resistance by many Northerners to emancipation and the extending of limited rights to the freedmen led many in the president's party to despair of success.

For his part, Sumner had serious reservations about another Lincoln term, but the alternative of a Democratic administration would threaten all that he hoped the war might

achieve. He believed that the president had "neither the facility nor dispatch" to defeat the Confederacy. The war
"should have been over long ago," he lamented. Yet if he had
doubts about Lincoln, he refused to join in any of the several
efforts to dump the president in favor of a more strongly committed antislavery advocate such as Chase or Frémont. He explained that he would "take no part in any of the
controversies. My relations with the Presdt. are of constant intimacy and I have reason to believe that he appreciates my reserve." As bleak as Lincoln's chances might appear, Sumner
preferred to stay with a known quantity with whom his relations were good and influence strong than to chance a
change.

Once the party renominated Lincoln, Sumner gave the candidate his whole-hearted support and confined his reservations to a few intimate friends. When in August military
setbacks made reelection even more uncertain, Sumner refused to join those who would have forced Lincoln's withdrawal. He explained to Lieber that he had refused "to sign
any paper or take part in any action" against the president.
He told Governor Andrew that "all who wish to preserve the
Union and to overthrow Slavery *must act together.*" Division
among Republicans was the surest way to improve the Democrat's election chances and jeopardize all that he stood for.
Only if Lincoln withdrew voluntarily would he consent to another nomination. Still, he no doubt agreed with George Ju-
lian of Indiana that "Old Abe is rather a burden than a help to
our cause."

Union military victories at the end of the summer combined
with a Democratic platform and candidate calling for compromise with the Confederacy ended any danger to Lincoln's
reelection. At a Faneuil Hall rally at the end of September,
Sumner argued that "in voting against Abraham Lincoln you
will not only vote against Freedom and for Slavery, but you
will vote against your country and for the Rebellion." In voting
for Democrat George McClellan "you will give the very vote

which Jefferson Davis would give were he allowed to vote in Massachusetts." Lincoln's substantial victory over McClellan in November meant that Republican war goals were now achievable. The president, in appreciation of Sumner's role in his reelection, could be expected to reward him for his support, and the senator could look forward to closer cooperation in the second term. The appointment of Chase as Chief Justice in December was one indication of such a trend. Still, Sumner could not help recalling privately his continuing reservations with the president on racial issues. He had moved slowly on emancipation and the use of black troops, and the senator feared that he might now resist his urgings for civil rights for the freedmen, including suffrage, as the nation moved from war to Reconstruction. Lincoln, he noted, had "no instinct or inspiration."

Sumner's ever-changing view of the president had also been revealed as both executive and legislative branches began to consider proposals for readmission of the seceded states. Already on record with his state-suicide theory, the senator had urged that the seceded states be considered as territories under exclusive congressional jurisdiction in order to expedite the destruction of slavery. Before the end of 1863, he had advanced his belief that "the moment any territory lapses under the *exclusive jurisdiction* of Congress, Slavery ceases." Congress could then establish the "terms of restoration" and "trample slavery out." In the process he challenged Lincoln's authority, in part because he feared the president's hesitancy on the granting of civil rights. In an article in the *Atlantic Monthly*, he argued that the chief executive's jurisdiction in seceded areas was based exclusively on martial law and did not even include the unilateral authority to appoint military governors. Legislative power during wartime equalled that of the executive and, most important, the constitutional requirement that guaranteed the states a republican form of government could only be implemented by Congress. Lincoln never responded directly to Sumner's challenge to his authority, but it was clear that he intended to maintain control of the implementation of Reconstruction.

The contrasting approaches to Reconstruction had surfaced by the end of 1863, when Lincoln announced that whenever one-tenth of a state's voters had taken an oath of future allegiance, its government could be reestablished. After abolishing slavery a state seeking readmission would be recognized by the president as restored to the Union. Six months later, Congress, with Sumner in the majority, responded with its own plan in the form of the Wade-Davis bill. It required that at least half of a former state's voters take an oath promising not only future but swearing past loyalty before it could reform a state government and apply to Congress for readmission to the Union. The state must also abolish slavery and repudiate its debts owed to those who had helped finance the Confederate war effort.

The battle was joined when the president allowed the Wade-Davis proposal to die without his signature, saying instead that the states being reconstructed could choose either his lenient plan or the more stringent one of Congress. For his part, Sumner had made his determination clear when Congress, in June 1864, rejected the efforts of Lincoln-backed delegations from Louisiana and Arkansas to win readmission. He spoke for many in insisting that Congress must restore each state "to its original position in the Union." The authority to admit states and therefore "to *readmit* them are vested in Congress" with "the approval of the President."

By the time Congress convened again in December 1864, Lincoln had been reelected and the end of the war appeared imminent. There was now an increased urgency that the president and the legislature formulate a mutually acceptable Reconstruction plan. But the power struggle continued when Lincoln urged congressional approval of states he considered already reconstructed. Unionist governments with his backing functioned in several of the former Confederate states through the winter, but these governments included no black participation. It was on that point that Sumner based his opposition. Lincoln's stance on black suffrage was not yet clear, and although he had suggested privately that African-American soldiers and the more educated might qualify to vote, it would be far short of the sweeping grant of guaranteed black suffrage that Sumner sought. The party's position in the postwar era must be biracialism, for the senator was convinced that only through it could full democracy finally be realized.

Furthermore, Sumner believed that if blacks were denied the vote, the states would not be "strong enough in loyalty and freedom" to be readmitted. Most important, government in reentering states must be based on the "consent of the governed." To Sumner that could only be achieved with suffrage for all African-American men. Without it, "the cause of human rights and of the Union itself will be in constant peril," and Congress would be sanctioning a return to power of the old white ruling class. After extended debate, the Senate dealt the president a defeat in late February by voting to postpone further consideration of Louisiana statehood.

Sumner and fellow radicals considered this a major victory, for by delaying a decision on Louisiana's readmittance they could assert congressional control, and there would now be time to "appeal to the sober second thoughts of the people." As he explained to Francis Bird: "Before the next Congress, the country can be rallied" to support suffrage for blacks. Not only was this a question of moral principle and equal justice, but it was, according to Sumner, politically practical. Without the votes of freedmen "we cannot establish stable govts in the rebel states. Their votes are as necessary as their musquets [*sic*] . . . Without them, the old enemy will reappear" and "put us all in peril again." He concluded: "The Nation is now bound by self-interest—aye *self defence*—to be thoroughly just."

Congress had thus administered a serious defeat to Lincoln and his plan of Reconstruction, and Charles Sumner had played a central role in that defeat. Fearing the president's anger and a possible break between the two, Sumner was pleasantly surprised that Lincoln took his defeat "with perfect good nature" and "cherished no feeling towards me on account of what I had done." In fact, the president understood the need to continue to work with radicals like Sumner, and he was moving toward a position of at least limited black suffrage. By late March, Sumner confidently predicted to Cobden that the president's "mind is undergoing change." In Sumner's eyes the issues of Reconstruction were clear: "Too much blood and treasure have been spent to allow these states to come back again until they are really changed." A fundamental political revolution was needed, for "*Union govts cannot be organized without the blacks.*" The degree to which the president and Congress would be able to agree toward this end remained unresolved as Congress adjourned and Lincoln began his second term.

When the president delivered his second inaugural address on March 6, 1865, relations between him and Senator Sumner were friendly and supportive. The president invited him to accompany him and Mrs. Lincoln to the inaugural ball that evening and even called for him in his carriage. There were frequent friendly letters between the senator and Mary Todd Lincoln, and in late March he attended an opera with the Lincolns. On the eve of Lee's surrender, he accompanied them to Richmond to tour the fallen city, and two days later, on April 10, Mary sent him the news that "Lee and his army were in our hands." Yet when the president again defended his Reconstruction efforts in Louisiana, Sumner unhappily told Chase that "I see in the future strife and uncertainty for my country and another hot controversy for myself."

Despite Sumner's misgivings about the president, Lincoln's death at the hands of the assassin John Wilkes Booth left the senator in a state of shock and disbelief. On receiving news of the tragic events at Ford's Theatre, Sumner rushed first to the White House, informed the president's oldest son Robert Todd of the shooting, and then went with the young Lincoln to the theatre. They reached the president's bedside within thirty minutes of the shooting and remained there until Lincoln's death the next morning. A bystander described the deathbed scene: "Sen. Sumner was seated on the right of the President's couch near the head, holding the right hand of the President in his own. He was sobbing . . . with his head bowed down almost on the pillow of the bed on which the President was lying."

Two days later Sumner helped organize a meeting of the small number of senators and representatives still in Washington and chaired the committee that helped plan funeral arrangements. He also wrote the group's resolution of respect, acknowledging "a martyr whose memory will become more precious as men learn to prize those principles of constitutional order and those rights, civil, political and human for which he was made a sacrifice." To the Duchess of Argyll he wrote of the president's "gentle and forgiving" nature, and that during his last days he had said "nothing harsh even of Jefferson Davis." Throughout the next difficult weeks, while Mary Lincoln remained in Washington, he called on her on several occasions to show his sympathy and friendship. In early May, she sent him Lincoln's cane in thanks for "your unwavering kindness" and as a memento "of the great regard he entertained for you."

Long after Lincoln's death, Sumner reminisced about the close alliance he had developed with the president. It was, he said, a friendship "of unbroken intimacy." To those who claimed that it was Seward who had been closest to Lincoln, the senator quoted the president as saying that "I have counselled with you twice as much as I ever did with him." Sumner also suggested that he had been told by numerous friends and cabinet members that the president "would have offered me the Dept. of State" when Seward stepped down after the war. The degree to which Sumner may have exaggerated their friendship cannot be known, but despite their ongoing differences on war and Reconstruction issues, the relationship had strengthened during the last six months of Lincoln's life.

Clearly, Sumner had lost a close friend, albeit one whose position on civil rights for African Americans was not as advanced as his.

As Andrew Johnson assumed office, Sumner remained optimistic over the future of the Reconstruction process and thankful for the role that Lincoln had played in bringing a successful conclusion to the war. The new president declared June 1 to be a day of commemoration for Lincoln, and officials in Boston invited Sumner to deliver that city's eulogy. The senator began by comparing the fallen president to George Washington. The two were "kindred in service," and "kindred in patriotism," each the leader "of his country at a great epoch of history." Emphasizing Lincoln's compassion and forgiving spirit, Sumner suggested that most important, he had "pronounced that great word by which slaves were set free." Indeed, as a part of the memorial service, Sumner had asked that a black chaplain deliver the benediction, for "it was for his race that Presdt Lincoln died." He included a lengthy review of the president's achievements in both foreign and domestic policy, areas in which his audience recognized Sumner's own significant contributions. The senator concluded his eulogy with a plea for black suffrage, for how else "shall the war waged by Abraham Lincoln be brought to an end, so as to assure peace, tranquility and reconciliation?" As he looked ahead to what he and many Republicans assumed would be close cooperation with Johnson, he concluded: "Liberty has been won. The battle for Equality is still pending."

CHAPTER FIVE

I Am Now Where I Have Always Been, in the Breach

The struggle for equality that Charles Sumner spoke of in June 1865 in his eulogy to Abraham Lincoln would dominate the remaining years of his life. Despite the tragedy of the assassination, the senator had reason for optimism. Indeed, the new president Andrew Johnson gave early indication of support for Sumner's Reconstruction philosophy, including equal rights for freedmen, and the Republican party appeared poised to complete the revolution in race relations. The states of the shattered Confederacy were on their knees and recognized that they must accept at least a degree of racial equality. Leaders in both the North and the South spoke of the need to reconcile their differences and proceed as a reunited nation. Moreover, Anglo-American relations had improved dramatically with the defeat of the Confederacy, and Sumner hoped for a favorable settlement of U.S. claims for damages caused by English-built ships. He also looked forward to a restoration of those personal friendships that had been jeopardized by the turmoil of war.

Sumner's goals, however, were not to be achieved easily. He had had little contact with Johnson before the controversial scene in early March that had found the new vice president drunk at the Lincoln-Johnson inaugural. Outraged at Johnson's behavior, Sumner at that early date had sought fellow Republicans in the Senate to demand Johnson's resignation or to urge his impeachment. His colleagues hesitated to make an issue out of one incident, and Johnson assumed the presidency in April. Nevertheless, Sumner initially feared the worst from the former slaveholder.

Their first meetings, however, allowed the senator to rekindle some optimism. A week after Johnson had taken his oath, Sumner and Chief Justice Chase met with him about the importance of black suffrage; they left him "confident that our ideas will prevail." Sumner remained in Washington until mid-May and had several more private conversations with the president. Their only difference appeared to be the best method for instituting black suffrage, the senator insisting on "*Federal authority*," and Johnson preferring that it "proceed from the people," apparently meaning the states. Johnson confidently believed that the issue of whether the central government or the states would have the authority to grant the right to vote to African Americans could easily be resolved. After a lengthy exchange, Sumner quoted Johnson as saying "there is no difference between us; you and I are alike." Sumner returned to Boston hopeful of a friendly and cooperative relationship with the new president.

Then suddenly at the end of May, Johnson issued a proclamation offering a pardon to all citizens of the former Confederacy, except those who had held leadership positions or owned taxable property valued at $20,000 or more. This rankled Sumner, for he believed that "all who have borne arms against their country" must be excluded from political participation. Moreover, former Confederates would jeopardize blacks' precarious place in the new society, and southern whites would keep their land as if no war had been fought. While agreeing that rebels should be spared "their lives" and not tried for treason, Sumner insisted that there must be property confiscation: How else "can we get lands for the freedmen?"

Even worse was Johnson's second proclamation establishing the procedure for North Carolina's readmittance to the Union, a plan that would likely set precedent for the other seceded states. Only those whites who had taken an oath of allegiance and received amnesty could vote for delegates to the state's constitutional convention, thereby excluding all blacks from the electorate. At first, Sumner was assured by Attorney General James Speed that the North Carolina requirement would be the exception, but subsequent proclamations for six other states confirmed the "madness" of Johnson's course.

Fearing that his goal of racial equality was in jeopardy, Sumner immediately wrote to members of the cabinet and fellow radicals in Congress urging a reversal of the Johnson policy. Although encouraged by Speed and Secretary of War Stanton, he received little sympathy from others in the cabinet. Complaining to Navy Secretary Welles of the questionable background and past loyalty of some of those appointed by Johnson to state offices, he urged that "the *rule of justice*" be followed and that loyal citizens, including the freedmen, must participate. Welles defended Johnson's action, admonishing Sumner not to become "denunciatory and intolerant." Believing that any bigotry rested with the president, Sumner prepared for battle, writing to Ben Wade and Thaddeus Stevens that "we must speak and act." Though still hopeful that "we shall succeed," Sumner now understood that it would be a struggle. Those committed to government by the consent of the governed must "be ready to declare the true doctrine," yet few lawmakers appeared concerned over Johnson's actions.

The summer months brought further evidence that Johnson was bent on ignoring Sumner's appeals and defying the Republican Congress. The president was determined to complete Reconstruction unilaterally and present legislators with an accomplished fact when they convened in December. Sumner of course opposed "reconstruction by *Executive action*," but Johnson refused to call Congress into special session and by mid-September had granted 13,500 pardons to rebel leaders.

Even worse, in Sumner's eyes, Johnson's provisional governor appointees could not "take without perjury" an oath of past loyalty, a requirement clearly intended by Congress.

Sumner attributed the president's reversal to the influence of former Confederates and their sympathizers. Accordingly, Johnson broke his ties with the Republican party and sought to restore his leadership among Democrats, North and South. To Sumner, presidential policy forfeited a golden opportunity for racial justice. He explained to English friend John Bright that "after the surrender of Lee," Southerners were ready "to accept the terms" of the federal government. "*The Presdt has changed all this*" and now the rebels were returning to "their old alliance with Northern democrats." In surrendering to Democratic demands that empowered former Confederate leaders and excluded blacks, Johnson had compromised "all that has been done." Only James Buchanan had made "an equal blunder."

Despite his discouragement, Sumner was not yet ready to give up on the president. In forwarding the petitions of southern blacks for the right to vote, he reminded Johnson "that the peace and tranquility of the country require that *they should not be shut out from it.*" He believed that it was too soon for Republicans to break with the president, for as he told Governor Edwin Morgan of New York, "*He is our Presdt.*; but precisely on this account . . . tell him plainly the blunder he has made, compromising all that has been done." Continuing correspondence with cabinet members further revealed the Sumner strategy, to persuade those around the president of the folly of Johnson's policy and urge them to counsel him accordingly. To Welles he argued that the war had overcome states' rights despite those who claimed that a state could not be forced to submit to the central government. The theory of states' rights was now being "set up against those safeguards and securities which are essential to peace and tranquility without which the war will have failed." He therefore believed that the positive changes brought about by the war were jeopardized by the Johnson approach to Reconstruction.

Sumner worked actively among his friends in and out of Congress to resist the president's policies. To Garrison, who remained hopeful that Johnson would change his course, Sumner asked: "Has not the time come for yr. voice," for "this criminal and cruel experiment of the Presdt must be exposed." Chase reported a less cordial president compared to their early May meeting and complained that Johnson showed little interest in his report on his recent tour of the South. Senator Wade expressed fear that the president was adamant and noted that "the salvation of the country devolves upon Congress and against the Executive." Sumner agreed that "the course of the Presdt is so absurd that he cannot force it upon Congress. It must fail."

Sumner summarized his Reconstruction goals in a late-August letter to Lieber:

1. Refer the whole question of Reconstruction to Congress.
2. Lead public opinion in the right direction.
3. Obey the existing laws of Congress which expressly exclude from public service any person who has sustained the rebellion.
4. Obey the Constitution which refuses to make any distinction of color.
5. Redeem the promises of the Declaration of Independence.

Publicly he repeated these points at the Massachusetts state Republican convention in Worcester in September and even called for an amendment guaranteeing black suffrage. On the latter point he could find few who agreed with him. As the time for the lawmakers to convene approached, Sumner argued that Congress must "assume jurisdiction of the whole subject of Reconstruction." In November, he urged the president—"as a faithful friend and supporter of your administration,"—to suspend a policy that "abandons the freedmen to the control of their ancient Masters." The stage was set for a presidential confrontation with the Republican Congress.

Returning to Washington in December, several days before

Congress convened, the senator had a two-and-a-half hour meeting with the president that confirmed his worst fears. As the two hotly discussed the issues, he found Johnson "ignorant, pig-headed and perverse," pursuing a policy which, if "not arrested this country would be ruined." It was a "painful" time because "he does not understand the case." The scene was aggravated because the president, in his ardor, unconsciously used Sumner's hat "as a spittoon!"

Sumner seized the initiative in the Senate on the first day of the session when he introduced a series of resolutions calling for equal suffrage based on the constitutional obligation of the national government "to guarantee to every State a republican form of government." Said he: "No government could be considered republican" where large masses of loyal citizens were excluded from the vote. In a Senate speech two weeks later he called on Congress to block the Black Codes of southern legislatures, which reinstituted a new form of slavery. He concluded: "I have spoken especially for the loyal citizens now trodden down by Rebel power and without representation on this floor. . . . In the name of God, let us protect them." Congress must assume jurisdiction and block readmission of states Johnson considered reconstructed. In praising his speech, a friend lamented that "you will have to fight your old battle over again." It would soon become clear that as had been the case since the 1840s, Sumner's proposed methods of securing racial equality were far in advance of most other Americans, including members of Congress from both the North and the South.

Congressional colleagues were not prepared to endorse his proposals and instead sought a more moderate program in the hopes of achieving a compromise with the president. Republican leaders agreed to a joint committee of fifteen to pursue such a goal. Chaired by Fessenden of Maine, it included few radicals and pointedly omitted Sumner in an effort to induce presidential cooperation. After extensive hearings the committee concluded that further legislation and a constitutional amendment were necessary to assure southern loyalty and protect the freedmen. By mid-February 1866, Congress took the initial step, with legislation extending the life of the Freedmen's Bureau and protecting civil rights. Presidential vetoes followed by a bitter attack on Sumner and other radicals as traitors soon convinced even moderates that compromise with Johnson was impossible and closer cooperation with the radicals would be imperative.

Still, Republicans remained far apart on the basic issues as debate developed on a proposed constitutional amendment that was designed to provide some guarantee of civil and political rights to freedmen and prevent a quick return to power of former Confederate leaders. The complex proposal dealt directly with civil rights by denying the states the power to deprive "any person of life, liberty or property" without due process of law. Most controversial was the evasion of a direct endorsement of black suffrage. Well aware that such a guarantee would bind northern states and antagonize white voters who had repeatedly rejected equal suffrage, the joint committee proposed only a proportional reduction in congressional representation to those states withholding the right to vote from African Americans. Most of the North still denied blacks suffrage, but, with only small black populations residing in their states, northern whites had little to fear from a proportional reduction in representation, the burden of such a penalty falling on the South.

Ever committed to his belief in equal suffrage, Sumner was quick to denounce this evasion and, in a four-hour address, labeled the provision "a delusion and a snare." To expect "the recent slave-master to confer suffrage without distinction of color" was folly, for "even the bribe offered cannot tempt him." He predicted accurately that the South would find ways to evade the requirement and still retain its political influence. Yet he antagonized moderates with his moralistic fervor by suggesting that their proposal, "after degrading the Constitution" and "borrowing an example from Pontius Pilate turns over a whole race to sacrifice." Said Sumner, "the equal rights of all" could be protected by simple legislation based on the constitutional authority of Congress to guarantee a republican form of government.

Strained feelings between Sumner and the moderates continued through the spring after his opposition led to an initial rejection of the amendment. Even his friend Chase had urged his support, believing it to be as advanced a proposal obtainable from Congress. Because larger Republican majorities were needed in the fall elections for Congress to overcome the president's vetoes, Sumner backed away from his open opposition to the amendment. Usually the idealist, in this case the senator recognized the need for compromise. Thus a modified and somewhat strengthened amendment went to the states, one that included the offending section on congressional representation as well as a section denying rebels the right to hold office. Congress, by two-thirds vote, could remove this disqualification. The proposed Fourteenth Amendment, clearly a compromise, became the basis of the Republican platform for the fall campaign.

While accepting the proposal for the sake of party unity, Sumner maintained his pressure for equal suffrage through separate legislation. In the process, his bitter attacks on the president won him few new friends in Congress, especially when he labeled Johnson's idealistic and distorted description of conditions in the southern states, included in a message to lawmakers, as a "white-washing document." Responding to those who called him "dogmatic," he noted that he could not "but press forward earnestly." If Congress was not yet prepared to legislate equal suffrage he would oppose the admission of any state that did not include it in its constitution. He even spoke against the admission of Colorado, where few blacks lived, because suffrage there was confined to whites, clearly "repugnant to the principles of the Declaration of Independence." Sumner assured his supporters that equal suffrage would be legislated for all states: "Whatever

Congress was able to do for civil rights, it can do for political rights."

Sumner also had accepted the proposed Fourteenth Amendment because by spring of 1866 he was worn down physically. He continually overworked himself while Congress was in session, rarely going to bed before midnight after an evening of study, and returning to the Senate early the next morning. His doctor warned that his "brain and nervous system [were] overtasked and suffering from my original injuries." Adding to his stress was his aging mother's deteriorating health. By mid-May he expected to be called home to be with her. He wrote to her faithfully and received regular updates on her status from friends and the attending physician, Dr. John Homans, who reported her growing weaker "both in body and mind." He arrived home four days before her death, and lamented that her demise left him "more than ever alone." His return to Washington in late June was bittersweet. He was free to return to his Senate duties and more financially secure because of the inheritance of his share of his mother's estate.

Relief Sumner's death precipitated a profound change in her son's personal life, but one that he had contemplated for some time. A bachelor for fifty-five years, in August, Sumner announced his engagement to Alice Mason Hooper, the widowed daughter-in-law of his House colleague Samuel Hooper. He had met the twenty-eight-year-old Alice during the war and, although taken by her beauty and charm, had developed only a casual relationship. Until now he felt that his financial condition had precluded marriage, but his mother's estate included the family home on Hancock Street and a modest sum of money. To his closest associates he admitted misgivings: "I tremble sometimes at the responsibility I assume." Long set in his bachelor ways and with his past insecurity in mind, he could not forget the "disappointment and sorrow" of earlier relationships with women.

A small private ceremony on October 17 conducted by the

Episcopal bishop of Boston was followed by a three-week honeymoon in Newport. As a wedding gift Sumner presented Alice with a gold and diamond bracelet valued at $475. The couple and her eight-year-old daughter Bell then moved to a rented home in Washington. Entertaining friends at dinner as he had as a bachelor brought him a measure of happiness, and the couple appeared to be adjusting readily to their life together.

The summer and fall of 1866 had also brought the senator the prospect of political success occasioned by his party's triumph at the polls. The one-sided victory pointed to an acceptance of the kind of Reconstruction policy Sumner advocated. Andrew Johnson had led the effort to mobilize Democrats behind him with an active role in the National Union convention in August. Calling for the immediate admission of the southern states, the platform failed to lure conservative Republicans who were upset by southern and presidential intransigence in rejecting the Republican plan. Race riots precipitated against blacks in Memphis and New Orleans in May and July led northern voters to conclude that the war had changed little in the South. The president's intemperate speeches during a campaign swing in September added to northern distrust, and Sumner noted that "people are disgusted." The returns allowed Republicans to retain their three-to-one margin in Congress. It was a Congress more willing than ever to impose a Reconstruction plan that was to Sumner's liking.

The holdover session of the Thirty-ninth Congress met from December to March, and Republican leaders arranged to have the new Fortieth Congress convene forthwith. This would provide continuity and the least delay in enacting their plan of Reconstruction over the expected Johnson vetoes. While not playing as central a role in the Reconstruction legislation as he would have preferred, because he had been denied a place on the joint committee, Sumner pressured Republicans into equal rights legislation. On the first day of the session he proposed a bill conferring suffrage on blacks in the District of

Columbia. Both houses agreed by mid-December, and the override of the Johnson veto came in early January, allowing Sumner to conclude that "here at least my ideas have prevailed." He continued to demand resistance to admission of states from Tennessee to Nebraska when their constitutions denied black suffrage. Here, too, he was partially successful.

With the southern states refusing to ratify the Fourteenth Amendment, even while being encouraged to do so by the president, Republicans of all persuasions were at last ready to agree with Sumner on the need for forceful action. After weeks of wrangling over details, Congress passed a Reconstruction bill dividing the South into military districts and requiring that states agree to manhood suffrage and ratification of the Fourteenth Amendment before being readmitted to the Union. Congress also passed the Tenure of Office Act, requiring Senate consent for the dismissal of cabinet officers and continuing in office any official dismissed by the president until the Senate confirmed a replacement. Sumner, having argued for an even more stringent policy, supported any bill that would limit the "presidential usurper menacing the Republic."

A second Reconstruction bill passed in late March established the machinery by which military leaders would register voters, black and white, to select constitutional convention delegates. Sumner was unhappy with the procedure because it employed military rather than civilian means to force compliance. He noted his preference "not to see new States born of the bayonet," yet rejoiced because Congress at long last had adopted his views on black suffrage for the former Confederacy.

At the same time, however, Congress refused to consider his bill to extend black suffrage to all states, for despite Northern legislators' desire to impose it on the states of the former Confederacy, few shared Sumner's commitment to equal rights everywhere. Senators failed to respond to his plea: "How can you look Rebel States in the face when you have required colored suffrage of them and fail to require it in the other States?" They found unconvincing his argument that "we are bound to guarantee a republican form of government through-out the whole country," not just in the South. Falling back on the rationale that secession had given Congress an authority it did not possess in loyal states, many Northerners were not yet ready to see the consistency of their colleague's arguments.

As the conflict between Johnson and Congress intensified, Sumner and his Republican associates viewed most of the cab-inet with deepening suspicion. Especially was this true of Sec-retary of State Seward, whom Sumner had distrusted ever since his appointment by Lincoln. As chairman of the Senate Committee on Foreign Relations, Sumner knew that it was only a matter of time before the two would clash again, as they had throughout the war years. In late 1866, he described the secretary as "more than usually perverse." When, therefore, in the midst of Johnson's vetoes of domestic legislation, Sew-ard surprised the committee by presenting to it a draft treaty providing for the U.S. annexation of Alaska, many assumed approval unlikely.

Initially caught off guard, Sumner responded to Seward's proposal with reluctance. Seward had signed the treaty on March 30, 1867, with the United States agreeing to pay Russia $7.2 million for what many Americans considered little more than a frozen wasteland. Sumner thought so little of the treaty at first that he even advised the Russian minister, Edward de Stoeckl, to withdraw it to avoid the embarrassment of Senate rejection. But Seward's effective lobbying convinced Sumner of the land's value, and the senator soon became an enthusi-astic booster of the treaty. Not usually an expansionist, Sumner nevertheless hoped for the eventual acquisition of Canada and believed that the annexation of Russian America would improve U.S. chances for the larger prize: "considerations of politics and comity" convinced him to support it. With char-acteristic enthusiasm and preparation, Sumner presented a three-hour Senate address that stressed Alaska's natural re-sources and commercial advantages as well as the advance in democracy achieved by eliminating the Russian monarchy from North America. Impressed with his arguments, the Senate quickly voted 37 to 2 to ratify. Sumner accurately told Longfellow that "my course had a decisive influence."

If Sumner could express some satisfaction over his role in the Senate, he could not say the same for his worsening marital relations. Although the couple's initial months together outwardly had appeared happy, it had been a trying adjustment for husband and wife. Long years as a bachelor had left the fifty-five-year-old Sumner set in his ways, and it was only with difficulty that he had adjusted to the social desires of his much younger, high-strung, and quick-tempered wife. Increasingly, he remained at home to read and study while she enjoyed Washington society without him. By March 1867, she was frequently seen in public with the young Prussian diplomat, Baron Friedrich von Holstein. That relationship, which was most likely little more than a flirtation, was the cause of great distress and embarrassment to Sumner. Even after the Baron's recall to Berlin, arguments increased between the Sumners. By the time of the couple's return to Boston in late May, they began occupying separate bedrooms. When Alice left for Lenox in June the public was not yet aware how incompatible she and her husband had become.

The next months for Charles Sumner were indeed miserable ones, as the press seized on rumors of his differences with Alice. Few journalists could resist speculalting about the von Holstein relationship or the rumors that Alice would file for divorce on grounds that Sumner was impotent. Surely there was incompatibility with regard to age and temperament if not sexual relations, with neither able to discuss their problems or even attempt to work out their differences. Perhaps he was preoccupied with Senate business and his sense of self-importance, but, in any event, he quietly watched as she left, never to see her again as she spent much of the next years in the most fashionable of European society. Personal relationships had never been easy for Sumner. Despite close friendships with Longfellow and Howe, he had frequently insulted and antagonized many of his male friends in the past. Relations with Alice, as they had indeed been with all women, had been even more difficult, a projection of Sumner's own personal unhappiness. Public success continued to contrast sharply with his private failures.

When, in the fall of 1867, Sumner sold the "old family house" in the fashionable neighborhood of Hancock Street, he felt truly "alone and homeless." Long discussions with Longfellow helped ease the break with Alice somewhat, with the poet noting, "he is in great sorrow." Efforts by Hooper to bring the estranged couple back together failed, and Sumner complained to Howe that Alice had made for him an "intolerable life with constant dishonor." Earlier in the year, Sumner had purchased a large home in Washington for $30,000, a sum ten times his Senate salary. The worry over the cost of the home, along with the expense of furnishing and maintaining it, had added to the stress in his marital relations. He now faced the unenviable task of either selling the home or moving into it alone. Lamented Sumner, "What can I do? Would that I were in some far off land?"

As tensions with Alice had increased during the spring and summer he had become more irritable in his relations with fellow senators. After Congress adjourned in July he publicly attacked several colleagues, most notably Senator Fessenden, for blocking his civil rights legislation. Finally he embarked on a long lecture tour in the fall to help defray the expenses of the new home, and then made his unhappy decision to occupy it alone. His return to Washington in December would allow him to bury himself in his public duties and try to forget the ordeal of the last months. He admitted "satisfaction in the idea of a house of my own so that I need not pack and unpack at the beginning and end of every session." Only time would ease the pain, and he sought "repose—such as I can hope to find in my solitude."

Not surprisingly, the press, led by the *New York Express*, would not leave him alone and during the fall began printing lurid accounts of his marital problems. Longfellow lamented to his friend that he could not imagine that "even American vulgarity could stoop so low." Holding Alice responsible for the rumors, Sumner reacted bitterly, explaining to Howe his decision to remain silent and not give political enemies further excuse to belittle him. Yet he concluded, "She is a bad woman." He now told friends that he had learned too late that she had engaged in extramarital affairs while married to her first husband. Although such stories were unsubstantiated rumors, Sumner now accepted them as fact.

Well into the next year, Sumner relived the painful memories of the past year and even considered for a time attacking Alice in print to let the public know the abuse to which she had subjected him. Toward the end of their relationship, he told a friend: "I never entered the carriage to drive to dinner that she did not treat me so that I was obliged to find relief in tears. All the time, day and night she was off with her paramour until my name was dishonored and she was a public scandal." By late 1868, he could finally accept the advice of friends not to "breathe your convictions, for you would then lose sympathy," which "you now inspire in your opponents as well as your true friends in Boston."

It was thus a long, lonely winter for the senator, and his solitude brought only partial relief. He invited numerous Boston friends to come visit him in his Washington home, which he had elaborately furnished with the art works he had acquired in Europe. Longfellow was unable to visit due to plans to take his family to Europe, and Sumner complained in self-pity: "You go abroad with joyous children, I stay at home alone with nobody to care for me." Palfrey did visit for a week in April, but when he left, Sumner continued "alone and morose." Nonetheless, occupying his own home did bring him some satisfaction and perhaps even a sense of freedom. Time and the onrushing political events of 1868 gradually allowed him to bury his memories of Alice. He rarely mentioned her again, and with the pain of the separation behind him, in 1873 he obtained an uncontested divorce on the grounds of her desertion.

Meanwhile, Congress consumed much of early 1868 with impeachment proceedings against Andrew Johnson, and Sumner's central role in the Senate's action forced him to put his personal problems aside. The senator was, as mentioned, an early advocate of the removal of the president, having first called for it after Johnson's behavior at the inauguration in March 1865. He also was among the first of the radical Republicans to abandon Johnson for his opposition to black equality and the sharing of Reconstruction authority with the Republican Congress. The president's bitter attack on him and other radicals in February 1866 cemented Sumner's hostile opinion of the man. Thus when a House investigation was authorized in January 1867, Sumner was in full support of impeachment.

Johnson, the Radicals believed, deserved to be removed for usurping the powers of Congress and defying lawmakers on Reconstruction issues. But because moderates dominated the House proceedings and because the Radicals could find no specific violations of the Constitution, the House rejected the proposal at the end of the year. Yet as Johnson's defiance of Congress intensified with his removal of Secretary of War Stanton and his efforts to force a replacement in violation of the Tenure of Office Act, the House finally impeached him in early 1868. The scene now shifted to the Senate for trial beginning on March 4, giving Sumner the opportunity to pursue what had become almost an obsession to see Johnson's removal.

Sumner's lack of objectivity was further conditioned by the realization that in the event of Johnson's removal, the president pro-tem of the Senate, Benjamin Wade, would assume the presidency. It was widely rumored that as president, Wade would ask Sumner to join his cabinet, perhaps as secretary of state. Sumner later asserted that the possibility had not appealed to him, but few were convinced. His denials notwithstanding, his vast experience in foreign affairs would have made him a logical choice, and the position would have been a fitting climax to his long career.

Nontheless, foremost was Sumner's desire to remove Andrew Johnson, whom he regarded as the most formidable obstacle to racial justice in the country. As he explained to English friends, Johnson was "now a full blown rebel." Under him "rebellion has been aroused anew." Thus Sumner insisted that the trial in the Senate should be a political rather than a purely judicial proceeding, for that would more likely assure the president's removal.

As the trial proceeded with great drama before crowded Senate galleries, Sumner pursued his efforts to promote a Johnson conviction. First he argued successfully to ensure Senator Wade a vote on all issues at the trial. Then he insisted that the presiding officer, Chief Justice Chase, not have the authority to decide disputes or to vote in order to break ties: he was determined that the jurist not block his goal of a political trial. Impeachment, he convinced his colleagues, was "a political proceeding before a political body with political purposes" aimed at "*expulsion from office*," not a criminal conviction. Johnson's crime, in Sumner's eyes, had been resistance to Republican Reconstruction, turning the veto power "into a weapon of offense against Congress . . . to beat down the just opposition which his usurpation had aroused." In illegally removing Stanton, Johnson had made the veto "an engine of tyranny."

The president's able defense team effectively countered the arguments of Sumner and other radicals by contending that an impeachment conviction could be pursued only for criminal offenses indictable in civil trials. Sumner had won the procedural points but failed to persuade two-thirds of the Senate of Johnson's guilt. In the end, seven moderate Republicans led by Fessenden, fearing the precedent of a political trial, accepted the defense's argument and joined with twelve Democrats to block conviction by a single vote. Though it had been a tense scene, to Sumner the outcome was the result of "tech-nicalities and quibbles" foisted on the timid by "the legal mind." In his view, one or two senators had been swayed "against their country at a crisis of history." He regarded the result "as a great calamity" against "unionists, white and black" in the South. Yet with Johnson's veto power now severely lim-ited, the congressional Reconstruction process progressed, and both parties looked ahead to the upcoming presidential election as a referendum on the Republican record.

When Congress adjourned, Sumner followed his usual habit of remaining in Washington after most had gone home, to catch up on correspondence and Senate duties neglected dur-ing the session. By August the summer heat finally drove him from the city; yet he returned to Boston reluctantly, for he now had no home there. With Longfellow traveling in Eu-rope, he could not find the seclusion and companionship he craved at the poet's summer retreat at Nahant. Having sold the family home, he lamented to think "how homeless I am in Boston." Reduced to taking rooms in a Boston hotel that looked out over a stable and a machine shop, he nonetheless now had ample, undistracted time to oversee his own reelec-tion to the Senate.

Sumner never seriously considered retirement, despite his declining health in the face of Senate battles. He was deter-mined to guide to completion his Reconstruction goals of racial equality and to obtain a fair settlement with Britain on damages done to Union shipping. Still the choice of most Massachusetts Republicans, he had first to beat off conser-vative opponents within the party and then help it to retain control of the legislature. Unconvincingly, he claimed indif-ference to the outcome, suggesting to Longfellow that "if the people of Massachusetts turn from me, I shall not complain. I have done my duty." Far from passive, he worked with Francis Bird and others to assure his renomination.

At the party's state convention it quickly became apparent that Sumner and his supporters had prepared well. The delegates overwhelmingly endorsed him for reelection, then campaigned effectively to retain control of the legislature, assuring the senator reelection when the lawmakers voted in January 1869. While not universally popular, Sumner continued to enjoy the support of a clear majority of Bay State voters. During the campaign he defended his record in behalf of equal rights for the freedmen, just as he had earlier attacked those "clinging to Slavery."

Sumner's and his party's theme in the presidential election was the need to prevent a return to slavery as represented by the black codes of the South. Fearing a resurgence of Democratic power, Republicans had quickly nominated military hero Ulysses S. Grant as their candidate. Though they loudly defended their Reconstruction program, Sumner was disappointed by their failing to endorse black suffrage, which they left to local decision "in all the loyal States." Sumner complained that opponents "will have a great opportunity" to expose the inconsistency of their insisting on it for the South. Still the majority of his party refused to accept his egalitarian vision. The Democrats chose Horatio Seymour, with Frank Blair as his running mate, and attacked Republican Reconstruction as "a flagrant usurpation of power" that was "unconstitutional, revolutionary and void." It appeared to Sumner that Democrats wanted to replace secession with nullification, with Blair demanding that the president declare the Reconstruction acts "null and void."

In a campaign address in late October, the senator defended the Republican's Reconstruction legislation but suggested it had done "too little." Most significant, it "should have secured a piece of land" for freedmen and "common schools open to all." Despite Ku Klux Klan violence in parts of the South designed to prevent blacks from voting, Grant swept to victory, demonstrating that at least in the North, Democrats remained out of step with the electorate. Heartened by the results, Sumner nonetheless lamented that the violence, spurred on by the "mischief of Andrew Johnson," revealed that "*the*

South is not civilized" and that continued vigilance was necessary.

In the short session of Congress before Grant's inauguration, Republicans concentrated on drafting a constitutional amendment to guarantee universal suffrage throughout the nation, something that they had been unwilling to address during the campaign. On this issue Sumner remained strangely at odds with his party as to the best way to accomplish the goal. He feared that the states would fail to ratify such an amendment, thus allowing former Confederate areas in which African Americans had recently been granted suffrage to reverse themselves and deny blacks the right. Instead he argued that Congress already possessed the authority to grant voting rights throughout the nation through the guaranty clause in the Constitution, making an amendment unnecessary. Party leaders disagreed, and by late February, Congress approved an amendment guaranteeing the right of universal male suffrage to submit to the states. Sumner played only a minor role in the debates and instead had unsuccessfully moved a substitute bill establishing voting rights through legislation. Thus when the Fifteenth Amendment was ratified a year later, the senator could claim little credit for the approval of one of his most cherished goals. He nonetheless could rejoice that political equality had been accomplished.

As the Reconstruction process neared completion, Sumner used the memories of the war to assist Abraham Lincoln's widow, Mary Todd. Having lost touch with her, he learned from friends that she was living near poverty in a dingy hotel in Frankfurt, Germany. Sumner knew of her shortcomings and rumored mental instability, but he could not "forget that she is the widow of our President," and he thus supported a pension of $5000 for her. When a House bill granting her $3000 reached the Senate in 1870, Sumner labored over the unanimous opposition of the Committee on Pensions until the Senate relented and gave the bill narrow approval. Mrs. Lincoln gratefully thanked him for "his kind perseverance."

Sumner also sought to preserve his own reputation. Visibly aging, he told friends of his "one solicitude . . . to print a revised edition of my speeches before I die." Proud of his oratory—his "life"—and its significance, he explained to Howe: "These speeches . . . illustrate the progress of the great battle with Slavery." He thus began collecting copies of his speeches and contracted with a Boston firm to direct their publication. Preparation of his *Works* would occupy his spare time until his death, when it remained unfinished. It was a laborious task that included lengthy explanatory notes and some editing, both for clarity and self-enhancement. The first of fifteen volumes was published in 1870, with Sumner exclaiming that if he could complete the project, he "should be ready to go"!

From the time of Grant's inauguration, Sumner shifted his focus from Reconstruction to foreign policy, believing that his time, energy, and senatorial influence could best be applied to the unresolved issues with Britain. His relationship with and attitude toward the president went through a rapid deterioration during Grant's first term, from friend and supporter to critic, and finally to outspoken opponent. Like many Republicans, the senator had come to appreciate Grant's willingness to engage the enemy, referring to him in late 1863 as a "military genius." The general's resistance to Andrew Johnson on Reconstruction issues further encouraged radicals, and Sumner thus had no hesitation in supporting him for president in 1868.

Like many politicians, Sumner also condescendingly believed that as a professional soldier Grant lacked the political skill necessary to lead the nation and the party effectively without strong advisers. Sumner egotistically but realistically assumed that he would play a key role among those who would influence Grant as president. Obviously he expected that this would be true concerning the remaining issues of Reconstruction, but, even more significant, he assumed that he would play a prominent role in foreign affairs. Never admitting disappointment that the new president had chosen

Hamilton Fish of New York to be his secretary of state, he nonetheless hoped to continue to influence, if not actually control, the nation's foreign policies from his position as chair of the Committee on Foreign Relations.

Sumner and Fish were good friends, and the senator believed that they could work together easily. The two men enjoyed similar intellectual interests, although the secretary, with vast experience in New York politics as a Whig, had never shared Sumner's commitment to racial equality. But since foreign policy rarely dealt with such issues, Sumner assumed that the normally reserved Fish, who had little experience in foreign policy, would yield to his judgment on most critical issues. Fish had promised as much, telling Sumner that as secretary he hoped to "rely upon your friendship and your experience and ability, for your support and aid to supply my manifold deficiencies."

Small wonder that Sumner expected to influence the Alabama Claims, a subject he had addressed in September 1863. After his anti-British speech of that date, he had said nothing, perhaps hoping that the end of the war and a more conciliatory British government would bring a diplomatic settlement. Domestic and personal problems also had left him little time for foreign issues during Johnson's presidency.

Sumner's silence did not, however, mean that he had dismissed his outrage over the damage done by British-built Confederate raiders, which he sincerely believed had prolonged the war. With the collapse of the Confederacy in the spring of 1865, Foreign Secretary Russell had again refused to admit any British violation of international law or to submit the U.S. claims issue to arbitration. Privately, Sumner poured out his disgust to his English friends, explaining to Cobden that the foreign secretary must bear "the responsibility of keeping alive" the controversy. He wrote to the Duchess of Argyll and to Bright that Britain must pay "our bill" and suggested that "two years of our war with its loss of life and treasure . . . to say nothing of indignities and brutalities and the loss of our commerce" must be recognized by Britain. Not yet ready to suggest what Britain's "alliance with slavery" would cost, he insisted that Lord Russell's uncompromising stand must change.

A possible way to end the impasse had occurred in mid-1866, when a new British government assumed power and Foreign Secretary Lord Edward Stanley replaced the militant Russell. Secretary of State Seward had insisted, however, that the basis for negotiations must include the consequences of Britain's error in having recognized Confederate belligerency, implying a financial responsibility for prolonging the war. Stanley stood firm, insisting that Britain would not negotiate the belligerency issue; rather, it would recognize only claims for specific damages done to Union shipping by the Confederate raiders. With Sumner and Seward in full agreement on U.S. willingness to enter arbitration only if "the whole case is submitted," discussions between the two countries again stalled. Despite a continued exchange of letters with persons abroad, Sumner was unable to convince even his friend Bright of the justice of the U.S. position. At the same time, however, he used his influence to block Senate consideration of several House-passed bills in support of the anti-British Fenian movement in Canada, measures that would have seriously jeopardized Anglo-American relations and future negotiations on the claims issue.

The resignation of Charles Francis Adams as U.S. minister to London in June 1868 and his replacement by Maryland Democrat Reverdy Johnson signified a change of course for the Johnson administration and Secretary Seward. With Johnson and Seward soon to leave office, they were eager for a quick settlement to the nagging issue, and in January 1869, the two nations signed the Johnson-Clarendon Convention. The agreement sought to create an arbitration commission to settle the claims issue but made no reference to Britain's responsibility for indirect damages or to a British apology for its Civil War role. The prospects for ratification of the treaty appeared dim from the outset, coming as it did from a discredited and lame-duck Democratic administration. That it was far from a satisfactory settlement even under ideal political conditions made a favorable recommendation from Sumner's committee even less likely, and indeed, it voted unanimously in February against ratification.

On the eve of the full Senate's overwhelming rejection of the treaty, Sumner delivered one of his most memorable speeches, demanding what was already a foregone conclusion—that the body reject the treaty and replace it with a stronger one. Sumner called the proposal "a snare" that "left untouched the painful sense of wrong planted in the national heart." The senator claimed that Great Britain owed the United States not only $15 million for direct damages done by the cruisers, but also for the costs of doubling the length of what had already been a two-year war:

> No candid person who studies this eventful period, can doubt that the Rebellion was originally encouraged by hope of support from England,—that it was strengthened at once by the concession of belligerent right on the ocean, . . . that it was quickened into frantic life with every report from the British pirates flaming anew with every burning ship; nor can it be doubted that without British intervention the Rebellion would have soon succumbed under the well-directed efforts of the National Government. Not weeks or months, but years were added in this way to our war, so full of costly sacrifice.

The implication was that Great Britain owed half of the more than $4 billion that the Civil War had cost the United States. "Everybody can make the calculation," concluded Sumner. Nor did he suggest how Britain might compensate the nation for such a huge sum. Later in the year Sumner suggested more directly what many assumed he had meant in the speech—that the cession of Canada to the United States would settle the debt!

The reaction to Sumner's speech was swift. The lopsided 54-to-1 Senate rejection of the Johnson-Clarendon Convention reflected his sentiments, and the great majority of Americans applauded his efforts. In contrast, the *London Times* labeled his address the worst kind of "despotism" from one "more responsible for the Civil War than any other." Although some feared that Britain had now been pushed to the brink of war with the United States, the British government's official response was more tempered. Prime Minister William Gladstone described Sumner "as our arch enemy," while the senator's good friend, the Duchess of Argyll, found his attack on her country "entirely unreasonable." Many in Britain saw it as an insult from a former friend that could only delay rather than facilitate a settlement of the dispute.

For his part, Sumner vehemently denied that he sought anything other than a peaceful settlement. To those who claimed he had been unnecessarily harsh, he explained that with the Senate poised to reject the treaty, "I was obliged to state the reasons." Defending his friendly intent, he noted that the Peace Society planned to publish his speech as "a peace tract" and challenged anyone to find in it "a single note of war." He suggested that a settlement should be left to diplomacy, although privately he came close to admitting an interest in Canada: "How the case shall be settled—whether by money, more or less—by territorial compensation,—by apologies . . . is an open question." Whatever his intent, neither side sought a quick resolution. Sumner explained to the Duchess that Grant would leave it to her government to reopen negotiations.

At the same time, President Grant and Secretary Fish were not pleased with Sumner's uncompromising stand, and a bitter dispute soon developed between them. Sumner had earlier used his influence to pressure the president and the secretary to appoint his Boston friend, historian John Lothrop Motley, as minister to Britain. An experienced but opinionated diplomat, Motley fully endorsed Sumner's view that Britain was responsible for both direct and indirect damages and was determined to advocate it in direct talks in London. In contrast, Fish regarded Sumner's position untenable and believed that England would flatly refuse to compensate the United States beyond the direct damages. Thus he carefully instructed Motley to base the U.S. case solely on the direct damages done by the British-built Confederate cruisers. At Fish's insistence, the cabinet approved instructions to Motley to omit any mention of the inflammatory indirect damages that the senator insisted upon.

In response, Sumner sternly reminded Fish that Congress would determine "how much shall be claimed and on what grounds." He threatened to use his influence to persuade the Senate accordingly and promised never to "be a party to a statement which abandons or enfeebles any of the just grounds of my country." His effort to force Fish to modify his instructions to Motley had quickly become part of a power struggle in which Sumner sought to seize control of the most critical foreign policy decisions. Originally assuming that he could persuade his old friend to his position, he became overbearing when Fish refused. A series of letters and personal confrontations resolved little, and Motley proceeded to push the Sumner view in London in defiance of Fish's instructions.

Upon hearing of Motley's disobeyance, Grant urged Fish to remove him, but the secretary persuaded the president to avoid what would amount to a direct challenge to Sumner. Instead he reprimanded his minister and transferred the site for further negotiations from London to Washington, where he could direct them personally. Fish explained his actions to Sumner by complaining that Motley's "rhetoric is strong" and "not consistent with the restraints of his position." Privately, he also feared that Motley's statements might leave Sumner in control of foreign policy.

By avoiding a direct confrontation, Fish had restored an uneasy truce between Sumner and the administration. Who controlled foreign policy remained unresolved, as did the whole dispute with Britain itself. Surely Sumner had not backed down even though the secretary had taken control of the negotiations. In a September speech to the Massachusetts state party convention, the senator suggested that the union of Canada and the United States was inevitable and that Americans could "never be indifferent to Canada." Remaining vague on when and how such a union might occur, he concluded that "the end is certain; nor shall we wait long for its mighty fulfillment." Sumner's remarks were clearly designed "to prepare the way for Canada."

Ironically, Sumner's interest in expansion northward contrasted sharply with his view of the Caribbean. This had become clear during the Johnson presidency, when he had blocked a treaty negotiated by Secretary Seward for the purchase of the Danish West Indies. Believing the islands to be of little value, the senator buried the treaty in his Foreign Relations committee. His attitude became much more evident when he resisted Grant's desire to recognize the belligerency rights of Cuban revolutionaries and annex Santo Domingo.

On the first of these issues Sumner was in full accord with Secretary Fish. A Cuban revolution against the Spanish rulers had begun in October 1868, thus becoming the first foreign policy crisis for Fish. The secretary, like Sumner, was opposed to recognition of Cuban belligerency, much less independence, in part because the insurgents controlled no ports or provinces and thus failed to meet the accepted rules of international law. Sumner's fears doubled when he realized that the president's motives had a dual purpose. Grant had not been eager to push for a British admission of error in according belligerency recognition to the Confederacy because he hoped the United States might now do the same in regard to Cuba.

For a time it had appeared that the Cuban issue could be avoided by U.S. diplomatic intervention, by which the island's independence would be purchased from Spain with the United States acting as financial guarantor. Even more pleasing to Sumner, Cuban slavery would have been abolished in the process. As he told Fish, "if accomplished completely, it will be one of the best things in our diplomacy." Unfortunately, the Spanish and the Cubans could not agree on the arrangement and the war continued. Meanwhile, with the House eager to approve recognition of Cuban belligerency, Sumner again used his influence to prevent his committee from endorsing such action, and Fish diverted Grant's attention, even persuading him to issue a U.S. neutrality proclamation with regard to Cuba in June 1870.

For the time being, Fish and Sumner had combined to avert a crisis with Spain. Although Sumner clearly hoped for Cuban independence and emancipation, he believed that "both are certain to come very soon" without the United States assuming "needless responsibilities." Such involvement, he and many others feared, could easily have followed recognition of Cuban belligerency. Unfortunately, with his attention turned from Cuba, the president assumed an even more contentious interest in Santo Domingo.

Grant's interest in annexing Santo Domingo emerged in 1869 for complex reasons, one of which was a desire to use the island as a refuge for the freedmen of the South, a black American state. The unstable black republic was then under the leadership of the corrupt President Buenaventura Baez. In danger of being overthrown and perhaps executed by Dominican and Haitian insurgents, Baez favored annexation. He thus worked with two American speculators who stood to make millions and who soon drew Grant's private secretary and close friend, Orville Babcock, into the scheme. Only by annexation could the three cash in on their vast land, mining, timber, and shipping interests on the island.

Suspicious of their motives, the highly moral Secretary Fish opposed any involvement, also fearing that the situation in Santo Domingo might require committing U.S. troops to the region. For the time being, however, he acquiesced in Grant's interest in return for the president giving him a free hand with regard to the delicate situation in Cuba and the Alabama claims issues. In July 1869, Grant sent Babcock to Santo

Domingo on a fact-finding mission. By December, Babcock had returned with a proposal of annexation in exchange for $1.5 million payment to Baez. He emphasized the wealth of the area and especially the commercial and strategic value of the splendid Bay of Samana. The president then secretly authorized U.S. naval vessels to prevent Baez's enemies from toppling his regime. He also ordered Fish to prepare a formal treaty of annexation for Senate confirmation, an effort that would require the cooperation of Charles Sumner.

With the proposal completed, rather than going through the normal protocol, Grant rushed to Sumner's home on the evening of January 2, 1870, seeking the senator's endorsement. The spectacle of the president coming unannounced to a powerful senator's home to plead his case was unprecedented and a measure of Grant's inexperience and Sumner's influence in foreign affairs. Dining at the time with two journalist friends, Sumner invited the president to join them. After they all discussed the treaty, a copy of which Grant had failed to bring with him, Grant came away with the impression that Sumner had promised his support, an opinion later confirmed by one of the journalists. Sumner's version of his comments was that he had never directly promised support; he recalled telling Grant: "I am an administration man, and whatever you do will always find in me the most careful and candid consideration." Sumner believed that he had committed himself only to study the issue, an honest misunderstanding. The incident would prove to be a major turning point in the Grant administration and in Sumner's political future.

A week later the State Department submitted the proposal to the Senate Committee on Foreign Relations, where it remained for two months of scrutiny. As Babcock and others testified, Sumner and most of his committee became deeply concerned about the treaty's irregularities and the unethical motives of Baez and his American friends. When one of the conspirators suggested that the annexation of Haiti and other Caribbean areas would follow Santo Domingo, Sumner's determination to oppose the treaty was reinforced. Already concerned about the loss of independence of a black republic and committed to the freedmen finding equality where they lived rather than being shipped off to a new frontier, Sumner was further disturbed by the questionable financial dealings underlying the scheme. He thus hoped to bury the treaty in committee rather than force a confrontation with the president. When the administration insisted on Senate action, the committee recommended rejection of the proposal by a five-to-two margin.

In a closed Senate session, Sumner took five and a half hours to explain his opposition. Citing the U.S. military and financial commitment that would be required to maintain peace in Santo Domingo, he stressed the negative ramifications of annexing other desired areas such as Haiti and the many financial and diplomatic improprieties involved in negotiating the Dominican treaty. Most important, he suggested that Santo Domingo was destined "by a higher statute" for blacks: "a right of possession by their sweat and blood mingling with the soil." The United States should support the Dominicans in their quest for an independent republic, for "to the African belongs the equatorial belt."

The Senate adjourned without taking action, but Grant realized his pet project was in jeopardy and in fury blamed Sumner. Two months of debate, pressure, and investigation followed as both sides sought Senate allies. Though many Republicans found Sumner's explanation convincing, they feared a break with the president. Grant's anger at Sumner accelerated, as did his pressure on other Republicans to support the treaty. Although unenthusiastic about the treaty, the loyal Fish tried repeatedly, albeit unsuccessfully, to dissuade Sumner from his opposition. Most radicals remained faithful to the president, but with moderates and Democrats opposed, the full Senate rejected the treaty on June 30 by a 28-to-28 vote.

Grant vowed to continue the struggle and sought revenge. The president was especially upset with Sumner's haughty and domineering manner and the fact that he, rather than the chief executive, appeared to be in control of foreign policy. To punish him for his treachery, he removed the senator's friend Motley as minister to Britain. Grant informed cabinet members that he would "not allow Mr. Sumner to ride over me." When Fish protested that it was Motley not Sumner whom he was hurting, the president snapped: "It is the same thing." When the secretary suggested that Sumner himself be offered the London post, Grant rejected the idea, intent on punishing the senator, who in turn refused to be silenced with such a diplomatic position. As the summer dragged on, Grant and Fish had difficulty in finding a suitable replacement for Motley; finally, former Ohio congressman Robert C. Schenck accepted the post.

In the Senate debates that followed, some supported the removal of Motley on the grounds that he was not American enough because he had lived abroad for so long. Sumner's arch enemy Roscoe Conkling of New York pointed out that Motley had violated Fish's instructions on the Alabama claims negotiations. But Sumner considered the removal "an act of sheer brutality" that had "nothing to do with Motley's role in London and everything to do" with his (Sumner's) having blocked the Santo Domingo treaty. The president, said Sumner, sought to annex St. Domingo through "punishment and reward . . . equally employed."

Sumner also assailed Fish for not coming to Motley's defense and consequently becoming "*a party to his removal.*" Fish's lengthy response defended his role and that of the president, stressing Motley's violation of instructions. A bitter exchange of letters between the senator and secretary continued into the fall with neither man backing down. Sumner finally lamented to Longfellow: "I long to leave this place. . . . It pains me to think that I belong to a government capable of doing such a thing."

When Congress adjourned, Sumner embarked on another extensive lecture tour to help meet the expenses of maintaining his Washington home. His feud with the Grant administration was never forgotten, however, and he occasionally included an off-the-record attack on the president. When Grant resumed his campaign for the annexation of Santo Domingo in his State of the Union Address of December 5, 1870, the battle was again joined. Efforts by Henry Wilson and others for a reconciliation between Grant and Sumner collapsed, the latter accelerating his attack in a bitter Senate exchange.

The occasion for Sumner's response to Grant was debate on a resolution introduced at the president's behest by Indiana Senator Oliver Morton to establish a special commission to visit Santo Domingo to gather more information. But the revival of the treaty's chances remained unlikely, and Sumner might better have remained out of this debate. Stubbornly, he entered the fray, refusing to avoid a struggle over a moral principle and angrily describing the commission as "a new step in a measure of violence." He reviewed the threat that annexation posed to Haiti's independence and charged that the actions of the U.S. navy were those of violence and war, contrary to international law and the Constitution. Labeling his speech "Naboth's Vineyard" after the Old Testament King of Samaria who had coveted the vineyard of his neighbor, he demanded that Grant cease bullying the Dominican people. Sumner noted that "the waters of a weak power were as sacred as those of France or England."

During the debate, Conkling, Morton, and others had proposed that Grant move next to force the senator's removal from his cherished position as chair of the Foreign Relations Committee. To this suggestion Sumner acted the part of the martyr, comparing the idea to the Kansas situation in the 1850s. Grant's interference with the committee, he charged, was similar to Buchanan's insistence on Douglas's removal from the Committee on Territories in 1858 for the purpose of carrying the Lecompton Constitution, and subjecting "a distant Territory to Slavery." The president, he said, "has fallen into the line of bad examples." The exchange intensified, with

Morton terming Sumner's abuse of Grant "unprovoked and indefensible" and Conkling suggesting that the committee should no longer be led by "a Senator who has launched against the Administration an assault" more wicked than that of any Democrat. The debate ended with a personal defeat for Sumner as the Senate approved the fact-finding commission to Santo Domingo. While the chances for an annexation treaty remained poor, Sumner's influence in foreign affairs was in jeopardy.

Animosity accelerated further when Fish answered Motley's charges that he had been removed to avenge Sumner's opposition to the treaty. Such a claim, said the secretary, had originated with Sumner, who was "personally, and vindictively hostile to the President." Sumner's reaction to this "deep sense of wrong" was to continue official contacts with Fish, but to give him "the cold shoulder" socially. Strained relations developed with another old friend when Howe, an expansionist, agreed to serve on Grant's Santo Domingo commission. In the midst of the rising tensions, Sumner suffered a recurrence of his old illness, angina pectoris. With severe pain in his chest and left arm, he stayed away from the Senate for a week. His dogged adherence to principle also threatened a possible loss of his senatorial power.

Sumner's rapid fall from power was confirmed when the Forty-second Congress organized in early March 1871. Senators Morton and Conkling, with backing from the administration, used Sumner's break with Fish as proof that his usefulness as chair of the Foreign Relations Committee had been seriously impaired. It was essential, they said, that the secretary of state work closely with the Foreign Relations chairman, and the Republican caucus, by a vote of 26 to 21, removed Sumner from the committee that he had chaired for ten years. Close friend and ally Schurz led his defense, but administration loyalists, long angered by Sumner's domineering control over diplomacy, had their way. Although it appeared unlikely that they could save the Santo Domingo treaty, difficult negotiations with Britain were set to resume, and they wanted Sumner's—like Motley's—negative influence removed.

Embarrassed but not chastened, Sumner said little publicly, but his removal produced a greater outpouring of support than even the beating by Brooks had in 1856. Although the opposition gloated over his fall, the Democratic *New York World* pronounced Grant "incompetent" and "pig-headed" and Longfellow spoke for many when he noted that people were "troubled and indignant." The "meanness and folly" of Sumner's removal made the poet "sad to think how this noble country is governed and misgoverned."

Through it all there were clearly other underlying issues that had led to Sumner's being unseated, for the more the Republican party changed, the more the senator remained committed to his old agenda. His foreign policy differences with party leaders were real, but his continuing insistence on racial equality became troublesome and tiring to many Republicans who were eager to deal with other domestic issues. Not sharing the strength of his commitment, they had begun to feel that his tenacity on racial issues had become a liability to continued Republican dominance. Therefore, opposing views on Caribbean policy was thus the immediate cause of the clash, but conflict over Sumner's egalitarian vision was also a critical factor.

Even though the president's Santo Domingo commission produced the expected favorable report, no amount of pressure from Grant could produce the necessary votes for ratification of an annexation treaty. In his message accompanying the report, Grant referred to "the censure of disappointed men" and to the unjust charges of corruption. In response, Sumner delivered a ringing attack on the methods of the administration behind the Santo Domingo scheme. In the end, the Senate again said no to annexation, and the president's pet project was dead, this time for good. Although Sumner's party had found his methods obnoxiously arrogant and deserving of censure, it was forced to agree with him that to the people of Santo Domingo the United States was "as a hawk to chickens."

Sumner's fall from influence was, as mentioned, in part a calculated effort by Fish to give himself a freer hand in negotiations with Britain. Since December, he had been in consultation with Sir John Rose, who was in Washington to seek an agreement on terms for more formal negotiations to follow. Fish knew that no settlement would be possible unless his country renounced any claim to Canada or for indirect war damages, conditions that Sumner would never have accepted.

Thus the secretary rejoiced when Senate Republicans touted the senator's inability to work with the State Department as the major reason for deposing him. In fact, Fish may have deliberately triggered Sumner's hostility by attacking Motley. In talks with Rose, he also pointedly emphasized Sumner's demand for "the withdrawal of the British flag from this hemisphere" as a reason for a more conciliatory attitude by England. Said Sumner in a January 1871 memo to Fish, British withdrawal "cannot be abandoned as a condition" for negotiation. With Sumner removed and Fish in full control of foreign policy, the way to an Anglo-American agreement had been made easier.

Within two months U.S. and British commissioners agreed on terms for the Treaty of Washington. The pact, which was signed on May 8, provided for a commission of five members, including one each from Britain and the United States, to settle the claims issue. Included was a British expression of regret for the escape of the Confederate raiders and a definition of the obligations of neutral nations. A neutral government must exercise "due diligence to prevent the fitting out, arming, or equipping," of ships designed to make war on a nation "with which it is at peace." The British in effect had surrendered their case and left it up to the tribunal simply to set the amount of damages owed. At the same time they had safeguarded themselves in regard to the actions of neutrals in future wars.

Long before Senate ratification, Sumner had reconciled himself to the treaty and, in a four-hour speech on May 19, called for its approval. He could do so without loss of face because in the Treaty of Washington the British expressed regret for what they had done and approved international rules for neutral nations, items to be "hailed with joy by the thinking men" of both nations. To Lieber he explained that "every point I made against" the Johnson treaty had been met. Sumner had never publicly called for Britain to surrender Canada and although he had demanded indirect damages, the treaty's silence on those issue allowed him to suggest that they had not been abandoned. And, even though deposed from his chairmanship, he had consulted with the British commissioners frequently and thus had played a highly visible role in the negotiations.

Privately, however, Sumner remained far from satisfied, and probably agreed with his friend, the international law expert George Bemis, who labeled the treaty "a miserable abortion; a wholesale sell and an ignominious surrender of everything valuable." Unhappy with the final terms, Sumner nonetheless believed that it met many of his cherished goals. He thus reluctantly joined with the majority for its 49-to-12 ratification vote. Stripped of power, the senator had little choice but to acquiesce in the best possible light.

Sumner played no role in the arbitration process, for Grant had appointed Charles Francis Adams to the commission that convened in Geneva in December. As a gesture to public opinion and to senators like Sumner, Fish allowed Adams to raise the indirect claims issue, but he gladly abandoned it when the British threatened to withdraw from the talks. Thereafter, the Senate overwhelmingly accepted a supplemental article to the treaty that excluded indirect damages. The final September award of $15.5 million to the United States represented the commission's decision on direct damages. Predictably, Sum-

ner voted no and complained privately to Bemis that "Fish
has sacrificed our case."

Long before this, Sumner had decided that further public
dispute with Secretary Fish would be futile. A year earlier he
had prepared a speech reviewing the abuse he had been subjected to by the secretary and Grant, but he had been talked
out of delivering it by friends who convinced him that it might
"recoil upon yourself." The country was no longer interested
in his complaints. Naively, he explained to a friend that "I hesitate to crush Mr. Fish although he has behaved very badly."
Realistically, he may have already decided on a complete break
with the administration as it drove for reelection.

The long struggle with Grant and Fish had taken a political
and physical toll on Sumner. He continued to overwork in
Congress, friends noting that he had aged visibly. Attacks of
angina pectoris became more common. Yet he remained determined to push for a civil rights bill to guarantee equality for
African Americans, still so obviously denied them in most parts
of the country, only to find resistance from Democrats, apathy
among fellow Republicans, and—most disheartening—a lack
of commitment from the administration. Having been forcibly
removed from a foreign policy role by Grant, Fish, and their
allies, he discovered that his influence on domestic issues had
declined accordingly. He recoiled as these same forces resisted his life-long battle for racial equality. Only by cleansing the
party of Grantism could its original goal be reestablished.

By late 1871, Sumner felt that the president's problems in
foreign policy and the corruption evident in his domestic policies might deny him renomination. Over the next months, as
party leaders coalesced around the chief executive, the senator
wrote privately that Grant was "*unfit*" and had made his office
a "plaything." The party must avoid "the suicidal folly of
renominating him." Yet publicly, Sumner remained silent for
the time being, not wishing to jeopardize his civil rights bill: "I
can do nothing by which the cause of the colored people is
any way weakened or compromised. I stand by them always."

Nor did he actively encourage Grant's many Republican opponents then forming the Liberal Republican movement. They gathered in a Cincinnati convention in early May to choose an alternate candidate and a platform stressing civil rights and civil service reform. They fully expected Democrats to join with them to oust the president. To pleas from Massachusetts friends that he speak out, assume a leadership role, and permit others to tout him for the presidency, the senator remained aloof. Knowing that his age, health, and unpopularity precluded such a role, he was reluctant to break with the party he had helped to form and been a leading member of for its entire history. A break with Republicans would likely reduce even further his already waning influence. Still hoping that Grant might "have the patriotism to withdraw and give us peace," he would maintain his silence until the nominations were completed; only then would he "take the position in which I can best serve the country and . . . the African race."

By mid-May, Grant's renomination was secure, and the Liberal Republicans had chosen Horace Greeley, with Democrats also prepared to support the New York editor. Grant's supporters, anticipating that Sumner might leave their party, had hoped to minimize the damage in Massachusetts by nominating his Senate colleague Henry Wilson for vice president. The two senators had exchanged awkward letters explaining their respective roles and remained "personal friends" despite strained relations during the campaign.

Sumner faced his dilemma squarely. At the end of the month he broke his silence with a strong Senate speech labeled "Republicanism vs. Grantism," which arraigned the president for nepotism, gift-taking, and the abandonment of the freedmen. By "forcibly intervening in Dominica and menacing war on Hayti," Grant had violated the Constitution by seizing Congress's power to declare war. He had abdicated the party's commitment to racial equality at home and had restructured the Republican party into his "personal party"; Republicanism became "Grantism" and party members became "Grant-men."

The senator refrained from publicly endorsing Greeley until the end of July, meanwhile facing a storm of protest from long-time Republican associates like Frederick Douglass, who feared that the Liberal Republican movement might permit the resurgence of southern Democrats. Even the usually apolitical Longfellow disagreed with his friend. Fearing that Democrats could not be trusted on racial issues, the poet warned: "They will deceive you if they can." Especially bitter were Sumner's exchanges with abolitionists Garrison and Gerrit Smith. The former ridiculed Sumner's claim that Greeley had been a life-long abolitionist, reminding him of the editor's opposition to the Free Soil movement. When Smith accused Sumner in a public letter of opposing the president out of personal anger, the senator countered that his opposition stemmed from "my deep sense of Genl. Grant's unfitness." Their acrimonious correspondence continued into August, with Sumner bestowing upon Smith "the exclusive honor of attacking an old friend without cause."

In a lengthy letter to the African-American community, Sumner broke his public silence during the summer by urging its support of Greeley because of the president's lack of "heartfelt sympathy" for civil rights. He labored to present Liberal Republicans as the true Republican party, composed of those who had gathered "for the sake of Reform and Purity in Government." This, even though some Liberal Republicans in the Senate, including Trumbull, had consistently opposed his civil rights bill! Republican opponents, Sumner claimed, had assembled to sustain Grant's "personal government and . . . pretensions." Hence the "surest trust" for blacks was in Greeley.

Sumner's dilemma in the 1872 campaign was indeed a tragic one for an aging senator committed to racial equality. Frustrated so long by Republican intransigence, he found the Liberal Republican record on civil rights little better. Nevertheless, weighing his options, he still felt that his principles were better sustained by supporting Greeley, though he confined his role to the writing of public letters in behalf of what soon appeared to be a hopeless cause. Much of his effort was a defense of his leaving the Republican party. House Speaker James G. Blaine condemned Sumner's association with southern Democrats, whom he described as secessionists and accomplices of Preston Brooks. Sumner retorted that it was primarily due to "Republican lukewarmness and a want of support in the President" that his civil rights bill had not become law.

Sumner had planned to speak at a Greeley rally in Faneuil Hall in early September, but friends convinced him that his delicate health would suffer further if he did so. Moreover, they suggested that his public support of Greeley would do the cause little good and only further aggravate tensions with Republicans with whom he must still deal in the Senate. Instead, they persuaded him to go to Europe and regain his strength for a renewed battle for civil rights. Sailing in early September, he released a public letter explaining that "recurring symptoms" had forced him to submit "most reluctantly" to the admonitions of friends and physicians that he take a restful trip. Still, he publicly endorsed Greeley, for the editor represented "a reformed civil service" as well as "reconciliation not only between the two sections but between the two races."

Sumner's two-month stay in Europe got off to a bad start when he received word from Francis Bird on his arrival in London that Massachusetts Liberal Republicans had nominated him for governor. He responded immediately: he "could not and would not serve as Governor," an office that would afford him no role in his struggle for federal civil rights legislation. "I must be left to my independence" in the Senate. Bird reluctantly acquiesced and released Sumner's letter pleading that his delicate health precluded his seeking the governorship. Finally free from any obligation to campaign, he traveled and visited European friends. He sailed for home in mid-November partially restored to health, aware of Greeley's crushing defeat, yet hopeful that Congress could be convinced to endorse his civil rights measure.

Unlike most Republicans in 1869, Charles Sumner believed the process of Reconstruction to be incomplete. As he viewed the growing segregation of southern schools, churches, railroads, and inns, he never ceased to agitate for equality. Late in the year he lectured throughout the Northeast on "The Question of Caste," stressing the importance of political and civil equality to end segregation and prevent separate castes for black and white. A scholarly appeal for the unity of the races and for full recognition of citizenship rights for freedmen, his address became the basis for his civil rights bill, first introduced in 1870.

Sumner's efforts also came in the face of rising agitation in the South that, under Ku Klux Klan leadership, sought social, economic, and above all, political control over southern blacks. As Klan violence at the polls and elsewhere mounted, with a death toll in the hundreds, Congress in May 1870 made interference with voting rights a federal crime. But with little initial effort by Grant and Attorney General E. Rockwood Hoar to enforce this law, further legislative action was necessary. The passage of two additional laws in early 1871 provided the necessary machinery to control Klan disturbances, and they brought a measure of peace to the South by 1872. Sumner had supported the use of federal intervention to enforce voting rights because no state could be permitted to "set up its local system against the universal law. Equality implies universality; and what is universal must be national."

But more than protection at the polls was necessary if true civil equality were to be established. Accordingly, in 1870, Sumner introduced his civil rights bill to prohibit discrimination in schools, juries, public accommodations, and on public transportation. In both 1870 and 1871, the proposal was sent to the Judiciary Committee and blocked by Chairman Trumbull.

Sumner's proposal finally got a full hearing on the Senate floor in early 1872, when he adroitly attached it as an amendment to a proposed amnesty for former Confederate leaders, a bill that had the backing of Grant and most Republicans. Sumner based its constitutionality not only on his usual appeal to the Declaration of Independence, but also to the clauses in the Thirteenth and Fourteenth amendments granting Congress the authority to enforce civil rights by necessary legislation. In order to use the Thirteenth Amendment as justification, he equated segregation with slavery, an interpretation that many rejected.

Sumner believed his legislation to be the "cap-stone or keystone; it is the final measure for the safeguard of our colored fellow-citizens." Many Republicans were unenthusiastic about backing such an explosive issue in an election year; and some doubted its constitutionality, since the Fourteenth Amendment banned only discrimination by states and not by individuals, corporations, or private organizations. They were especially leery of the desegregated school guarantee and questioned whether the equal protection clause of the Fourteenth Amendment applied to public education.

Sumner urged his amendment as the logical extension of the approach he had made in the Boston school case of 1849, noting that "even if accommodations are the same, as notoriously they are not, there is no equality." As he had argued almost a quarter of a century earlier, he pointed out that separate schools were "an ill-disguised violation of the principle of Equality." For black children, preventing equal access denied them "preparation for the duties of life," while for whites "the prejudice of color is nursed when it should be stifled." Attaching his proposal to the amnesty bill was fitting, for "each is a measure of reconciliation intended to close the issues of the war." In February 1872, his amendment passed, but it died when the amnesty bill failed to receive the necessary two-thirds vote required by the Fourteenth Amendment. Grant's failure to encourage its passage had provided Sumner with yet an additional reason to break with his party during the campaign of 1872.

If Sumner had difficulty still being a loyal, albeit discredited, Republican, he would find it even more of a problem after having supported Horace Greeley. As Congress convened, an aging Sumner, "bending under physical weakness and tried by aches and ailments," was nonetheless determined to press the civil rights issue anew. Unable to understand why so few were interested, he asked, "Where are the friends whom I have helped and whose cause I have never failed to champion?" He concluded, "I have not changed. I am now where I have always been, in the breach." In fact he had returned to Congress only "in fidelity to that Bill."

Not surprisingly, his efforts in early 1873 to attach his proposal to related bills was ruled out of order or not acted on. Finally, in January 1874, he made what he feared might be his final effort, only to find his bill sent again to the Judiciary Committee. Such delaying tactics, said Sumner, would deny "my desire," which was "to close forever the great question . . . so that there shall be no such words as 'black' or 'white' but that we shall speak only of citizens and of men." Tragically, the Senate was still delaying at the time of his death in March 1874. Two months later it passed the measure with several senators supporting it more as a gesture to Sumner's memory than out of a commitment to the bill. House passage did not come until February 1875, with the desegregated school section deleted. The measure, which, like its fallen sponsor, was far ahead of its time, was nonetheless a fitting tribute to Sumner, although few were surprised when the Supreme Court ruled much of it unconstitutional in 1883.

If congressional Republicans relented in their attacks on Sumner after his death, they were not going to make his lot any easier while he was still among them. In December 1872, he introduced a bill designed to "promote national unity and good-will among fellow citizens" of the North and South. It would have required that the names of battles between Americans be removed from the Army Register and from regimental colors. He believed that excluding such names would help put the Civil War in the past. During the war, Sumner, with the approval of military leaders and with little controversy, had won approval of a ban on placing any picture of a battle between Americans in the capitol. But if Sumner saw the regimental flag issue as a gesture for sectional peace, many Republicans interpreted it as a slap at General Ulysses S. Grant, the soldier-president. Not only was the bill rejected, but it was assailed in Congress and especially in Massachusetts.

Within two weeks of the bill's introduction in Congress, the Massachusetts House passed a motion censuring Sumner, claiming the bill to be "an insult to the loyal soldiery of the nation." To some, Sumner sought "the overturn of soldiers' gravestones, the ploughing up of national cemeteries . . . and the obliteration of Union victories from histories and school books." Sumner had not only miscalculated the strength of Union veterans but also the opposition of those Massachusetts Republicans who sought to embarrass and perhaps unseat him as his Senate term neared its end. Sumner professed not to "comprehend this tempest." Claiming only a desire to bind up the nation's wounds, he felt he "deserved better of Mass." The state "which led in requiring all safe-guards for Liberty and Equality" should have the "honor of leading in reconciliation." Poet John Greenleaf Whittier and others of his old friends organized a petition drive in his behalf, but the legislature failed at first to rescind its action. Finally in February 1874, the censure was repealed with the announcement of it read in the United States Senate one day before Sumner's death.

Sumner's fall from influence in Washington corresponded with the decline of radical influence, which he symbolized. It came at the same time as the decline in his health, which had been evident to his closest friends since 1870. The angina attack he experienced in 1872 at the height of his confrontation with the Grant administration was merely the outward manifestation of a rapidly accelerating aging process. Although apparently recovered from his caning in 1856, Sumner had never regained the robust health he had enjoyed in his youth and early middle age. Friends like Longfellow were especially solicitous of him, and the poet constantly pleaded with him to ease up on his Senate activities and to return to New England more often to relax. In the midst of the Santo Domingo crisis, Longfellow urged his friend to visit him in Cambridge "and take possession of the southwest chamber overlooking the meadows and the sunset. There you shall have uninterrupted quiet . . . Let Santo D. go." But the senator rarely heeded such advice, insisting each year on remaining in Washington well into the summer, after Congress had adjourned, until the heat finally drove him north.

When his health problems intensified in 1872, he had heeded the advice of doctors and friends by taking his trip to Europe to escape the pressure of a very stressful presidential campaign. But his return in December brought little relief, as he plunged back into renewed efforts for his civil rights legislation. Again, friends urged him to lighten his work schedule, Phillips reminding him not to waste his strength on everyday duties. Phillips could not help wondering if Sumner's departure for Washington in December was a final parting: "Years and something more cruel than years, narrow the circle, and the narrower it becomes we must draw the closer together." The spring of 1873 found Sumner weaker but experiencing "ups and downs." He told Longfellow that he was again suffering "those great pains in the heart which make life intolerable," and in April, he described himself as "feeble, very feeble." By early summer he had recovered sufficiently to look forward to a return to Boston with health restored "after a winter and spring of considerable trial."

By the end of the summer, Sumner was strong enough to plan another lecture tour to ease his embattled financial condition. Unpaid bills from his European trip, the costs of publishing his speeches, and the continued upkeep of his Washington home continued to bore in on him greatly.

Friends begged him to reconsider, but he could find "no senatorial way" of easing his debt. This despite Congress's having recently voted itself a salary increase with a "Salary Grab" $5000 bonus to those currently in office. Although it would have virtually erased his debt, he found the act abhorrent to his principles and returned his bonus to the Treasury. Nor would he relent in his drive to complete publication of his *Works*, which he regarded as an essential conclusion to his career. Only after accepting a loan from a close friend was he able to cancel his lecture tour, giving him both relief and despondency. Feeling he still had something to say about racial justice, he lamented: "This is the saddest act of my life."

Sumner began his final session in Congress in December 1873 with mixed feelings. His health was stronger and it appeared likely that the Massachusetts legislature would soon rescind its censure of him. His prospects for election to a fifth term in the Senate by the legislature to be chosen the following fall had improved, and he remained determined to push again for civil rights. But death continued to close his circle of friends, and he could not help but reflect on his own future. Chief Justice Chase died in May 1873, and scientist Louis Agassiz passed away in December. College friend and former law partner George S. Hillard had suffered a stroke, and Sumner could only lament to Longfellow that their "little circle is growing smaller and I am on the way to solitude." He appeared increasingly lonely in Washington, writing a stream of letters to friends inviting them to dinner or to stay with him for a longer visit. But most of all he was tired of politics and often appeared just to be going through the motions. He found politics "more than ever distasteful" and concluded, "I am not of the stuff for these strifes."

Sumner's death on March 11, 1874, thus came as no surprise to those aware of his decline in body and spirit. On the eighth, he suffered a severe attack of angina, compounded by a bladder problem. On the tenth, he attended a brief Senate session and wrote several letters, one expressing anger that

Boston Republicans, led by Howe, planned a testimonial dinner in honor of Dominican dictator Baez: "If he comes to Boston he ought to be driven out by an indignant public sentiment." After dining at home with two close friends, servants heard a heavy fall from his bedroom. Doctors and close friends were summoned. As he lay close to death, he entreated Judge Hoar: "You must take care of the civil rights bill,—my bill . . . don't let it fail." A final spasm brought a peaceful end early the next afternoon.

Tributes poured in at the time of his funeral and after, but perhaps none more meaningful than that of Longfellow. In describing the public grief, he noted that "the nation's loss is great and irreparable." He sadly concluded that Sumner's friends "shall feel his loss more and more as the days go on." Before a funeral service in the Senate, his body was placed in the capitol rotunda. It was then carried to Boston, where 40,000 mourners viewed the coffin at the State House. Funeral services at King's Chapel were followed by public tributes at a ceremony that featured Schurz as the chief speaker. In recalling his dedication to racial equality, Schurz concluded that Sumner's mission was "to march ahead of his followers, when they were afraid to follow." The Senate set aside a day in late April for further eulogies where his life was reviewed. Several noted his emphasis on "the ideal over the practical," and his unwillingness to compromise, but he was remembered best as "the undoubted leader of the political opposition to slavery."

To Rise Up Alone

Charles Sumner was a man well in advance of his times, opposing slavery and school segregation before the Civil War in a way that few in his own state, much less the nation, were willing to endorse. After the war, in fighting for racial justice and civil rights, he again led the North by his continued efforts to complete the struggle long after most had abandoned it for more familiar and comfortable issues. Led to reform originally by anger over society's injustices, his ongoing and deep commitment to the causes of antislavery and racial equality quickly became the driving forces that dictated his every action from the early 1840s until his death in 1874. Carl Schurz summed up Sumner's achievements in his determination "to rise up alone for what he thought right when others would not rise with him."

Sumner's achievements were many. In attacking the growing military spirit of the 1840s he raised issues that few were prepared to face. More significant, he joined with other young Whigs to demand that their party resist slavery's expansion, and, when it refused, he played a central role in forming the Free Soil party dedicated to the containment of the South's peculiar institution. Accelerating his efforts in this direction, he helped form the Republican party in the mid-1850s and then pushed it relentlessly to a stronger antislavery stance until the Civil War finally brought abolition. Throughout the years of war and Reconstruction he kept the question of equal rights foremost in the face of massive resistance and apathy. His commitment to civil rights for blacks brought the nation closer to his egalitarian vision than it had ever been before.

In advocating reform, Sumner was an impractical moralist who rarely understood the need for compromise. As such, he antagonized opponents and exasperated friends. His unwillingness to see anything other than his own perspective and his self-assuredness, self-importance, and self-righteousness left foes angered and friends in disbelief. Perhaps a degree of insecurity drove him to attempt to complete the publication of his *Works* before his death; perhaps, too, it resulted in a martyr complex inviting wrath, ridicule, and disdain as proof of his self-worth and higher purpose.

Sumner personified the scholar in politics. His Harvard education and extensive reading in the classics and history initially led him to a life of intellectual pursuit. Unsuited for the everyday drudgery of the law, he entered politics through reform, first with an attack on the military complex and then through a life-long commitment to racial justice. Eventually his moral values overtook his interest in books. At first deeply unhappy to leave his study, he remained committed to scholarly reading and research and learned to combine it with reform and politics. His closest friends were as apt to be men of letters as they were reformers in politics.

During his twenty-three years in the Senate, Sumner could be as politically minded as any of his colleagues. His partisanship—first as a Free Soiler and then a Republican—served as a means to advance moral ends. Rarely satisfied with the compromising tendencies of presidents or congressmen, he remained a stern voice of conscience. He prodded Abraham Lincoln into a more advanced stance on slavery and race relations, yet rarely appreciated the president's need to keep the support of all Northerners. Among the first to recognize Andrew Johnson's lack of commitment to equality, he berated those who refused to push for his impeachment. By far his most trying relationship involved Ulysses S. Grant. Sumner's commitment to moral correctness and Grant's insistence on personal goals led each to loath the other and to the senator's fall from political power.

Yet Charles Sumner could be truly compassionate to those who opposed his views. While many Northerners sought vengeance on Southerners over the crimes of war, Sumner sought humane treatment of Confederate prisoners. When his friends wished the worst for Preston Brooks, Sumner viewed his assailant with a calmness that belied his hatred of slavery. His advocacy of relief for Mary Todd Lincoln was in the face of the desire of most to dismiss her as unimportant and mentally unstable. Finally, his efforts at sectional reconciliation through the removal of the names of Civil War battles from regimental flags wrought him only disdain and censure from Union war veterans and fellow Republicans.

Despite his egotism and self-righteousness, Sumner is best remembered as the moral conscience of the North. While most in his state and section preferred to ignore slavery in the South and segregation in the North before the war, he boldly took up the cause of African Americans nationwide, calling on all Americans to recognize their own and their nation's commitment to the principles of the Declaration of Independence. Continuing his efforts during the war, he demanded emancipation and the opportunity for blacks to fight for their freedom. In the uneasy peace that followed, Sumner continued his relentless drive for racial equality, antagonizing many, but endeavoring—even in defeat—to try to convince Americans of the justice of his cause. Even with all of his flaws he remains as relevant today as he was in the nineteenth century. Indeed, Americans continue to struggle with the issues he championed.

BIBLIOGRAPHICAL ESSAY

Charles Sumner wrote and spoke as prolifically as anyone of his era, thus giving those interested in pursuing his career an abundance of material. At the same time the sheer volume of the Sumner correspondence and speeches complicates the biographer's task. Any such biography is largely dependent on the massive collection of letters to and from the senator, which is housed at Harvard University's Houghton Library. It is also available in the eighty-five reel microfilm collection, *The Papers of Charles Sumner* (1988), edited by Beverly Wilson Palmer. More than nine hundred of Sumner's most significant letters have been published in *The Selected Letters of Charles Sumner*, 2 vols., (1990) also edited by Palmer. In addition, *The Works of Charles Sumner*, 15 vols. (1870–1893) that Sumner worked on so exhaustively during his last years is an invaluable source of his speeches. Readers should use these volumes with care, however, because Sumner altered his writings, sometimes for clarity and other times to portray himself in a better light. Therefore, wherever accessible, the original words, available in the *Congressional Globe* and sometimes in pamphlet form, are more reliable.

Numerous other manuscript collections of Sumner's contemporaries, some of which are published or on microfilm, are also invaluable in reconstructing Sumner's life. Among the most important are those of Salmon P. Chase, Joshua Giddings, Charles Francis Adams, and Hamilton Fish. Published works include: *The Letters of Henry Wadsworth Longfellow*, 5 vols. (1966–1982) edited by Andrew Hilen; *The Letters of William Lloyd Garrison, 1805–1879*, 5 vols. (1970–1979), Walter M. Merrill and Louis Ruchames editors; and *The Collected Works of Abraham Lincoln* (1953), edited by Roy P. Basler. Also important as a primary source are the newspapers of the day, which were always partisan and sectional but nonetheless reveal the spirit of the era. Most important is the Boston press, which included the *Evening Transcript, Morning Post, Daily Advertiser, Daily Whig, Courier,* the *Commonwealth,* and Garrison's *The Liberator.* New York papers of relevance include Horace Greeley's *Daily Tribune,* as well as the *Times, Evening Post,* and *Evening Sentinel.* An anti-Sumner British perspective is found in the London *Times.* Numerous southern journals present a vehement rejection of everything for which Sumner stood.

Biographies of Charles Sumner have gone through a historiographical cycle common to biographies of others of his era; the early ones are filled with praise, while those written in the twentieth century are more apt to display sharp criticism. Sumner's earliest interpreters, several of whom were contemporaries and even close friends, made little attempt to be objective and stressed his positive personality traits, including generosity and compassion. Modern students cannot discount these early biographies but should treat them with care. This is especially true of the most valuable of the early efforts, Edward L. Pierce's authorized biography, *Memoir and Letters of Charles Sumner,* (4 vols., 1878–1893). Pierce was a Massachusetts Republican who directed the Port Royal Reconstruction experiment in South Carolina and was fully committed to Sumner's program of land distribution and equal rights for the freedmen. As a member of the Massachusetts legislature and lieutenant of Sumner, he sometimes found fault with his subject's actions, but rarely questioned his motives and goals. Nonetheless his closeness gave him a unique perspective, and he thus wrote with valuable insight into Sumner's activities. His massive study also includes Sumner correspondence and thus is a valuable primary source.

By the time the final volumes of Pierce's study were published in 1893, the tide of opinion regarding Sumner and his colleagues had begun to reverse itself. Once seen as a positive force, if not actually heroes, by the turn of the century the champions of racial equality were viewed as dangerous fanatics and meddlers who needlessly tampered with the South's peculiar institution. They were pictured as forcing on the South an "experiment" in race relations that could not help but fail because of supposed black inferiority. Among the newly decreed villains, few suffered more than Charles Sumner, as the literature of the first half of the twentieth century reflected the segregated society and racist views of most white Americans. Interpreters dismissed him out of hand, a revisionist trend verified by Louis Ruchames in "Charles Sumner and American Historiography," *Journal of Negro History*, 38 (1953), 139–160.

By midcentury, as the nation entered into the early stages of the civil rights revolution, historians still held a consensus view of the nineteenth century, which either minimized Sumner's significance or continued to berate it. Thus Avery Craven could equate Sumner with William L. Yancey, Robert B. Rhett, and John Brown "and their 'fellow travelers'" who "made war inevitable." [*The Civil War in the Making 1814–1860*, (1959), p. 114] Allan Nevins implied that Sumner deserved Preston Brooks's assault because of the "deplorable taste" and "pure rant" of his "Crime Against Kansas" speech. [*The Ordeal of the Union*, II (1947), 440], while a quarter century later, David Potter could still argue that Sumner's speech alternated "between pompous rectitude and studied vilification." [*The Impending Crisis, 1848–1861* (1976), 210] In contrast, a more positive appreciation of the reformer and civil rights activist was also emerging, as seen in the collection of essays edited by Martin Duberman, *The Antislavery Vanguard: New Essays on the Abolitionists* (1965).

Because of the harshness of his message Sumner did not always share in the generally positive revisionism accorded mid-nineteenth-century reformer-activists by the 1960s. Many historians lauded the results of the antislavery crusade and

Reconstruction legislation, but the reputation of some of the key participants continued to receive mixed reviews. Along with William Lloyd Garrison, Sumner fit into this category. Ruchames reminds us that Arthur Schlesinger, Jr., described him as "the frigid Sumner," S. E. Morison called him a "complete doctrinaire," while Richard Hofstadter dismissed him as "a haughty and impatient abolitionist." [p. 139–40]. Because of his confrontational style, many seemed more willing to emphasize Sumner's sometimes abrasive personality and rhetoric than his moral commitment and real achievements.

Significantly, David Donald combined both approaches in his two-volume biography, the first and only one since 1910. Donald spent more than two decades researching and writing *Charles Sumner and the Coming of the Civil War* (1960) and *Charles Sumner and the Rights of Man* (1970) and produced a remarkable study that Sumner scholars and students alike must consult. In more than one thousand pages, Donald's biography provides a detailed portrait of every phase of his subject's life.

While generally well received by historians, Donald's prize-winning volumes have come under attack by those who argue that he stressed the negative side of Sumner's personality and record. They have suggested that Donald failed to appreciate Sumner's emphasis on the immorality of slavery and segregation. Instead, Donald explained Sumner's commitment in terms of a personal crisis. As a young man troubled by a lack of goals, his attention was directed by friends to prison reform, to pacifism, and finally to slavery. Critics have accused Donald of stressing Sumner's arrogance, insensitivity, and egotism, while failing to see his moral courage, integrity, and dedication. So said Louis Ruchames in "The Pulitzer Prize Treatment of Charles Sumner," *Massachusetts Review*, II (1961), 749–769, Paul Goodman's "David Donald's *Charles Sumner* Reconsidered," *New England Quarterly*, 37 (1964), 373–387, and Gilbert Osofsky, "Cardboard Yankee: How not to Study the Mind of Charles Sumner," *Reviews in American History*, 1 (1973), 595–605.

Donald's psychohistorical study of Sumner was an out-growth of his controversial assessment of New England abolitionists, "Toward a Reconsideration of Abolitionists," in *Lincoln Reconsidered: Essays on the Civil War Era* (2nd ed., 1962), [pp. 19–36]. These antislavery advocates, he argued, used the crusade primarily as a means to regain the status that their forebears had enjoyed. Donald's biography of Sumner was thus a part of a short-lived adherence to a controversial approach that was influenced as much by a psychological methodology as it was by the civil rights era.

Each of Donald's critics recognizes his exhaustive primary research in the first modern biography of Sumner. Appreciative of the volumes as a scholarly achievement, they nevertheless point out that Sumner can not be effectively evaluated without a greater acceptance of his moral commitment. Rather than finding deep psychological problems as explanation for his interest in reform, Sumner should be seen as calling attention to a racial situation that most white Americans preferred to ignore. Sumner and his reformer allies forced them to recognize and deal with slavery and racism, the paramount achievement of all abolitionists. This was perhaps best recognized, according to Osofsky, by Sumner's contemporary and collaborator Carl Schurz in his *Charles Sumner: An Essay*, (Arthur R. Hogue, ed., 1951).

Among the most important secondary sources are the numerous biographies of Sumner's contemporaries. Many of Sumner's abolitionist friends, most of whom avoided politics, have been the subject of special interest among biographers. Two biographies by James B. Stewart are especially useful: *Wendell Phillips, Liberty's Hero* (1986) and *William Lloyd Garrison and the Challenge of Emancipation* (1992). Biographies of antislavery advocates who became involved in politics, first in the Liberty or Free Soil movements and then in Republican ranks include: Stewart, *James R. Giddings and the Tactics of Radical Politics* (1970); Jonathan Messerli, *Horace Mann: A Biography* (1972); Frank O. Gatell, *John Gorham Palfrey and the New Eng-*

land Conscience (1963); Martin Duberman, *Charles Francis Adams* (1960); and Frederick J. Blue, *Salmon P. Chase: A Life in Politics* (1987).

Many of Sumner's closest friends were reformers or writers involved in pursuits other than antislavery. The most useful of their biographies in understanding Sumner include: Edward Wagenknect, *Longfellow: A Full-Length Biography* (1985); Frank Freidel, *Francis Lieber, Nineteenth Century Liberal* (1947); and Harold Swartz, *Samuel Gridley Howe, Social Reformer, 1801–1876* (1956). The man who shaped much of Sumner's early life is the subject of Kent Newmyer's *Supreme Court Justice Joseph Story: Statesman of the Old Republic* (1985).

Among Sumner's Senate friends were two whose biographies present a Sumner perspective. Hans Trefousse, *Carl Schurz: A Biography* (1987) is an effective presentation of Sumner's closest associate during the Reconstruction era. Sumner's Massachusetts colleague Henry Wilson is the subject of: Ernest McKay, *Henry Wilson, Practical Radical: A Portrait of a Politician* (1971) and Richard W. Abbott, *Cobler in Congress: The Life of Henry Wilson, 1812–1875* (1972).

Sumner's frequently stormy relations with the presidents during the Civil War and Reconstruction are described effectively in William McFeeley's *Grant: A Biography* (1981); Hans Trefousse, *Andrew Johnson: A Biography* (1989); and Stephen Oates, *With Malice Toward None: The Life of Abraham Lincoln* (1977). Because of the senator's close relationship with Mrs. Lincoln, Jean H. Baker's *Mary Todd Lincoln: A Biography* (1987) is useful. Sumner's central role in foreign policy after 1860 make biographies of the two secretaries of state especially relevant: Glyndon Van Deusen, *William Henry Seward* (1967) and Allan Nevins, *Hamilton Fish: The Inner History of the Grant Administration,* (1937), the latter of which presents an excessively negative bias against Sumner.

Two surveys add insight into Sumner's role in the critical issues of his times. They are James M. McPherson, *Ordeal By Fire: The Civil War and Reconstruction,* 2nd ed. (1992), and Eric

Foner, *Reconstruction* (1988). More specialized monographs for the antebellum years include: Kinley Brauer, *Cotton Versus Conscience: Massachusetts Politics and Southwestern Expansion, 1843–1848* (1967); Frederick J. Blue, *The Free Soilers: Third Party Politics, 1848–54* (1973); and William Gienapp, *The Origins of the Republican Party, 1852–1856* (1987). Ronald P. Formisano's *The Transformation of Political Culture: Massachusetts Parties, 1790s–1840s* (1983) provides an understanding of the vast political changes occurring in the two-party system in Sumner's home state during the first half of the nineteenth century. Two studies dealing with the rise and significance of the public lecture, so critical to Sumner's career, add insight to our understanding of his age: Kenneth Cmiel, *Democratic Eloquence: The Fight Over Popular Speech in Nineteenth Century America* (1990); and Donald M. Scott, "The Popular Lecture and the Creation of a Public in Mid Nineteenth Century America," *Journal of American History* 66 (1980), 791–809.

Domestic issues during the Civil War and Reconstruction are dealt with by Brooks D. Simpson, *Let Us Have Peace: Ulysses S. Grant and the Politics of War and Reconstruction, 1861–1868* (1991) and Dale Baum, *The Civil War Party System: The Case of Massachusetts, 1848–1876* (1984). Sumner's role in foreign affairs, especially as chairman of the Senate Committee on Foreign Relations, is studied in a number of important works: Charles Tansill, *The United States and Santo Domingo, 1798–1873, A Chapter in Caribbean Diplomacy* (1938); Norman Ferris, *The Trent Affair* (1977); Gordon H. Warren, *Fountain of Discontent, The Trent Affair and Freedom of the Seas* (1981); Robin W. Winks, *Canada and the United States: The Civil War Years* (1960); and Adrian Cook, *The Alabama Claims: American Politics and Anglo–American Relations, 1865–1872* (1975).

Relevant secondary articles dealing specifically with Sumner's activities in the antebellum years include: Bill Ledbetter, "Charles Sumner: Political Activist for the New England Transcendentalists," *The Historian* 44 (1982), 347–63; Laura A. White, "Was Charles Sumner Shamming, 1856–1859?" *New*

England Quarterly, 37 (1960), 291–324; Frank Freidel, "Francis Lieber, Charles Sumner, and Slavery," *Journal of Southern History* 9 (1943), 75–93; Leonard Levy and Harlan Phillips, "The *Roberts* Case: Source of the Separate But Equal Doctrine," *American Historical Review* 56 (1951), 510–18; and Beverly Wilson Palmer, "Towards a National Antislavery Party: The Giddings-Sumner Alliance," *Ohio History* 99 (1990). Issues relevant to Sumner's Civil War and Reconstruction activities are dealt with in Victor H. Cohen, "Charles Sumner and the *Trent* Affair," *Journal of Southern History* 23 (1956), 205–19; and James M. McPherson, "Grant or Greeley? The Abolitionist Dilemma in the Election of 1872," *American Historical Review* 71 (1965), 43–61.

INDEX

Charles Sumner and the Conscience of the North
Copy editor, Andrew J. Davidson
Production editor, Lucy Herz
Typesetter, Point West, Inc.
Printer, McNaughton & Gunn, Inc.

About the author: Frederick J. Blue, born in Staten Island, New York, received a B.A. from Yale University and a Ph.D. from the University of Wisconsin; he is currently Professor of History at Youngstown State University. Professor Blue's other books include *The Free Soilers: Third Party Politics, 1848–54* (1973) and *Salmon P. Chase: A Life in Politics* (1987). He has also authored numerous other articles on antislavery politics.